Nonprofit Financial Management

Nonprofit Financial Management

A Practical Guide

CHARLES K. COE

WILEY

John Wiley & Sons, Inc.

Published by John Wiley & Sons, Inc., Hoboken, New Jersey.
Published simultaneously in Canada.

Library of Congress Cataloging-in-Publication Data:

Coe, Charles K.
  Nonprofit financial management : a practical guide / Charles K. Coe.
       p. cm. – (Wiley nonprofit authority series)
  Includes index.
  ISBN 978-1-118-01132-4 (hardback); 978-1-118-08815-9 (ebk);
978-1-118-08861-6 (ebk); 978-1-118-08862-3 (ebk)
  1. Nonprofit organizations–Finance.   I. Title.
  HG4027.65.C64 2011
  658.15–dc22

                                                      2011004109

Printed in the United States of America.

10 9 8 7 6 5 4

This book is dedicated to the students in my Nonprofit Financial Management classes, whose care for others gave me the impetus to write this book.

Contents

Who this Book Is For

The genesis for this book came from my students in a nonprofit financial-management course. Many of them work in or volunteer for nonprofit organizations. They have a deep passion for their cause and the people they serve. They hunger for knowledge that can enable them to use their scarce financial resources as efficiently as possible. Few, though, have a financial background, which is the case for most nonprofit managers. In 2009, there were 1,617,447 nonprofit organizations in the United States, 714,000 of which—about 44 percent—had gross receipts of less than $25,000. Such an organization typically has an executive director who is knowledgeable about the mission and has experience in service delivery and, perhaps, fundraising, but with little financial expertise. Though appropriate for a nonprofit of any size, this book is especially useful for the nonprofit whose executive director and Board have relatively little experience in financial management.

If you are an instructor, go to www.wiley.com/college (search for the book title) for additional classroom tools including PowerPoint slides, cases, and testing materials, to use alongside the content presented in this book.

Acknowledgments

My most sincere appreciation goes to those who gave their time to review and comment on the book. Nancy Kwansnich, the assistant vice president, Branch Banking & Trust Company, who specializes in nonprofit banking services, reviewed the chapters on cash flow management, investments, and banking. Her long experience working with nonprofits of all sizes gave valuable insights into the particular cash management needs of nonprofits. Also shedding light on cash management was a team of professionals in the city government of Raleigh, North Carolina, namely, Perry James, the finance director; Jerrae Williams, the treasury manager, who has experience as a nonprofit banking specialist; and Jordan Topal, the investments and cash manager, who shared his wisdom about investments and referred me to *The Essentials of Treasury Management,* 2nd ed., the bible for financial professionals.

From the accounting and auditing world, two people were tremendously helpful. Kristen Hoyle, Audit Partner with the firm Thomas, Judy and Tucker, has audited nonprofits for many years and has graciously served on the boards of many nonprofits. Kristen reviewed the chapters relating to accounting, auditing, internal control, and evaluating financial condition. Also providing most valuable input in these areas was Mig Murphy Sistrom, CPA. Mig served as finance director for a nonprofit with an annual budget over $10 million. She now provides accounting and tax services exclusively to nonprofits and teaches in the Nonprofit Management Program at Duke University.

Anita White, administrative officer, Haven House, helped me to understand the myriad funding sources that a nonprofit can receive. Exhibit 6.12 in Chapter 6, Prepare and Manage the Budget, indicates the varying length, fiscal years, payment periods, and reimbursement time of Haven House's various funding sources. Cheryl Perry, procurement and risk service manager for the town of Cary, North Carolina, reviewed the chapters on purchasing and managing capital assets.

Students in my Nonprofit Financial Management class for the fall semester contributed significantly to the effort. Caroline Gibson contributed the notes to the financial statement problem; Kristen Feneley contributed material on contracting with hotels. My son, Lincoln, prepared many of the spreadsheets in the accounting and financial analysis chapters. Charlene Reiss contributed two very useful budgeting cases, as did Johanna Foster with the Wake County Community Service Department. Michael Riley, working as a graduate student, helped with the instructors' website materials. Mac McGee again exhibited his editing mastery to get the book in decent shape.

CHAPTER 1

Introduction

Background on Nonprofits

There are over 1.6 million nonprofits in the United States. They are diverse in size and mission, ranging from human service organizations to advocacy groups to religious organizations. They are growing rapidly in number. From 1995 to 2005, the nonprofits registered with the Internal Revenue Service (IRS) grew by 27 percent.[1] They are important economically, contributing 7.2 percent of the paid jobs and 6.6 percent of the total wages in the United States (see Exhibit 1.1).

Although nonprofits are extremely diverse in size in mission, each one must have a sound financial management system.

There are three types of nonprofits: *charity, foundation,* and *other.* In 2009, there were about 957,000 charities and 113,000 foundations registered with the IRS as 501(c)(3) organizations ("501(c)(3)s"). The "other" group includes 501(c)(4) registered mutual benefit organizations (e.g., medical plans, civic leagues, and advocacy organizations) and about 350,000 religious organizations not required to register with the IRS, although about half chose to do so.

All nonprofits are exempt from income taxes on their mission-related income, but only 501(c)(3)s can receive *tax-deductible* donations. A 501(c)(3) organization cannot support or oppose anyone running for public office but can engage in a political campaign consistent with its purpose. Most 501(c)(3)s can spend no more than 20 percent of their resources on lobbying. Exhibit 1.2 shows the types of public charities.

Board of Directors

Nonprofit governance and management rests on three legs: the Board of Directors (Board), the chief executive officer (CEO), and the staff. Board members nominate and elect fellow members. Board members have civil immunity for the official actions they take, as do volunteers, but the law

EXHIBIT 1.1   Charities' Employment

Category	Number	Percent of U.S. Economy
Paid workers	9.4 million	7.2%
Volunteer workers (FTEs)	4.7 million	3.9%
Total workforce	14.1 million	11.1%
Wages	$321.6 billion	6.6%

Source: Lester Saloman and S. Wojciech Sokolowski, *Employment in America's Charities: A Profile* (Baltimore: Johns Hopkins Center for Civil Society Studies, 2006).

does not protect Board members from criminal, intentionally malicious, or reckless conduct. Board meetings are not subject to open-meeting laws, as government meetings are; however, Board members must exercise care, loyalty and obedience. Board members should:

- Determine the nonprofit's mission and issue the mission statement
- Select, support, and review the performance of the CEO
- Contribute time and resources to the nonprofit
- Raise funds
- Conduct business ethically and professionally
- Make well-informed, engaged decisions
- Adopt the budget
- Oversee the management of funds
- Adopt a human-resource policy

EXHIBIT 1.2   Number of Reporting Public Charities by Subsector

Subsector	Number of Organizations	Percent of Total
Arts, culture, and humanities	125,170	7.7%
Education	216,021	13.3%
Environment and animals	58,209	3.6%
Health	101,458	6.3%
Human services	410,028	25.3%
International and foreign affairs	20,737	1.3%
Public and societal benefit	359,160	22.3%
Religion-related	231,858	14.3%
Other	94,806	5.9%
Total	1,617,447	100.0%

Source: Urban Institute, National Center for Charitable Statistics, *Core Files* (2007–2008).

- Follow laws
- Serve on a committee
- Promote the organization's image

The mission statement should succinctly reflect the nonprofit's core values. The Board should adopt the mission statement with input from the CEO, the staff, and stakeholders such as clients, members of the organization and community members. Board members should contribute both time and resources to the nonprofit. Some Board members have needed skill sets. For instance, a Board member who is a certified public accountant (CPA) or has a strong business background can serve on the Finance Committee or even volunteer as the chief financial officer (CFO). Likewise, a Board member who is a lawyer can provide legal advice. Board members should visibly participate in fundraising activities, contributing their own funds, and ask community members to contribute.

Boards with many members typically break down into subcommittees and each Board member should have an office or committee responsibility. As the policymaking body, the Board adopts policies, including the annual budget. This book discusses an array of financially related policies. For reference to these and other policies, the organization Boardsource offers downloadable policies in 48 topic areas, including 13 financial management policies (see http://www.boardsource.org/?Bookstore/).

Management

The second leg is the CEO, either volunteer or paid, who carries out the Board's policies. There is no single package of education and experience necessary to be a successful CEO. She (or he) may be an experienced professional with a graduate degree in public, nonprofit or business administration. Absent a management degree, she may have extensive nonprofit working experience as a program manager or CEO. She may even be a volunteer with limited nonprofit experience.

The CEO should facilitate the Board's interaction with herself and the staff. The CEO should seek broad Board involvement in setting policy. In serving the Board, the CEO should:

- Orient new members
- Help craft a mission statement
- Help adopt a strategic plan and envision change
- Prepare the budget for the Board's adoption
- Manage the budget during the fiscal year
- Provide financial and programmatic information
- Tout the organization's accomplishments to the community

In theory, the Board makes policy decisions that the CEO carries out. In practice, however, many Boards heavily depend on the CEO to engage more in policymaking. This is often because many Boards have an unwieldy size. For instance, 47 percent of the Boards in Indiana have 10 or more members; 19 percent have between 15 and 29 members.[2] Another reason for strong CEO influence is Board member turnover. Often, Board members limit themselves to three-year terms.

In addition to Board-related responsibilities, many CEOs are extensive boundary-spanners, interacting with a host of stakeholders, including funders, community leaders, service recipients, volunteers, and staff members. A typical CEO must be entrepreneurial and should be thankful to deal with less red tape and enjoy more flexibility than do government managers.[3]

Staff

The third leg of the stool is the staff. Many nonprofits have an all- or mostly all-volunteer staff. Volunteers are motivated to serve because of a nonprofit's good works. The CEO and the Board should consistently laud the efforts of volunteers and staff members and compensate staff equitably. The CEO should:

- Follow best practices with regard to hiring and disciplinary action
- Orient new employees
- Build a high-performance management team
- Train employees to do their job
- Treat employees fairly
- Give performance feedback throughout the year, not just at annual performance review

Finances

Most reporting nonprofits have small budgets. Indeed, 44.6 percent had annual expenses less than $100,000 (see Exhibit 1.3). Large nonprofits, with expenses of more than $10 million, account for only 3.7 percent of nonprofits, but a whopping 82.7 percent of total expenses.

Nonprofits have three main revenue sources. The main revenue, fees for services and goods, includes items such as Medicare and Medicaid reimbursements, ticket sales and tuition payments (see Exhibit 1.4). The second principal revenue source, private contributions, includes grants and contributions from foundations, individuals and corporations. Other revenue sources are government grants, investment, and other income.

EXHIBIT 1.3 Number and Expenses of Reporting Public Charities

Expenses	Percent of Total Charities	Percent of Total Expenses
$10 million or more	3.7%	82.6%
$5 million to $9.99 million	2.6%	5.5%
$1 million to $4.99 million	11.4%	7.5%
$500,000 to $999,000	8.5%	1.8%
$100,000 to $499,000	29.2%	2.0%
Under $100,000	44.6%	0.6%
Total	100.0%	100.0%

Source: Urban Institute, National Center for Charitable Statistics, NCCS-Guide Star National Nonprofit Research Database: Special Research Version (2005).

The revenue picture changes significantly when looking only at human service nonprofits, of which there are eight types: (1) crime and legal, (2) employment and job related, (3) food and nutrition, (4) housing and shelter, (5) public safety and disaster preparedness, (6) youth development, (7) community development, and (8) human service multipurpose organizations. These nonprofits depend far more heavily on government grants (see Exhibit 1.5).

Financial Management Organization

The National Association of Schools of Public Affairs and Administration (NASPAA) has issued guidelines for graduate professional education in nonprofit organizations, management and leadership.[4] One such guideline

EXHIBIT 1.4 Sources of Revenue for Reporting Public Charities

Sources of Revenue	Percent of All Charities	Percent of Charities Excluding Hospitals and Higher Education
Fees for services and goods	70.4%	53.5%
Private contributions	12.3%	23.3%
Government grants	9.0%	17.0%
Investment income	5.4%	2.3%
Other Income	2.9%	3.9%
Total	100.0%	100.0%

Source: Urban Institute, National Center for Charitable Statistics, *NCCS-GuideStar National Nonprofit Research Database: Special Research Version* (2005).

EXHIBIT 1.5   Sources of Revenue Human Service Nonprofits

Funding Source	Number of Nonprofits	Largest Funding Source
Government (federal, state, or local units)	19,657	60%
Donations (individual, corporate, foundations, federated giving)	6,124	19%
Fees (public and private) for services	5,179	16%
Other	1,663	5%
Total	32,623	100%

Source: The Urban Institute, *National Survey of Nonprofit Government Contracting and Grants* (2010).

requires graduate education to cover in its curriculum budgeting and re-source management, including general accounting practices and budget management, risk management, contract monitoring, supervision of grant projects, and reporting to government agencies, philanthropic foundations, and other funding agencies. To perform these functions, nonprofits organize differently, depending on their size and resources.

Organizational Options

Very small nonprofits rely on a volunteer to do the accounting. Somewhat larger ones have a full- or part-time bookkeeper with some accounting experience and usually structure themselves as shown in Exhibit 1.6. A still larger nonprofit can hire a CFO with an accounting degree and perhaps is a CPA as shown in Exhibit 1.7.

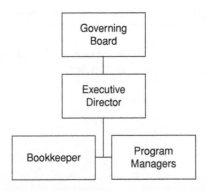

EXHIBIT 1.6   Organization with a Bookkeeper

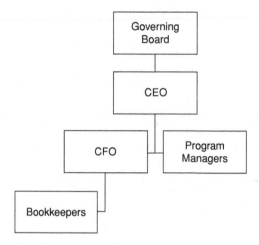

EXHIBIT 1.7   Organization with a CFO

Conclusion

Nonprofits are extremely diverse with regard to their size, mission, funding sources, and organizational structure; however, one constant remains. Each nonprofit should have a *sound* financial management system with which it can be accountable to its funders and perform capably. This book is designed to assist all nonprofits, from the smallest to the largest and most financially sophisticated, to manage their finances responsibly and professionally.

CHAPTER 2

Account for Transactions

Staffing Structure

Depending on their size and complexity, nonprofits can staff the accounting and financial management function in several ways. Large, relatively complex nonprofits are more likely to have an in-house certified public accountant (CPA). Small, less complex nonprofits can have a non–accountant administrative staff member handle the day-to-day bookkeeping operations and have the books periodically reviewed and adjusted by a CPA adviser. Alternatively, the entire accounting function might be outsourced to a CPA adviser. For organizations that do not need an in-house CPA, outsourcing the accounting work often ensures competency at a lower cost than paying a full-time employee. Regardless of the staffing approach, it is helpful for any nonprofit to have a finance professional, preferably a CPA, on its Board.

Even with a strong staffing structure, it is imperative that the Board and chief executive understand (1) basic accounting terms and (2) the accounting process.

Basic Accounting Terms

The accounting profession, like all others, has its jargon, understandable to accountants but "Greek" to others. Common terms include:

- Fiscal year
- Generally accepted accounting principles
- Basis of accounting
- Chart of accounts
- Functional expense cost allocation
- Single- and double-entry accounting
- Capitalization and depreciation

- Federal grant indirect cost allocation
- Accounting and fundraising software

The Fiscal Year

The fiscal year, sometimes erroneously called the "physical year," refers to the 12-month period that the nonprofit selects as its accounting year. A nonprofit may choose any 12-month period for its fiscal year. This decision is usually made when the nonprofit initially applies for its tax exemption, using IRS Form 1023 or 1024. Some nonprofits, at the time they are formed, establish their fiscal year to coincide with the grant year or fiscal year of their first funder. For instance, the federal government's fiscal year runs from October 1 to September 30. The fiscal year of states and most local government units is July 1 to June 30. Other funders typically have a fiscal year ending either June 30 or December 31, but some have a different fiscal year.

If the organization has a major program or event that ends at a certain time each year, the fiscal year-end might ideally be shortly after it is completed. For instance, an organization whose primary activity is to work with schools during the academic year might choose to end its fiscal year on July 31, when staff will have more time to close the books in preparation for the year-end audit.

Generally Accepted Accounting Principles (GAAP)

GAAP refers to the set of rules used to record transactions and prepare financial statements. The Financial Accounting Standards Board (FASB), a private organization supported by the Financial Accounting Foundation, sets the standards for nonprofits and private sector firms. Since July 1, 2009, these rules are collectively organized into a system called the *Accounting Standards Codification* (ASC). ASC did not change the rules; it merely reorganized them. GAAP is organized into about 90 topics, each of which includes subtopics, sections, and subsections. Exhibit 2.1 indicates three principal Statements of Financial Accounting Standards (SFAS) and the ASC reference.

Generally, non-CPAs need not be familiar with specific passages of ASC, but it is incumbent upon every organization's management and Board of Directors to maintain a level of familiarity with the basic accounting principles sufficient to exercise their fiduciary duties.

Nonprofit leaders who have worked in the sector since before the mid-1990s may be familiar with the term *fund accounting*, which once was the method nonprofits used to account for contributions. Using fund accounting, nonprofits would account for contributions without regard to donor

EXHIBIT 2.1   Accounting Standards

Topic	SFAS Standard	ASC Reference
Accounting for contributions	SFAS 116	ASC Section 958-605-25
Required financial statements	SFAS 117	ASC Subtopic 958-205
Investments in debt and equity		
Securities	SFAS 124	ASC Subtopic 958-320

intent and would record money only when received. In contrast, GAAP now require contributions be grouped into three categories of net assets, depending on a donor's intent.

1. *Permanently restricted.* Assets, such as endowments, land, and artwork, that the donor permanently restricts. In an endowment, the nonprofit must keep intact the corpus of the gift in perpetuity and can spend only investment income.
2. *Temporarily restricted.* Funds temporarily restricted to a particular use, (e.g., a contribution to be used only by a donor-specified program or campaign or only at or after a certain time.
3. *Unrestricted.* Funds free of donor-imposed restriction, such as unrestricted contributions grants.

Exhibit 2.2 shows where to record different types of transactions in a net asset account.

Basis of Accounting

The basis of accounting specifies how to record and report income and expenses. There are three bases of accounting:

1. Cash accounting
2. Accrual accounting
3. Modified cash accounting

The *cash basis* of accounting, similar to making a checkbook entry, records income when cash is received and records expenses when they are paid. The *accrual basis* of accounting, in contrast, records income when *earned* and expenses when *incurred*. For example, using the accrual basis, a foundation award of $25,000 is recorded at the time the grant is announced though the funds are not received until later. Similarly, an expense is recorded when it is obligated in the form of a purchase order or contract, though the bill is not paid until later.

EXHIBIT 2.2   Net Asset Accounts

Transaction	Unrestricted Asset	Temporarily Restricted Asset	Permanently Restricted Asset
An individual sends a check for $2,000 to support the nonprofit's general operations.	X		
An individual donates $1,000 to pay four students to participate in a camp run by the nonprofit.		X	
A local government grants $50,000 for a building campaign.		X	
An individual gives $150,000 to provide scholarships in perpetuity to two students from the interest on the principal.			X
A special events auction raises $30,000 for the nonprofit.	X		
A foundation awards a $10,000 grant for a three-year period.		X	

Cash accounting, though simpler and less expensive than accrual, inaccurately reflects the financial position. Revenues are *understated* by the amount of awarded grants not yet received and by program-service revenues receivable. On the other hand, the available balance in accounts is *overstated* by the amount of purchase orders and contracts for which the nonprofit is obligated. Exhibit 2.3 shows how the available balance changes with cash and accrual accounting. Assume a nonprofit has $100,000 in unrestricted net assets but has billed for grant reimbursements for $50,000 and has $30,000 in outstanding purchase orders and contracts, what is the amount of unrestricted net assets in an accrual versus cash basis accounting system?

EXHIBIT 2.3   Cash vs. Accrual Accounting

	Accrual Basis	Cash Basis
Unrestricted net assets	$100,000	$100,000
Outstanding grant reimbursements	+60,000	
Outstanding purchase orders and contracts	−40,000	
Unrestricted net assets	$120,000	$100,000

Moreover, cash accounting does not comply with GAAP, which means that the auditor cannot give an unqualified opinion that the financial statements comply with GAAP. To comply with GAAP, all but the smallest nonprofits must use accrual accounting.[1] There are two ways to perform accrual accounting:

1. Accrual accounting throughout the fiscal year
2. Cash accounting during the fiscal year but convert to the accrual basis at the end of the fiscal year for financial reporting

Year-round accrual accounting requires more expertise than cash accounting. The other option, to convert from cash to accrual at fiscal year-end, is less expensive but does not afford an accurate financial picture during the fiscal year. A nonprofit with an experienced accounting professional can make the year-end conversion from cash to accrual; however, nonprofits without such expertise must pay a CPA advisor, not their auditor, to make the conversion. Making the conversion from cash to accrual would compromise the independence that an auditor must have to audit the financial statements.

Some nonprofits use a third basis of accounting, the *modified cash basis*, which records some transactions on a cash basis and others on an accrual basis. For example, unpaid bills are recorded on an accrual basis but uncollected income on a cash basis.

The Chart of Accounts

A *chart of accounts* (COA) is a list of uniquely numbered accounts, typically arranged in order of their appearance in the financial statements. Nonprofits are not required to follow a standard chart of accounts. While suitable for large nonprofits, the Unified Chart of Accounts, with over 1,200 accounts, is too complex for medium- and small-sized ones. In designing the accounting system, each nonprofit, regardless of size, should ensure that its COA meets its *particular* reporting needs. Adopting a rigid COA that cannot be easily changed can lead to future reporting problems if the account structure cannot produce reports in a needed format. The COA should be flexible enough to permit changes. For instance, the account codes may need modification to add cost and revenue centers. Most nonprofits need assistance from a CPA to design their COA.

What follows is an explanation of the accounts in a COA. *All* nonprofits must file annually one of three Form 990s with the IRS.[2] Thus, explained below are the accounts in IRS Form 990, which fall into five classifications:[3]

Type of Accounts	Location in IRS Form 990
Asset accounts	Part X
Liability accounts	Part X
Net-Asset accounts	Part X
Revenue accounts	Part VIII
Expense accounts	Part IX

Assets Accounts (Found in Part X of IRS Form 990)

An asset is something owned or pledged, including the accounts described in Exhibit 2.4.

EXHIBIT 2.4   Assets Accounts

Assets Account	Line on 990	Explanation (Line)
Cash	1	Cash held including "petty cash" and cash in non-interest-bearing bank accounts but not cash held in investment accounts
Savings and temporary cash investments	2	Short-term investments readily convertible into cash (e.g., U.S. Treasury Bills, saving accounts, money market funds)[4]
Receivables	3–7	Money owed from pledges and grants (line 3), accounts receivable (line 4), officers and key employees (line 4), other qualified persons (line 6), and notes and loans (line 7)
Inventories for sale or use	8	Materials, goods and supplies held for future use or sale
Prepaid expenses and deferred charges	9	Short- and long-term prepayments of expenses
Land, buildings, and equipment	10a	Cost of land, buildings, and equipment held at the end of the year
Accumulated depreciation	10b	Accumulated depreciation of the assets reported on line 10a
Investments	11–13	Investments in publicly traded securities (line 11), other securities (line 12), other programs (line 13)
Intangible and other assets	14–15	Nonmonetary, nonphysical assets such as mailing lists and copyrights (line 14) and other assets (line 15)

EXHIBIT 2.5 Liabilities Accounts

Liabilities Account	Line on 990	Explanation
Accounts payable and accrued expenses	17	Accounts payable to suppliers, service providers, property managers, and other independent contractors
Grants payable	18	Unpaid portion of grants and awards the nonprofit is committed to pay other organizations or individuals
Deferred revenue	19	Revenue received but not earned (e.g., membership dues collected in advance)
Tax-exempt bond liabilities	20	Obligations to state or local units who have issued debt on behalf of the nonprofit (e.g., tax-exempt bonds and certificates of participation)
Escrow-account liability	21	Amount held in an escrow or custodial account for other individuals or organizations
Payables to officers and key employees	22	Unpaid balances of loans payable to current and former officers, directors, key employees, and trustees
Secured mortgages and notes payable to unrelated third parties	23	Total amount of mortgages and notes payable to financial institutions and other third parties
Unsecured notes and loans payable	24	Unsecured notes and loans payable to financial institutions and other third parties
Other liabilities	25	All other liabilities not reported in lines 17 to 24

Liabilities Accounts (Found in Part X of IRS Form 990)

A liability is an obligation to provide a good or service, including the accounts described in Exhibit 2.5.

Net Assets (Fund Balance) Accounts (Found in Part X of IRS Form 990)

Net assets accounts reflect the difference between assets and liabilities, including those shown in Exhibit 2.6.

Statement of Revenue Accounts (Found in Part VIII of IRS Form 990)

The three revenue accounts are (1) contributions, gifts, and grants, (2) program revenues, and (3) other revenues including those in Exhibit 2.7.

EXHIBIT 2.6   Net Assets Accounts

Net Assets (Fund-Balance) Accounts	Line on 990	Explanation
Unrestricted net assets	27	Assets neither temporarily nor permanently restricted by donors
Temporarily restricted net assets	28	Donors' restrictions may require that funds be spent (1) after a specified date (time restriction), (2) for a specified purpose, or (3) both
Permanently restricted net assets	29	Assets such as land and artworks donated with the stipulation that they be (1) permanently used and preserved for specific a purpose or (2) invested to provide a permanent source of income (e.g., a permanent endowment fund)
Capital stock, trust principal and current	30	Corporations or trusts that do not follow ASC Subtopic 958 enter the balance of capital stock, trust principal, or current funds
Paid-in or capital surplus, or land, building or equipment fund	31	Corporations or trusts that do not follow ASC Subtopic 958, enter the amount paid in excess of par or stated value of stock issued but not yet recorded or cancelled
Retained earnings, endowment, accumulated income or other funds	32	Corporations or trusts that do not follow ASC Subtopic 958, enter the balance of retained earnings

Another revenue source, uncommon among most nonprofits, is *unrelated business income* (UBI), which is income from businesslike activities not substantially related to a nonprofit's tax-exempt purpose. For instance, money gained from renting space in its building to a private firm is considered UBI, as is revenue from advertising in a nonprofit's publications. On the other hand, a church's renting space to another church is not a UBI activity. UBI is subject to state and federal income taxes. Sometimes nonprofits, ignorant of UBI provisions, fail to report UBI. If in doubt about whether revenue is UBI, the nonprofit should consult a CPA adviser. Moreover, a nonprofit can usually offset UBI by reporting related expenses. For example, rent paid on a building can be offset by the renter's pro rata share of utilities, taxes, mortgage, and insurance. The CPA adviser can help to identify offsetting expenses.

EXHIBIT 2.7   Revenue Accounts

Revenue Accounts	Line on 990	Explanation
Contributions, gifts, grants and other similar revenue	1a	Contributions received indirectly from the public received from federate fundraising agencies such as the United Way
	1b	Membership dues and assessments
	1c	Contributions from fundraising events
	1d	Contributions by related organizations
	1e	Government grants
	1f	All other contributions, gifts, grants, and similar amounts not included above
	1g	Noncash contributions (e.g., donated stock and cars)
Program revenues	2a–2e	Enter the five largest sources of program revenues
	2f	Enter all other revenue earned from (1) services delivered, (2) investments, (3) unrelated trade or business activities, (4) sale of inventories
Other revenues	3	Investment income from savings, temporary cash investments, dividend and interest income from stocks and bonds
	4	Investment income from investing tax-exempt-bond proceeds
	5	Royalties received licensing the ongoing use of property to others
	6	Rental income from investment property
	7	Sale of assets other than inventory
	8	Fundraising income from fees, ticket sales, or other events
	9	Gaming income
	10	Gross receipts from sales of inventory items

Statement of Functional-Expense Accounts (Found in Part IX of IRS Form 990)

Expenses use up assets or incur liabilities. Expense accounts record when cash is expended and capital assets are depreciated. There are three functional expense categories. A *program service expense* furthers the nonprofit's tax-exempt purposes and can include unrelated business or trade activities. A *management and general expense* relates to overall operations and management (e.g., the CEO's expenses not related to program services and fundraising). A *fundraising expense* is incurred in soliciting gifts and grants. The functional expense accounts are shown in Exhibit 2.8.

EXHIBIT 2.8   Functional Expense Accounts

Expense Accounts	Line(s) on 990	Explanation
Grants	1–3	Grants to governments, other organizations, individuals in the United States, and individuals outside the United States.
Benefits to members	4	Benefits to members but not to officers and employees, which are reported on lines 8 and 9
Salaries, other compensation, employee benefits	5–10	Compensation to current officers, directors, and key employees (line 5); compensation to disqualified persons who receive an excess benefit from the nonprofit (line 6); employee compensation (line 7); employer's share of pension plans for the year (line 8); other employee benefits such as insurance and health (line 9); employer payroll taxes (line 10)
Professional fundraising fees	11e	Fees for professional fundraising services
Fees for services	11a–g	Management, legal, accounting, and lobbying
Advertising and promotion	12	Advertising, including Internet link sites and signage
Office	13	Supplies, telephones, postage, mailing, equipment rental, bank fees, etc.
Information technology	14	Hardware, software, support services, website design, virus protections, and security services
Royalties	15	Royalties, license fees and other fees that permit the use of intellectual property such a patents and copyrights
Occupancy	16	Use of office space or other facilities, including rent, utilities, insurance, taxes and mortgage interest
Travel	17	Transportation costs (e.g., fares, mileage allowances, meals, lodging)
Payments for travel or entertainment of Federal, state and local officials	18	Report amount for a particular official only if the annual aggregate expense exceeds $1,000 per year
Conferences, conventions and meetings	19	Facility rentals, speakers' fees, printed materials, building rental, etc.
Interest	20	Annual interest expense, excluding interest attributable to rental property
Payments to affiliates	21	Payments to an affiliated state or national organization
Depreciation and amortization	22	Depreciation or amortization of leasehold improvements and intangible assets
Insurance	23	Insurance other than attributable to rental property

Functional Expense Cost Allocation

To prepare the Statement of Functional Expenses, a nonprofit must track its three types of expenses, which include:

1. *Program expenses.* Expenses related to the delivery of program services, such as salaries and fringe benefits for program personnel
2. *Management and general expenses.* Expenses needed to support program activities but not incurred directly in program or fundraising activities (e.g., the salary and wages of the CEO and his or her staff paid for managing the nonprofit)
3. *Fundraising expenses.* Expenses related to a fundraising activity such as postage and paper for a direct-mail funds solicitation

Some expenses are easy to categorize. For instance, the salaries of people who work only on programs are clearly program related; however, other expenses are not so easy to allocate. For instance, the CEO, and his or her staff, may do program- and fundraising-related work in addition to their management and general activities. For such work, they should keep a time log, recording their time on a daily, weekly, or monthly basis. Unlike their private-sector counterparts, they do not need to keep hourly records. The federal government requires that time spent on its grants be recorded at least monthly, which is also the requirement that auditors usually set. The functional expense allocation is reported in the Statement of Activities discussed in Chapter 5, "Evaluate Financial Condition." Exhibit 2.9 is an example of a time log.

To allocate fringe benefits, the percentage spent on pensions, social security, health care, and other fringe benefits is multiplied by the hours worked on program, management, and general and fundraising activities. Allocate utilities, office expenses, rent, or building loan payments base on the relative amount of square footage used by each activity as follows:

Space-Related Expenses	
Rent	$25,000
Utilities	6,000
Janitorial Service	3,000
Office Supplies	2,000
Total	$36,000

EXHIBIT 2.9 Monthly Time-Log Hours Worked

Employee _____

Date _____

Month	Jan.	Feb.	March	April	May	June	July	Aug.	Sept.	Oct.	Nov.	Dec.
Program 1												
Program 2												
Program 3												
Program 4												
Total Program												
Management & General												
Fundraising												
TOTAL HOURS												

Cost Center	Square Footage	Percent of Total Square Footage	Cost Allocation
Administrative Office	300	15%	$5,400
Development Office	200	10%	3,600
Program 1	600	30%	10,800
Program 2	400	20%	7,200
Program 3	500	25%	9,000
Total	2,000	100%	$36,000

Single- and Double-Entry Accounting

There are two types of accounting:

1. Single-entry accounting
2. Double-entry accounting

Similar to keeping a checkbook, single-entry accounting records only one-half of a transaction as either an expense or income. Dating back to the Roman Empire, the double-entry accounting system was first described by Luca Pacioli, the "father of accounting," in his mathematics textbook. Instead of using additions (+) and subtraction (−) symbols, a transaction uses the symbol DR (Debit) or CR (Credit). In double-entry accounting, every financial transaction affects the accounts in two ways. A debit value is recorded on the left side of a ledger for asset and expense transactions. A credit value is recorded on the right side of a ledger, for liability, gain and equity transactions. Keeping debits and credits in separate columns allows each to be recorded and totaled independently. The cardinal accounting rule is: *Debits must always equal total credits.*

Capitalization and Depreciation

GAAP permits prorating the cost of a capital asset over its estimated useful life. This accounting method, known as *capitalization*, permits the organization to spread out expenses over their useful life. Capital assets include property (land), plant (buildings), and equipment. To be considered a capital asset, the item must have a relatively high value and long life. The nonprofit's board establishes these limits. The federal government requires that nonprofits capitalize projects with a life of one year or longer and a value over $5,000. Most nonprofits, however, set a lower limit of typically $500.

An item with a value of less than $500, or a life of less than one year, is expensed, rather than capitalized. A capitalized asset is depreciated over its useful life in one of several ways. The most common, the straight-line method, assumes the asset will depreciate equally over its life. For example, a nonprofit may buy a vehicle for $22,000 with an expected life of five years and resale value of $2,000. The annual depreciation would be $4,000:

Purchase price	$22,000
Less resale value	−2,000
Divided by five-year useful life:	$20,000/5
Annual depreciation expense:	$ 4,000

The straight-line depreciation method is not always appropriate because some assets deteriorate more quickly in their later years of use. For instance, aging buildings or pieces of equipment require more maintenance in their latter years. In such cases, the *accelerated depreciation method* charges more depreciation expense in the early years but less in the later ones.

Federal Grant Indirect Cost Allocation

If a nonprofit receives more than $500,000 in federal grants, the auditor must conduct the audit in accordance with Office of Management and Budget (OMB) Circular A-133. Nonprofits have the option of charging federal grants for the indirect services that the nonprofit provides to grants. To be eligible to charge a federal agency for indirect expenses, nonprofits must allocate expenses in accordance with OMB Circular A-122, *Cost Principles for Nonprofit Organizations.* The federal government approves a *cost allocation plan* (CAP) that sets an indirect cost rate (percentage) that the nonprofit can charge against a grant. The CAP allocates indirect costs to each program based on federally approved criteria, such as those shown in Exhibit 2.10.

The federal agency from which the nonprofit receives the most grant funds approves a nonprofit's CAP.

EXHIBIT 2.10   A-133 Allocation Criteria

Indirect Costs	Allocation Basis per Program
Human Resources	Number of employees
Rental of Office Space	Square footage occupied
Printing	Number of copies made
Motor Pool	Miles driven or days used

EXHIBIT 2.11   Accounting Software Capabilities

Function

Allocate indirect costs
Allocate budgets by program
Prepare financial statements
Integrate accounting with fundraising/membership applications
Account for grants with different fiscal years
Account for grants that last longer than 12 months
Convert from cash to accrual accounting at the fiscal year-end

Accounting and Fundraising Software

There are three types of software:

1. Accounting software
2. Fundraising software
3. Combined accounting and fundraising software

Among the commonly used accounting software packages are Quick-Books for Nonprofits, QuickBooks Pro, Peachtree, Sage MIP Fund Accounting, Kinters FundWare, Blackbaud, and Financial Edge.[5] The accounting software should be able to perform the functions shown in Exhibit 2.11.

The fundraising software should be able to perform the functions shown in Exhibit 2.12.

A nonprofit that does considerable fundraising is more likely to use a combined accounting and fundraising software package.

To choose a software package, some nonprofits form a selection committee typically comprised of key stakeholders, including the CFO and the development director. A CPA adviser, not the auditor, can also assist with the selection process. The committee conducts a *needs assessment*, specifying

EXHIBIT 2.12   Fundraising Software Capabilities

Function

Track donors' donations and pledges
Maintain donor-information file (e.g., address, attributes, relationships)
Track fundraising activities of particular campaigns and appeals
Print acknowledgments, invitations, announcements, and solicitations
Generate queries for mailings and reports
Generate donor reports that track restrictions

the functions the software must perform. In conducting this assessment, the committee should ask fellow nonprofits about their experiences using the software under consideration. The website, www.techsoup.org/, an excellent resource, offers free and reduced-price software. In selecting the package, the committee should weigh not only the initial purchase price but also the future *operating costs*. Too often overlooked are the future costs of maintaining, upgrading, and converting software.

Accounting for Transactions

The accounting system records financial transactions in three documents:

1. Source documents
2. Journals: books of original entry
3. Ledgers: books of final entry

The accounting records provide an *audit trail,* which allows each accounting transaction to be traced back to its source document. The seven steps of the accounting cycle are now discussed in the following sections.

Step 1   Receive and File Source Documents

The accounting cycle begins with the submission of a *source document,* such as a bill, invoice, receipt, deposit slip, purchase order, check or receiving report. Local and state laws dictate how long to retain source documents.

Step 2   Record in Journals: Books of Original Entry

The information in source documents is entered (posted) into a *journal.* This step is known as making a *journal entry.* A journal is a book of original entry since it is the first record of a transaction. A journal chronologically lists financial transactions. Organizations with a high volume of transactions usually post entries daily. Organizations with fewer transactions may post entries weekly or even monthly if the accounting system is manual. A journal entry includes:

- The year, month, and day of the transaction
- The source document number (e.g., the check number)
- An explanation of the transaction
- The account(s) debited and by what amount
- The account(s) credited and by what amount

The debited and credited accounts are also noted on the source document to provide a reference should the transaction need to be checked. The most common journals are:

- *Cash disbursements journal*
- *Cash receipts journal*
- *Accounts receivable journal.* Each funder, customer, or contractor who owes money
- *Accounts payable journal.* A list of the bills and invoices owed to vendors
- *General journal.* A list of financial transactions not included in the other journals

Exhibit 2.13 is an example of a journal.

Step 3   Post Journal Entries to Ledgers: Books of Final Entry

To prepare the monthly and year-end financial reports, the journal entries are summarized in a *ledger*, which lists all transactions for each account. The ledger is a collection of individual accounts. A manual accounting system has a separate ledger page for each account. An automated system codes transactions by account, eliminating the need for separate ledger pages. The principal ledger, the *general ledger*, has "control accounts" that summarize the more detailed accounts posted to subsidiary ledgers. The most common subsidiary ledgers are:

- *Payable ledger.* Balances for each person or business owed money
- *Receivables ledger.* Balances owed by each individual or business
- *Payroll ledger.* Payroll information on each employee
- *Operating ledgers.* Detailed accounting for revenues (revenue ledger) and expenses (expenses ledger)
- *Property records ledger.* Value of land, buildings, and equipment

The timing of a journal entry depends on whether the accounting system is automated or manual. A manual system normally posts transactions at month-end in order to prepare the interim monthly financial report. Posting occurs only once because more frequent posting is too time-consuming. In contrast, an automated accounting system posts transactions daily.

Each ledger account on the balance sheet starts with the prior accounting period's balance. The balance at the end of the next accounting period is the new balance. Exhibit 2.14 is a sample general ledger.

EXHIBIT 2.13 Sample Journal

Date	Description of Entry	Account Names and Numbers	Document Number	Debit	Credit
8/8/2009	Office Supplies	Office Supply Expense 6300	July Office Supplies	$150	
		Accounts Payable 2100			$150
8/10/2009	First Nat'l Bank Loan	Cash 1000	Loan - FNB #1	$2,000	
		Notes Payable 2200			$2,000
8/15/2009	July Telephone Bill	Accounts Payable 2100	7/31/2009 Telephone Bill	$200	
		Cash 1000			$200
8/20/2009	City of Smithville Grant	Grants Receivable 1500	Grant # 35	10,000	
		Grants from Local Govts 4050			10,000
8/25/2009	August Electric Charges	Utilities Expense 6200	8/09 Electric Due 9/09	$125	
		Accounts Payable 2100			$125
8/31/2009	August Payroll	Salaries 6100	Payroll 8/2010	$3,000	
		Payroll Taxes 6150		$375	
		Cash 1000			$3,375

EXHIBIT 2.14 Sample General Ledger

Account:	Cash	Account Number:		1000
Date	Description of Entry	Debit	Credit	Balance
8/1/2009	Beginning Balance			$5,000
8/10/2009	First Nat'l Bank Loan	$2,000		$7,000
8/15/2009	July Telephone Bill		$200	$6,800
8/31/2009	August Payroll		$3,375	$3,425

Account:	Grants Receivable	Account Number:		1500
Date	Description of Entry	Debit	Credit	Balance
8/1/2009	Beginning Balance			$2,500
8/20/2009	City of Smithville Grant	$10,000		$12,500

Account:	Accounts Payable	Account Number:		2100
Date	Description of Entry	Debit	Credit	Balance
8/1/2009	Beginning Balance			$350
8/8/2009	Office Supplies		$150	$500
8/15/2009	July Telephone Bill	$200		$300
8/25/2009	August Electric Charges		$125	$425

Account:	Notes Payable	Account Number:		2200
Date	Description of Entry	Debit	Credit	Balance
8/1/2009	Beginning Balance			$6,000
8/15/2009	August Loan Payment		$2,000	$4,000

Account:	Grants from Local Govts	Account Number:		4050
Date	Description of Entry	Debit	Credit	Balance
8/5/2009	Community Growth Foundation		$4,500	
8/17/2009	Urban Community Foundation		$6,350	$10,850

Account:	Salaries	Account Number:		6100
Date	Description of Entry	Debit	Credit	Balance
8/30/2009	Payroll	$3,375		$3,375

Step 4   Prepare the Monthly Year-to-Date Trial Balance

After completing the journal entries and ledger postings, the bookkeeper or a CPA adviser prepares at month-end a *trial balance* in order to check the accuracy of the entries and prepare the monthly report. The trial balance lists the general ledger accounts with their debit balances in the left-hand column and credit balances in the right-hand column. Accounts are listed in their order in the chart of accounts. If manual bookkeeping is used, an *unadjusted trial balance* is prepared to determine whether the books are in balance. If in balance, the debit column will equal the credit column (debits equal credits). If not in balance, more work is needed to determine the cause of the error. Potential errors could be a one-sided entry (only a debit or credit) or a posting mistake for an account receivable. If an accounting software package is used, the books will always be in balance. Then, the trial balance is reviewed for the accuracy and completeness of the account balances.

Step 5   Prepare Adjusting Entries

Accrual basis accounting requires accounting for events that occur in different accounting periods. For example, a nonprofit is billed for a service in the last week of the accounting period, but the invoice is not received until after the month ends. The transaction must then be recorded as both an expense and a fee payable, so a journal entry must be made. Exhibit 2.15 is a sample adjusted trial balance.

EXHIBIT 2.15   Sample Trial Balance

Account	Debit	Credit
Cash	$3,425	
Accounts Receivable	$1,000	
Grants and Contributions Receivable	$12,500	
Equipment	$2,000	
Accumulated Depreciation		$1,000
Accounts Payable		$425
Loans and Notes Payable		$4,000
Net Assets		$6,500
Foundation Grants		$10,850
Salaries	$3,375	
Payroll Taxes	$175	
Occupancy Expense	$250	
Interest Expense	$50	
	$22,775	$22,775

Step 6   Prepare the Monthly Financial Statements

The revenue and expense account balances from the adjusted trial balance are used to prepare four statements:

1. The statement of financial position
2. The statement of activities
3. The statement of cash flows
4. The statement of functional expenses

In practice, though, most nonprofits do not prepare a monthly statement of cash flows. As stated earlier, most nonprofits use a cash basis during the year, converting to accrual at year-end. Moreover, most nonprofits that use the accrual basis do not prepare the statement because time-consuming manual adjustments are required.

Step 7   Make Year-End Closing Entries

To maintain the auditor's independence, the nonprofit adjusts accounts, closing revenue and expense accounts to net assets (equity), debiting the revenue accounts for the account balance and crediting the expense accounts for the account balance.

For Further Reading

Jackson, Peggy. *Sarbanes-Oxley for Nonprofits*. Hoboken, NJ: John Wiley & Sons. 2005. Discussion of SOX provisions that do and should apply to nonprofits.

McLaughlin, Thomas. *Streetsmart Financial Basics for Nonprofit Managers* 2nd ed. Hoboken, NJ: John Wiley & Sons, 2002. A very readable, conversational introduction to accounting and budgeting.

Ruegg, Debra, and Lisa Venkatrathnam. *Bookkeeping Basics*. St. Paul, MN: Fieldstone Alliance, 2007. Oriented to a basic accounting level for bookkeepers, nicely explains accounting basics, financial statements, and basic internal controls.

Sumariwalla, Russy, and Wilson Lewis. *Unified Financial Reporting System of Not-for-Profit Organizations*, 2nd ed. San Francisco: Jossey-Bass, 2008. Recommends a unified chart of accounts that can be used to prepare IRS Form 990 and funder reports to the United Way, governments, and foundations.

Zeitlow, John, Jo Ann Hankin, and Alan Seider. *Financial Management for Nonprofits*. Hoboken, NJ: John Wiley & Sons, 2007. Excellent overview, including discussions of accounting basics, financial statements, cash budgeting, capital budgeting, cash management, investments, and risk management. Includes suggested report forms.

CHAPTER 3

Create the Internal Control System

In 1992, the Committee of Sponsoring Organizations (COSO), commonly known as the Treadway Commission, issued a report, *Internal Control—Integrated Framework*, which established a widely accepted definition of internal control:

> *Internal control is a process, affected by an entity's board of directors, management and other personnel that provides reasonable assurance regarding the achievement of objectives with regard to the effectiveness and efficiency of operation, reliability of financial reporting, and compliance with applicable laws and regulations.*[1]

The COSO system is designed to provide reasonable assurance regarding:

- The effectiveness and efficiency of operations
- The reliability of financial reporting
- Compliance with applicable laws and regulations

The COSO approach has five features:

1. A control environment
2. An assessment of the likely occurrence and severity of each type of risk
3. Internal controls
4. An information/communication system
5. An effectiveness monitoring system

In conducting an audit, generally accepted auditing standards (GAAS) do not require that the auditor specifically look for internal control deficiencies, but the auditor must report any internal control weakness found in the course of the audit. Statement on Auditing Standards (SAS) No. 115, *Communicating Internal Control Related Matters in an Audit*, requires the auditor to communicate, in writing, to management and those charged with governance significant deficiencies and material weaknesses identified in the audit. The auditor may find three types of deficiencies:

1. A *control deficiency* exists when the design or operation of a control does not allow management or employees, in the normal course of performing their assigned functions, to prevent or detect misstatements on a timely basis.
2. A *significant deficiency*, or combination of control deficiencies, that adversely affects the nonprofit's ability to initiate, authorize, record, process, or report financial data reliably in accordance with GAAP such that *more than a remote likelihood* of a misstatement in financial statements exists.
3. A *material weakness* is a significant deficiency, or combination of significant deficiencies, that results in more than a remote likelihood that a material misstatement of the financial statements will not be prevented or detected.

The auditor considers both the likelihood and magnitude of misstatement in the financial statements. To comply with SAS No. 112, the auditor needs to be knowledgeable about the COSO framework.[2]

Create a Control Environment

Surprisingly, an unsuspected, highly trusted employee, with no hint of past impropriety, is most likely to commit a fraudulent act.[3] If not too greedy, the perpetrator can continue his or her larcenous behaviors for a long, even indefinite period. Thus, the control environment is the cornerstone for preventing and detecting illegal acts. The Board, Chief Executive, and the management team set the tone. They must "walk the walk," not just "talk the talk." The organization must maintain an unwavering commitment to the highest ethical standards. Employees should be competent and committed to service excellence. The Board should be independent of management and actively engage in policymaking. Finally, truthful and open communication, both written and oral, should flow up, down, and across organizational boundaries. Exhibit 3.1 describes the features and recommended practices of a top-notch control environment.

Such a control environment is more likely to detect and limit fraud, abuse, and questionable accounting and auditing practices. SAS No. 99, *Consideration of Fraud in a Financial Statement Audit*, defines fraud as "An intentional act that results in material misstatement in the financial statements."

EXHIBIT 3.1   Control Environment List

Feature	Recommended Practice
Integrity and Ethics	Adopt codes of conduct regarding conflicts of interest and expected ethical behavior.
Commitment to Competence	Adopt job descriptions that define tasks.
	Base the job description on a job analysis.
	Conduct background checks on job applicants under consideration for sensitive positions.
	Conduct exit interviews with persons fired for disciplinary reasons.
	Give progressive discipline to try to rehabilitate poor performers.
	Give ongoing performance feedback, not just an annual performance review.
Board of Directors	Keep the Board independent from management.
	Provide the Board timely and sufficient information.
Management Style	Meet frequently with the management team.
	Be fiscally conservative.
	Manage by "walking around."
Organizational Structure	Structure the organization to ensure the ready flow of information.
	Hire managers with the needed knowledge and experience.

The difference between an error (e.g., sloppy accounting) and fraud is a matter of *intent*. An error is unintentional; fraud is intentional. Examples of types of fraud are shown in Exhibit 3.2.

Persons commit fraud when they are in the fraud triangle, which includes (1) opportunity, (2) financial pressure, and (3) rationalization, as shown in Exhibit 3.3.

Opportunities can include: (1) weak internal accounting controls, (2) lack of separation of duties, and (3) absence of an external audit. Financial pressures can result from (1) addictions (e.g., drugs, gambling, shopping, and sex), (2) outstanding loans, (3) a marital affair, and (4) declining nonprofit revenues (e.g., lower giving). Persons can then find almost any excuse to rationalize their action, including

- "They unfairly passed me over for a promotion."
- "I am just not appreciated."
- "Person X is getting more paid more than I. It's just not fair."
- "My boss is unfair to me."
- "I'll pay it back as soon as I can."

EXHIBIT 3.2   Types of Fraud

Fraud	Examples
Lapping	Steal money by crediting a payment by customer A only after customer B makes a payment.
Steal Receipts	Not credit receipts to their proper account.
Steal Duplicate Payments	Steal a duplicate payment by not giving the customer a refund.
Inventory Theft	Steal supplies and equipment from motor vehicle centers and warehouses.
Use Assets for Personal Purpose	Use automobiles, computers, phones, and other equipment for personal use.
Vendor Payment	Overpay vendors for goods not received and for inferior goods.
	Receive a *kickback* from a vendor that may be cash, subsequent employment, and a gift.
Payroll	Pay a terminated, "ghost" employee for work not performed.
	Pay for inflated work hours and overtime not worked. Steal paychecks and divert payroll withholdings.
Travel Reimbursement	Overcharge for travel expenses.
Health Claims	Overpay a health care provider.
Retirement Benefits	Overfund pension benefits, use pension fund, and over withhold pension payments.

EXHIBIT 3.3   The Fraud Triangle

Assess Risks

The next step is to identify the risks, in and outside the organization, that threaten the organization as shown in Exhibit 3.4.

Of these risks, depending too much on a key individual stands out. Often, the person who commits fraud is the least expected. He or she often has a long work history with the nonprofit, allowing the person to earn trust and find flaws in the internal control system. The perpetrator works long hours and is reluctant to take a vacation or share accounting duties. Indeed, fraud perpetrators are often discovered when circumstances (e.g., an illness or accident) force them to be away from their work.

To avoid overlooking significant risks, estimate the significance of each risk and assess the likelihood of it occurring.

Create Controls

To manage risks, establish controls over:

- Staffing
- Accounting
- Information management
- Travel
- Physical assets

Staffing Controls

Risk can occur after a staffing change and when unclear lines of authority cause organizational confusion. Exhibit 3.5 is a list of ways to mitigate staffing risks.

EXHIBIT 3.4   Internal Control Risks

Type of Risk	Description
External Risks	New legislation or regulation
	Economic downturn
	Natural disaster
	Competition
	Changing customer needs
Internal Risks	Changed operating environment
	Change in management responsibilities
	Overdependence on key individual(s)
	New or revamped information systems
	Unclear job responsibilities

EXHIBIT 3.5   Staffing Controls List

Risk	Remedial Action
Staffing Changes	Hire qualified replacements.
	Provide the training and continuing education to perform tasks well.
	Adopt a policies and procedures manual.
Organizational Confusion	Maintain a current organizational chart.
	Establish clear lines of authority for each transaction.
	Eliminate duplicative functions.
	Separate accounting functions.

Accounting Controls

The most serious risk of losing accounting control occurs when the same person performs overlapping accounting functions. For instance, the same person should not:

- Approve a purchase order
- Make the purchase
- Receive the vendor invoice
- Maintain accounts payable records

Large organizations, with several accounting employees, have no problem separating accounting duties. However, separation is challenging in a small nonprofit with only one or two employees. In such a nonprofit, a Board member may be called on to separate duties. Exhibits 3.6 through 3.8 show how separate cash management, payroll disbursement, and non-payroll disbursement in organizations with one or two employees and including a Board member.

Though separation of duties most often can prevent fraud, it is less effective stopping *collusion*, which occurs when *two* or more persons conspire to steal assets.

Information Technology (IT) Controls

Weak controls over the information management system pose these risks:

- Improper input of data
- Lost data
- Unauthorized persons gaining access to the IT facility

A. **Duties**
1. Bank notifies board member of unusual items, like insufficient funds.
2. Make wire transfers.
3. Review bank accounts for proper collateralization.
4. Receive unopened bank statement.
5. Reconcile bank statements monthly:
    (a) Deposits
        (i) Compare dates and amounts of daily deposits on the bank statement with the cash receipts journal.
        (ii) Examine bank transfers to determine if both sides of the transaction were recorded on the books.
    (b) Disbursements
        (i) Account for the sequence of check numbers including voided checks.
        (ii) Examine cancelled checks for authorized signatures, irregular endorsements and alterations.
B. **Separation of Duties**
1. If one position:
    (a) Staff member performs duties 2 & 5 above.
    (b) Board member performs duties 1, 3, & 4 above.
2. If two positions:
    (a) CEO performs duties 2 & 3 above.
    (b) Other staff member performs duties 5 above.
    (c) Board member performs duties 1 & 4 above.

EXHIBIT 3.6   Separation of Cash Management Duties

A. **Duties**
1. Hire personnel setting salary rates and working hours.
2. Prepare personnel file from authorization papers and updates.
3. Review and approve (by signature) time sheets and leave records.
4. Prepare checks from authorized salary and time sheets and review work.
5. Review payroll for reasonableness and sign checks for first signature.
6. Review payroll and sign checks for second signature.
7. Distribute checks.
B. **Separation of Duties**
1. If one position:
    (a) Staff member performs duties 2, 3, 4, & 5 above.
    (b) Board member performs duties 1, 6, & 7 above.
2. If two positions:
    (a) CEO performs duties 3, 5, & 7 above.
    (b) Other staff member performs duties 2 & 4 above.
    (c) Board member performs duties 1 & 6 above.

EXHIBIT 3.7   Separation Payroll Disbursement Duties

A. **Duties**
   1. Initiate purchase.
   2. Type purchase order (at least original and one copy).
   3. Review and approve purchase order by signing preaudit certification.
   4. Sign off on copy of purchase order for receipt of goods after comparing purchase order to goods received.
   5. Match invoice to copy of purchase order and compare goods received to invoice (mathematically check footings).
   6. Prepare and review check.
   7. Review documentation and sign check.
   8. Present purchase order, receipt report, invoice, check, addressed and stamped envelope for second signature.
   9. Review supporting documentation, sign check, mail check to vendor, and return supporting documentation to accounting clerk.

B. **Separation of Duties**
   1. If one position:
      (a) Staff member performs duties 1, 2, 4, 5, 6, 7, & 8 above.
      (b) Board member performs duties 3 & 9 above.
   2. If two positions:
      (a) CEO performs duties 1, 3, 7, & 8 above.
      (b) Other staff member performs duties 2, 4, 5, & 6 above.
      (c) Board member performs duty 9 above.

EXHIBIT 3.8   Separation of Non-Payroll Disbursement Duties

- Unauthorized access to sensitive employee and customer information
- Funds and personal information stolen by a hacker

Exhibit 3.9 is a list of IT controls over: (1) data input, (2) data recovery, (3) access to the IT facility, and (4) access to employee records.

IT personnel should regularly back up data, storing it at a secure, remote location. Ensure computers and the software against damage or loss.

Travel Expense Controls

News media accounts abound and describe in vivid detail:

- Unjustifiably high expenses
- Trips ("junkets") to exotic location without justification
- Trips paid for by vendors to gain favor

Data Input Controls
☐ Assign separate access codes to each user.
☐ Keep a transaction data log, including the originating terminal, message ID, transaction type, time of day when the transaction was logged, and a copy of the transaction record.
☐ Establish a procedure to identify and reprocess rejected data.
☐ Establish a procedure to verify that the check and voucher numbers match.
☐ Require the initiating department to maintain control over turn-around transmittal documents, record counts, and dollar totals.
☐ Retain source documents long enough to permit identification with output records if needed.

Data Recovery Controls
☐ Follow a Board-adopted disaster recovery plan.
☐ Maintain back up files to be able to reconstruct records.
☐ Establish a procedure for retaining/copying master files and reconstructing damaged or destroyed files.
☐ Establish a procedures to use another data center during an emergency situation.

Separate the Duties of:
☐ Data input
☐ Data processing
☐ Data review

Facility Access Controls
☐ Restrict physical access to the computer center.
☐ Restrict physical access to online terminals.

Employee Record Controls
☐ Assign every user a unique user ID password.
☐ Periodically change the user password.
☐ Keep user passwords secret from other users.

Upon Termination of an Employee
☐ Deny access to computer, data, programs, etc.
☐ Inform other employees of the employee's termination.
☐ Delete the employee's user ID and password from the system.

EXHIBIT 3.9   IT Controls List

The Board should thus adopt a travel reimbursement policy, clearly spelling out the procedures for making a travel request, asking for a travel advance, and travel reimbursement as shown in Exhibit 3.10.

Physical Assets Controls

Physical assets must be safeguarded from theft and misuse. An inventory of assets is taken at least annually and an asset custodian is responsible for the custody and safekeeping of assets. Chapter 10, "Manage Capital Assets and the Inventory," discusses in detail how to safeguard assets.

Create an Information/Communication System

An effective communication system is the *most important* feature of the COSO system because, surprisingly, about 50 percent of all fraud cases are discovered by tips from employees.[4] Each employee should look out for suspicious behavior by a fellow employee such as:

- Living beyond his or her means and buying extravagant items (e.g., a fancy car, costly travel, extensive clothes, etc.)
- Having a costly addiction (e.g., gambling, shopping, drugs)
- Never taking a vacation

The person with his or her nose always to grindstone may simply be a model employee. However, sometimes it is because a person cannot afford to be absent lest his or her larcenous scheme be detected. Ensure that all tips are kept *confidential*. Exhibit 3.11 is a list of ways to create an effective communication system.

Monitor Effectiveness

The last step in the COSO internal control system is to evaluate its effectiveness by analyzing the:

- Interim and year-end financial reports
- Auditor's management letter
- Internal control and compliance report
- Budgeted versus actual revenue and expense report

Travel Policy
☐ Establish a policy regarding how to (1) make a travel request, (2) receive a travel advance, and (3) receive reimbursement for expenses (e.g., mileage, food, lodging, airfare, ground transportation).

Travel Advance Procedures
☐ Separate the duties of:
   ☐ Approving the travel advance
   ☐ Maintaining the records on the advance
☐ Set a ceiling on the amount of the advance.
☐ When an advance is given, create a record in a subsidiary receivables ledger.
☐ Ensure the employee submits original receipts that cover the amount of the advance.

Travel Expense Reimbursement Procedures
☐ Authorize a person to approve travel reimbursements.
☐ Only reimburse preapproved travel.

EXHIBIT 3.10   Travel Expense Control List

The auditor's *management letter* is especially telling. As discussed in detail in Chapter 4, "Manage the Audit," the management letter details the weaknesses found in internal controls and management practices found during the course of auditing the financial statements. The auditor recommends how to control these weaknesses and takes note in the ensuing audit if the nonprofit has not taken remedial action.

Information System Controls
☐ Enforce a Board-adopted policy protecting whistleblowers from retaliation.
☐ Establish a process for employees and the public to report suspected improprieties.
☐ Ensure the confidentially of all tips.
☐ Implement employees' and customers' suggestions to improve information flow.
☐ Ensure that information is timely and accurate.

EXHIBIT 3.11   Communication Network List

For Further Reading

Nonprofit Risk Management Center. *Healthy Nonprofits: Conserving Scarce Resources through Effective Internal Controls*. Washington, DC, 1996. Extremely comprehensive explanation of safeguarding cash, managing payroll, and employment-related expenses and accounting for contributions.

CHAPTER 4

Manage the Audit

A nonprofit can have three types of audits: internal, performance and financial. Some larger nonprofits have an in-house auditor who conducts *internal audits* to evaluate the efficacy of internal controls and to evaluate program' performance. A *performance* or *operational* audit evaluates the effectiveness of a program or programs. In the third and most common type, the *financial audit,* a certified public accountant (CPA) auditor renders an opinion as to whether the financial statements adhere to generally accepted accounting principles (GAAP). A financial audit is recommended but not required *unless*:

- A funding agency requires it as a condition of being awarded funds.
- A nonprofit receives over $500,000 in federal or state funds in a fiscal year. In which case, the nonprofit must undergo an A-133 audit, discussed later in more detail.
- A bank requires it due to its loan covenants.

If not required, a nonprofit should weigh the benefits of a financial audit. The cost is the expense of the audit itself, which can be quite burdensome to a nonprofit with a small budget. The benefits include:

- Increased donors' confidence in the nonprofit's financial management system
- Compliance with accounting standards
- Stronger internal controls because the auditor is required to report any significant deficiencies if observed in the course of the audit

In practice, 67 percent of nonprofits had a financial audit conducted in 2004 and 2005. Ninety-one percent with annual expenses over $500,000 had an audit, but only 43 percent with annual expenses less than $100,000 had an audit.[1,2] Small nonprofits are less apt to have an audit because of its cost. Better Business Bureau (BBB) Wise Giving Allowance, a consumer interest group, recommends a nonprofit with annual gross income exceeding $250,000 should have an audit.[3]

A nonprofit that cannot afford an audit has four less expensive but less thorough options:

1. *Member review.* A Board member with an accounting/auditing/finance background voluntarily reviews accounting procedures, records, and/or or selected areas of concern.
2. *Compilation.* The CPA compiles the financial information recorded by the nonprofit into a set of financial statements but does not verify balances or review internal controls. Generally, a compilation costs about one-half the cost of an audit.
3. *Independent review.* More extensive than a compilation, but less complete than an audit, the CPA renders no opinion on the financial statements but issues a letter stating whether a nonprofit complies with GAAP. Generally, a review costs about two-thirds the cost of an audit.
4. *An agreed-upon procedure(s).* The CPA evaluates an accounting procedure or procedures (e.g., payroll, bank statement reconciliation, handling cash receipts). The cost depends on the procedure or procedures evaluated.

The financial audit is unquestionably the most important report for evaluating fiscal condition. A snapshot of the financial condition as of the last day of the fiscal year, the audit process has three steps that are discussed in the following sections:

1. Designate the audit coordinator
2. Select the auditor
3. Conduct the audit

Designate the Audit Coordinator

The first step is to designate an audit coordinator, usually the CFO, to manage the audit process. If the nonprofit is large enough, it should form an *audit committee* to assist with the process. The audit committee can be a subset of Board members, community members with accounting expertise, or a combination of both. Using an audit committee has shown to reduce financial reporting problems.[4] Twenty percent of nonprofits, mostly large-sized, formed an audit committee.[5] About 50 percent of them have expenditures over $10 million; only 15 percent of them have expenditures less than $100,000. The Sarbanes-Oxley Act (SOX), enacted by Congress to correct the abuses shown by the Enron scandal, requires that private sector firms form an audit committee. The SOX provisions, shown in Exhibit 4.1, are useful guide to nonprofits wishing to form an audit committee.

EXHIBIT 4.1   Audit Committee List

SOX Provisions

At least one financial expert (e.g., a CPA) must be on the committee.

Prohibit the audit firm from providing non-\audit services that conflict with the auditing function, including bookkeeping, design, or implementation of financial information systems, actuarial services, human resource functions, investment advising and legal services related to the audit.

Prohibit the audit firm from conducting the audit if the nonprofit's CEO or CFO was employed by the firm in the previous year.

Select the audit firm and oversee its operations.

Require the audit firm to report directly to the committee, not to the CEO.

Prohibit the audit committee from accepting any compensation from the audit firm.

Institute a process to encourage employees to report unethical accounting practices.

The audit committee should not include management.[6] The committee members should be able to read and interpret financial statements. After reviewing the financial statements with the auditor, the committee reports their status to the full Board, highlighting significant findings and recommendations and drafts a response to the management letter if one was submitted.

Select the Auditor

As with any professional service, the best way to select an auditor is with a *request for proposals* (RFP). To find the best firm, you should cast the net widely, seeking as many qualified firms as possible. Use a ranking system to weigh firms' technical qualifications. Do not select the auditor based on price. Though price is important, paramount is whether an auditor has extensive nonprofit audit experience. Such experience is essential because nonprofit auditing differs from governmental and commercial auditing as follows:

- Nonprofits follow different accounting standards than do firms and governments.
- Nonprofits often must allocate indirect costs.
- All but very small nonprofits must prepare IRS Form 990.
- Nonprofits must comply with unique federal, state, and local government reporting requirements.

Exhibit 4.2 lists provisions to include in an RFP with reference to:

- The audit firm's qualifications
- The auditor's scope of work

EXHIBIT 4.2   Audit Request for Proposal (RFP) List

RFP Provision

Audit Firm's Qualifications
Identify the partner, manager, and accountant in-charge to be assigned to the audit.
The nonprofit's audit coordinator reserves the right to approve persons that the
    audit firm would like to substitute for those identified in the RFP response.
At least one partner or principal will supervise the work.
Provide the names of nonprofits who can be contacted about their experience with
    the firm's work.

Scope of Work: (The Auditor Shall Prepare for the Nonprofit)
Financial statements audited in accordance with GAAS
Tax filings for IRS Form 990
An opinion on the financial statements

The Work Schedule
The auditor will complete the audit in a timely fashion (e.g., 60–90 days).
The auditor will hold an exit interview with the CEO and CFO before the financial
    report is presented to the Board.

Services the Nonprofit Will Provide to the Auditor
Books closed in a timely fashion
A reconciliation of the monthly bank accounts
Schedules of assets, liabilities, investments, and accrued interest
The insurance in force
Copies of the budget, budget amendments, grant agreements, contracts, leases,
    and minutes with fiscal significance
Confirmation forms and letters authorizing the auditor to obtain financial
    information from organizations with whom the nonprofit conducted business
Clerical services, such as preparing and mailing conformation forms and document
    reproduction
Authorization to communicate with the previous auditor and with agency
    personnel to explain procedures or resolve problems
Copies of Board and committee minutes
Copies of grant and contract awards and proposals

- The work schedule
- The services the nonprofit provides the auditor

The CPA, not the nonprofit, usually prepares the IRS Form 990 because
the firm has software that expedites the process. The fee can be part of the
audit fee or a separate bill. The price for preparing IRS Form 990 varies with
(1) the number of schedules to complete and (2) how much time the auditor
must spend with the client clarifying data. Exhibit 4.3 is a sample Audit RFP

The Board of Directors of [Name of Nonprofit] invites qualified independent auditors with sufficient non-profit accounting and auditing experience to submit a proposal.

Contract Period

The nonprofit will continue the relationship with the auditor for no less than three years based on an annual negotiation after the completion of the first year contract. However, the nonprofit reserves the right to request proposals at any time following the first year of this contract.

Requirements

The audit will encompass a financial and compliance examination of the financial statements, supplementary information and compliance reports. The audit must be conducted in accordance with generally accepted auditing standards; Government Auditing Standards, issued by the Comptroller General of the United States; the Single Audit Act Amendments of 1996; Office of Management and Budget Circular No. A-133, Audit of States, Local Governments, and Non-Profit Organizations including revisions published in Federal Register June 27, 2003; and any other applicable procedures for the audit of a nonprofit's financial statements prepared in accordance with GAAP.

The independent auditor will be ultimately responsible for the preparation, typing, proofing, printing, and copying of the financial statements, supplementary information and compliance reports. The auditor will submit a draft of the financial statements for review by [Name of Nonprofit]'s CFO in time to allow completion of the financial statements no later than [Date].

At a preplanning conference, the audit firm will provide the CFO with a list of the information needed for the audit. Thereafter, periodic conferences will be held during the conduct of the audit, as well as an exit conference prior to the completion of fieldwork. Some meetings will be conducted with [Name of Nonprofit] audit committee.

The audit firm will furnish to the audit committee 30 copies of the audit report, the management letter, and other applicable reports within the period cited above. Should circumstances arise during the audit that require work in excess of the original estimates, the additional costs will be negotiated prior to commencement of the work.

The Selection Process

Submit proposals by [Date]. The Audit Committee will review and evaluate the proposals, selecting the firm that best matches experience and cost

EXHIBIT 4.3 Sample Audit RFP

expectations. Cost will be an important but not the sole determining factor in the selection process. [Name of Nonprofit] reserves the right to reject any or all bids, waive technicalities, and be the sole judge of suitability of the services for its intended use.

Information Requested

The audit firm should provide the following:

- Copy of the firm's most recent peer review letter
- Description of the relevant educational background and experience of assigned individuals in auditing nonprofit organizations
- Names, addresses, and telephone numbers of personnel of current and prior nonprofit audit clients who may be contacted for a reference
- Proof of insurance to cover claims
- Description of the audit team and the approximate percentage each will spend on the audit
- A tentative schedule for completing the audit
- The costs for the audit ending [Fiscal Year] and the estimated costs for [Subsequent Two Fiscal Years]

Costs

A. Personnel: Itemize the following for each category of personnel (partner, manager, senior, staff accountants, clerical, etc.): (1) Estimated hours doing onsite interim work, year-end on-site work, and work in the auditor's office, (2) the rate per hour for each person, and (3) the total personnel cost
B. Travel: Itemize transportation and other travel costs
C. Supplies and materials: itemize
D. Other costs

Time Schedule

The request for proposal package will be mailed by [Date]. A proposals signed by authorized officials is due by the close of business on [Date]. Early in October, the Audit Committee will make a recommendation to the Board of Directors, who will award the contract.

Assistance Available to Auditor

The [Name of Nonprofit] will pull and refile records and prepare and mail all necessary confirmations and will complete the year-end trial balance.

EXHIBIT 4.3   (*Continued*)

for a fictional nonprofit. Notice in the RFP a three-year contract period. The auditor has start-up costs to learn the nonprofit's policies and procedures, which can be amortized over a multiyear contract period. However, the nonprofit should also seek competition regularly to ensure the highest quality audit.

Notice that the sample RFP asks the CPA to provide its most recent *peer review letter.* The American Institute of CPAs requires that the work of each CPA firm be reviewed by a comparable firm. A firm specializing in nonprofit auditing, for instance, would be reviewed by a firm with nonprofit expertise. Exhibit 4.4 (see page 50) is a sample peer review letter.

Non-Audit Services

In addition to rendering an opinion on the financial statements and preparing Form 990, the auditor may perform non-audit-related services. To maintain independence conducting the audit, the audit profession distinguishes between the allowable and unallowable services. The allowable services, shown in Exhibit 4.5 (see page 51), are those that the auditor can perform in addition to the audit.

Selection Criteria

The lowest-priced proposal is not the best if the auditor has inadequate expertise. The best way to do this is to check the references of nonprofits that the firm has audited. After selecting a firm, the nonprofit and auditor enter into a contract that takes the form of an engagement letter. Exhibit 4.6 (see page 52) is a sample engagement letter.

Conduct the Audit

Auditing is highly technical and like any professionals, auditors have their own jargon, difficult for the layperson to understand. At the end of this chapter, is a glossary, explaining auditing and accounting vernacular. The audit process has the five steps shown in Exhibit 4.7 (see page 55).

Let us discuss each step in the following sections.

Plan the Audit

To prepare for the audit, the audit coordinator, and the audit committee if there is one, plan the upcoming audit. They review:

- The results of last year's audit
- The engagement letter

[CPA Peer Review Firm's Letterhead]
[Date]

To: [Name of CPA Under Peer Review]

We have reviewed the system of quality control for the accounting and auditing practice of [Name of CPA] [Referred to as Firm] in effect for the year ended [Date]. A system of quality control encompasses the firm's organizational structure, the policies adopted, and procedures established to provide it with reasonable assurance of conforming with professional standards. The elements of quality control are described in the Statements on Quality Control Standards issued by the American Institute of CPAs (AICPA). The firm is responsible for designing a system of quality control and complying with it to provide the firm reasonable assurance of conforming with professional standards in all material respects. Our responsibility is to express an opinion on the design of the system of quality control and the firm's compliance with its system of quality control based on our review.

Our review was conducted in accordance with standards established by the Peer Review Board of the AICPA. During our review, we read required representations from the firm, interviewed firm personnel, and obtained an understanding of the nature of the firm's accounting and auditing practice, and the design of the firm's system of quality control sufficient to assess the risks implicit in its practice. Based on our assessments, we selected engagements and administrative files to test for conformity with professional standards and compliance with the firm's system of quality control. The engagements selected represented a reasonable cross-section of the firm's accounting and auditing practice with emphasis on higher-risk engagements. Prior to concluding the review, we reassessed the adequacy of the scope of the peer review procedures and met with the firm's management to discuss the results of our review. We believe that the procedures we performed provide a reasonable basis for our opinion.

In performing our review, we obtained an understanding of the system of quality control for the firm's accounting and auditing practice. In addition, we tested compliance with the firm's quality control policies and procedures to the extent we considered appropriate. These tests covered the application of the firm's policies and procedures on selected engagements. Our review was based on selected tests. Therefore, it would not necessarily detect all weaknesses in the system of quality control or all instances of noncompliance with it. There are inherent limitations in the effectiveness of any system of quality control and therefore noncompliance with the system of quality control may occur and not be detected. Projection of any evaluation of a system of quality control

EXHIBIT 4.4   Sample Peer Review Letter

> to future periods is subject to the risk that the system of quality control may become inadequate because of changes in conditions, or because the degree of compliance with the policies or procedures may deteriorate.
>
> In our opinion, the system of quality control for the accounting and auditing practice of the firm has been designed to meet the requirements of the quality control standards for an accounting and auditing practice established by the AICPA and was complied with during the year then ended to provide the firm with reasonable assurance of conforming with professional standards.
>
> [Name of Peer Review Firm]

EXHIBIT 4.4 *(Continued)*

EXHIBIT 4.5 Allowable and Unallowable Non-Audit Services

Allowable Services	Unallowable Services
▪ Make an accounting data entry with no coding or decision making. ▪ Transmit payroll information to a third party, *if* the third party subsequently receives client approval. ▪ Generate unsigned checks based on client-provided information. ▪ Install an off-the-shelf accounting package. ▪ Train client's employees on the control and information management systems. ▪ Establish an IT system, totally unrelated to accounting records and financial statements.	▪ Change transactions without client approval. ▪ Prepare source documents. ▪ Change source documents without client approval. ▪ Authorize transactions. ▪ Sign checks. ▪ Authorize payments. ▪ Approve payments. ▪ Take custody of funds. ▪ Design or install a client's financial information system. ▪ Operate a client's local area network (LAN) system. ▪ Supervise client's personnel in operating the information system.

[CPA Firm's Letterhead]
[Date]

[Name and Address of Nonprofit]

We are pleased to confirm our understanding of the services we are to provide for [Name of Nonprofit] for the year ended [Date]. We will audit the statement(s) of financial position of [Name of Nonprofit] as of [Date], and the related statements of [Insert Statements Audited] for the year then ended. We will also prepare the Organization's federal and state information returns for the year then ended.

Audit Objective

The objective of our audit is the expression of an opinion about whether your financial statements are fairly presented, in all material respects, in conformity with U.S. generally accepted accounting principles. Our audit will be conducted in accordance with auditing standards generally accepted in the United States of America and will include tests of your accounting records and other procedures we consider necessary to enable us to express such an opinion. If our opinion is other than unqualified, we will discuss the reasons with you in advance. If, for any reason, we are unable to complete the audit or are unable to form or have not formed an opinion, we may decline to express an opinion or to issue a report because of this engagement.

Audit Procedures

Our procedures will include tests of documentary evidence supporting the transactions recorded in the accounts, tests of the physical existence of inventories, and direct confirmation of receivables and certain assets and liabilities by correspondence with selected individuals, funding sources, creditors, and financial institutions. We will also request written representations from [Name of Nonprofit] attorneys as part of the engagement, and they may bill you for responding to this inquiry. At the conclusion of our audit, we will require certain written representations from you about the financial statements and related matters.

An audit includes examining, on a test basis, evidence supporting the amounts and disclosures in the financial statements; therefore, our audit will involve judgment about the number of transactions to be examined and the areas

EXHIBIT 4.6   Sample Audit Engagement Letter

to be tested. We will plan and perform the audit to obtain reasonable assurance about whether the financial statements are free of material misstatement, whether from (1) errors, (2) fraudulent financial reporting, (3) misappropriation of assets, or (4) violations of laws or governmental regulations that are attributable to the Organization or to acts by management or employees acting on behalf of the Organization.

Because an audit is designed to provide reasonable, but not absolute, assurance and because we will not perform a detailed examination of all transactions, there is a risk that material misstatements may exist and not be detected by us. In addition, an audit is not designed to detect immaterial misstatements or violations of laws or governmental regulations that do not have a direct and material effect on the financial statements. However, we will inform you of any material errors and any fraudulent financial reporting or misappropriation of assets that come to our attention. We will also inform you of any violations of laws or governmental regulations that come to our attention, unless clearly inconsequential. Our responsibility as auditors is limited to the period covered by our audit and does not extend to any later periods for which we are not engaged as auditors.

Our audit will include obtaining an understanding of the [Name of Nonprofit] and its environment, including internal control, sufficient to assess the risks of material misstatement of the financial statements and to design the nature, timing, and extent of further audit procedures. An audit is not designed to provide assurance on internal control or to identify deficiencies in internal control. However, during the audit, we will communicate to you and those charged with governance internal-control-related matters that are required to be communicated under professional standards.

We may from time to time, and depending on the circumstances, use third-party service providers in serving your account. We may share confidential information about you with these service providers, but remain committed to maintaining the confidentiality and security of your information. Accordingly, we maintain internal policies, procedures, and safeguards to protect the confidentiality of your personal information. In addition, we will secure confidentiality agreements with all service providers to maintain the confidentiality of your information and we will take reasonable precautions to determine that they have appropriate procedures in place to prevent the unauthorized release of your confidential information to others. In the event that we are unable to secure an appropriate confidentiality agreement, you will be asked to provide your consent prior to the sharing of your confidential information with the third-party service provider. Furthermore, we will remain responsible for the work provided by any such third-party service providers.

EXHIBIT 4.6 *(Continued)*

Management Responsibilities

You are responsible for making all management decisions and performing all management functions; for designating an individual with suitable skill, knowledge, or experience to oversee the tax services and any other services we provide; and for evaluating the adequacy and results of those services and accepting responsibility for them.

You are responsible for establishing and maintaining internal controls, including monitoring ongoing activities; for the selection and application of accounting principles; and for the fair presentation in the financial statements of financial position, changes in net assets, and cash flows in conformity with U.S. generally accepted accounting principles. You are also responsible for making all financial records and related information available to us and for the accuracy and completeness of that information. Your responsibilities include adjusting the financial statements to correct material misstatements and confirming to us in the management representation letter that the effects of any uncorrected misstatements aggregated by us during the current engagement and pertaining to the latest period presented are immaterial, both individually and taken together, to the financial statements taken as a whole.

You are responsible for the design and implementation of programs and controls to prevent and detect fraud, and for informing us about all known or suspected fraud affecting [Name of Nonprofit] (1) management, (2) employees who have significant roles in internal control and (3) others where the fraud could have a material effect on the financial statements. Your responsibilities include informing us of your knowledge of any allegations of fraud or suspected fraud affecting [Name of Nonprofit] received in communications from employees, former employees, grantors, regulators, or others. In addition, you are responsible for identifying and ensuring [Name of Nonprofit] complies with applicable laws and regulations and for taking timely and appropriate steps to remedy any fraud, illegal acts, or violations of contracts or grant agreements that we may report.

Engagement Administration, Fees, and Other

We understand that your employees will prepare all cash, accounts receivable, and other confirmations we request and will locate any documents selected by us for testing. [Name of CPA Firm] is the engagement partner and is responsible for supervising the engagement and signing the report or authorizing another individual to sign it. We expect to begin our audit on approximately [Date] and to complete your information returns and issue our report no later than [Date].

EXHIBIT 4.6   (*Continued*)

We estimate that our fees for these services will range from $[ ] to $[ ] for the audit and $[ ] to $[ ] for the information returns. You will also be billed for travel and other out-of-pocket costs such as report production, word processing, postage, etc. Additional expenses are estimated to be $[ ]. The fee estimate is based on anticipated cooperation from your personnel and the assumption that unexpected circumstances will not be encountered during the engagement. If significant additional time is necessary, we will discuss it with you and arrive at a new fee estimate before we incur the additional costs. Our invoices for these fees will be rendered each month as work progresses and are payable on presentation. In accordance with our firm policies, work may be suspended if your account becomes [Number] days or more overdue and will not be resumed until your account is paid in full. If we elect to terminate our services for nonpayment, our engagement will be deemed to have been completed upon written notification of termination, even if we have not completed our report. You will be obligated to compensate us for all time expended and to reimburse us for all out-of-pocket expenditures through the date of termination. We appreciate the opportunity to be of service to you and believe this letter accurately summarizes the significant terms of our engagement. If you have any questions, please let us know. If you agree with the terms of our engagement as described in this letter, please sign the enclosed copy and return it to us.

[Name of CPA Firm]

EXHIBIT 4.6 *(Continued)*

- The major audit progress milestones
- The nonprofit's responsibilities for the audit, known as the *provided-by-client* ("PBC") list

After this review, the audit coordinator and audit committee meet with the auditor to review the contract's expectations regarding the steps and timing of the audit.

EXHIBIT 4.7   The Audit Process

Audit Step	Conducted By
1. Plan the audit	The nonprofit
2. Prepare the financial statements	The nonprofit
3. Prepare the audit program	The auditor
4. Audit the financial statements	The auditor
5. Prepare the financial reports	The auditor

Prepare Financial Statements

The nonprofit's key responsibility, of course, is to close the books in a timely fashion and to provide the financial statements to the auditor. The auditor can assist with the preparation, but only if such assistance is *provided as a matter of convenience*. That is, the nonprofit must have someone who could have prepared the statements. Should a nonprofit lack this ability, it can hire a second CPA firm to prepare the statements. The financial statements preparation list, shown in Exhibit 4.8, indicates:

- How to manage the project
- The accounting records to reconcile
- The transactions to review and verify
- The duties to separate in preparing the statements

EXHIBIT 4.8   Financial Statements Preparation List

Procedures

Project Management
Assign responsibilities for closing the general statements and financial statement worksheets.
Adopt a schedule with target dates for closing the general ledger and financial statement worksheets.
Adopt a policy concerning year-end cut-off of accounting transactions.
Maintain trial balances, adjustments, and supporting work papers to support closing the general ledger and financial statement preparation.
Prepare all cash, accounts receivable, and other confirmations.

Year-End Reconciliation of:
Investments to control accounts
Amounts designated for subsequent year's expenses to budget authorizations
Financial statements to the general ledger

Review and Verify
Transactions subsequent to balance sheet update for proper classification
Revenue accounts to identify possible deferred revenue
Investment earnings calculations and accruals
Accumulated leave records
Capital asset inventory records
Retained earnings for restrictions/reservations
Bank reconciliations

Separate the Duties of:
Preparing and reconciling financial statements
Preparing and reviewing journal entries
Preparing and reviewing supporting worksheets and schedules
Performing and reviewing reconciliations

Prepare the Audit Program

The auditor prepares a program prior to conducting the audit. Generally Accepted Auditing Standards (GAAS) require that the auditor thoroughly understand the work environment, being particularly sensitive to the risk of material misstatement in the financial statements. To gain this overall perspective, the auditor preliminarily examines:

- Laws and regulations
- Accounting, budgeting, and financial reporting policies and procedures
- The prior audit's work papers
- The organization's structure
- The assignment of financial responsibilities
- Financial reports, forms, and the chart of accounts
- Computer hardware and software

Based on the preliminary examination, the auditor prepares an *audit program*, which is the design to obtain sufficient evidence to afford a *reasonable basis* for the audit opinion. The audit program specifies the tests the auditor will make of:

- Internal controls
- The information technology system
- Legal compliance
- Financial systems
- Human resource systems

The auditor obtains an organization chart of the nonprofit and a detailed flowchart or narrative of the accounting process. The auditor then "walks through" selected transactions to determine whether controls are reliable or need further testing.

Audit the Financial Statements

The auditor next implements the audit program, which details the procedures and transaction sampling process. The American Institute of Certified Public Accountants (AICPA) requires that the auditor follow the 10 Generally Accepted Auditing Standards shown in Exhibit 4.9.[7]

In 2007, the AICPA issued eight more standards, known as the "Risk Management Standards," which require that the auditor fully understand the control environment, especially the current economic situation and organizational climate.[8] To test for audit compliance, the auditor examines material accounts, which include cash, accounts receivable, investments, fixed

General Standards

1. Have the necessary technical training and proficiency to perform the audit.
2. Maintain independence in mental attitude in all matters related to the audit.
3. Use due professional care during the audit and preparation of the report.

Field Work Standards

1. Adequately plan the work and properly supervise employees.
2. Assess the risk of material misstatement of the financial statements due to error or fraud.
3. Obtain audit evidence by performing audit procedures sufficient to afford a reasonable basis to express an opinion regarding the financial statements under audit.

Reporting Standards

1. State whether the financial statements are in accordance with GAAP.
2. Identify the circumstances in which GAAP were not consistently observed.
3. State when the informative disclosures were not reasonably adequate.
4. Express an opinion regarding the financial statements as a whole, if an opinion cannot be expressed, state the reasons why.

EXHIBIT 4.9   Generally Accepted Auditing Standards

assets, account balances, trial balance totals, financial statement amounts, expenses, and encumbrances. For example, the auditor selects a sample of validated deposit slips and bank statements to:

- Determine whether deposits were made as reported
- Trace the deposit record to the monthly bank statement to verify that the deposit tickets coincide with the bank statement
- Examine the internal controls to verify the accurate receipt and deposit of funds

The auditor records test results in *work papers*, which include schedules, analyses, transcriptions, memos, confirmation results of specific accounts, and income statements as well as:

- The results of the internal controls review
- Evidence that the auditor met GAAS auditing standards
- Evidence the auditor properly tested transactions
- An explanation of how the auditor treated audit exceptions
- An explanation of the auditor's significant findings and recommendations

---

EXHIBIT 4.10   Audit Preparation List

Audit Preparation Procedures

Examine Documents
Insurance policies
Loans and notes payable
Invoices
Correspondence from your attorney

Examine Financial Records
Year-to-date general ledger
Bank statements
Statements for investment and cash accounts
Year-end trial balance and financial statements

Prepare Work Papers
Liabilities Schedules
Year-to-day salaries and payroll taxes
Loans and notes payable
Salaries payable
Employee vacation earned but not used

Assets Schedules
Accounts receivable
Depreciation
Allowance for doubtful accounts

Other Schedules
Grants and contributions receivable
Rent expense for the year

Exhibit 4.10 is a list of audit preparation procedures including:

- The documents to examine
- The financial records to examine
- The work papers to prepare including schedules of liabilities, assets, and other accounts

SAS 114

SAS 114, or *Statement on Auditing Standards No. 114, The Auditor's Communication with Those Charged with Governance,* was issued in response to the accounting scandals of the 1990s and early 2000s. Intended to ensure better communication between the auditor and the governing board, SAS 114 requires the auditor to include:

- A discussion of the auditor's responsibilities under generally accepted auditing standards
- An overview of the planned scope and timing of the audit
- Significant findings from the audit

These communications may be either oral or written. However, the auditor must communicate in writing significant findings from the audit when, in the opinion of the auditor, an oral communication would insufficiently explain the significant findings. The written communication is called the "SAS 114 letter," an example of which is shown in Exhibit 4.11.

SAS 115

SAS No. 115, *Statement on Auditing Standards No. 115, Communicating Internal Control Related Matters in an Audit*, requires the auditor to evaluate the seriousness of internal control deficiencies. The auditor may find a *significant* deficiency in the design or operation of internal control that could adversely affect the nonprofit's ability to record, process, summarize, and report financial data. An aggregation of significant deficiencies can constitute a *material weakness*, which poses a high risk of a material misstatement in the financial statements. Material weakness examples include:

- Not segregating accounting duties
- Not having a written accounting policy manual
- Inadequately safeguarding assets
- Insufficiently supervising journal entries, bank account reconciliations, ledger entries, etc.

The communication, formerly known as a *management letter*, now known as a Communication of Significant Deficiencies or Material Weaknesses or the SAS 115 letter, is for the sole use of the Board and management. In the communication, the auditor recommends corrective action. However, the Board can release it to the public. Indeed, some funding agencies *insist* on seeing it as condition of funding. Funders will look to see if a nonprofit has redressed deficiencies noted in the prior year's communication. If the auditor does not identify a weakness, the auditor does not prepare a

[CPA Firm's Letterhead]
[Date]

[Name and Address of Nonprofit]

We have audited the financial statements of [Name of Nonprofit] for the year ended [Date], and have issued our report thereon dated [Date]. Professional standards require that we provide you with the following information related to our audit.

Responsibility under U.S. Generally Accepted Auditing Standards and OMB Circular A-133

Our responsibility, as described by professional standards, is to express an opinion about whether the financial statements prepared by management with your oversight are fairly presented, in all material respects, in conformity with U.S. generally accepted accounting principles. Our audit of the financial statements does not relieve you or management of your responsibilities.

In planning and performing our audit, we considered [Name of Nonprofit]'s internal control over financial reporting in order to determine our auditing procedures for the purpose of expressing our opinion on the financial statements and not to provide assurance on the internal control over financial reporting. We also considered internal control over compliance with requirements that could have a direct and material effect on a major federal program in order to determine our auditing procedures for the purpose of expressing our opinion on compliance and to test and report on internal control over compliance in accordance with OMB Circular A-133.

As part of obtaining reasonable assurance about whether [Name of Nonprofit]'s financial statements are free of material misstatement, we performed tests of its compliance with certain provisions of laws, regulations, contracts, and grants, noncompliance with which could have a direct and material effect on the determination of financial statement amounts. However, providing an opinion on compliance with those provisions was not an objective of our audit. Also, in accordance with OMB Circular A-133, we examined, on a test basis, evidence about Charter School's compliance with the types of compliance requirements described in the "U.S. Office of Management and Budget (OMB) Circular A-133 Compliance Supplement" applicable to each of its major federal programs for the purpose of expressing an opinion on [Name of Nonprofit]'s compliance with those requirements. While our audit provides a reasonable basis for our opinion, it does not provide a legal determination on [Name of Nonprofit]'s compliance with those requirements.

EXHIBIT 4.11   Sample SAS 114 Letter

Planned Scope and Timing of the Audit

We performed the audit according to the planned scope and timing.

Significant Audit Findings

QUALITATIVE ASPECTS OF ACCOUNTING PRACTICES   Management is responsible for the selection and use of appropriate accounting policies. The significant accounting policies used by [Name of Nonprofit] are described in Note 1 to the financial statements. No new accounting policies were adopted and the application of existing policies was not changed during the year ended [Date]. We noted no transactions entered into for which there is a lack of authoritative guidance or consensus. There are no significant transactions that have been recognized in the financial statements in a different period than when the transaction occurred.

Accounting estimates are an integral part of the financial statements prepared by management and are based on management's knowledge and experience about past and current events and assumptions about future events. Certain accounting estimates are particularly sensitive because of their significance to the financial statements and because of the possibility that future events affecting them may differ significantly from those expected. There were no sensitive estimates affecting the financial statements.

DIFFICULTIES ENCOUNTERED IN PERFORMING THE AUDIT   We encountered no significant difficulties in dealing with management in performing and completing our audit.

CORRECTED AND UNCORRECTED MISSTATEMENTS   Professional standards require us to accumulate all known and likely misstatements identified during the audit, other than those that are trivial, and communicate them to the appropriate level of management. Management has corrected all such misstatements. In addition, none of the misstatements detected because of audit procedures and corrected by management were material, either individually or taken together, to the financial statements taken as a whole.

DISAGREEMENTS WITH MANAGEMENT   For purposes of this letter, professional standards define a disagreement with management as a financial accounting, reporting, or auditing matter, whether or not resolved to our satisfaction, they could be significant to the financial statements or the auditor's report. We are pleased to report that no such disagreements arose during the course of our audit.

EXHIBIT 4.11   *(Continued)*

MANAGEMENT REPRESENTATIONS   We have requested certain representations from management that are included in the management representation letter dated [Date].

MANAGEMENT CONSULTATIONS WITH OTHER INDEPENDENT ACCOUNTANTS   In some cases, management may decide to consult with other accountants about auditing and accounting matters, similar to obtaining a "second opinion" on certain situations. If a consultation involves application of an accounting principle to the [Name of Nonprofit]'s financial statements or a determination of the type of auditor's opinion that may be expressed on those statements, our professional standards require the consulting accountant to check with us to determine that the consultant has all the relevant facts. To our knowledge, there were no such consultations with other accountants.

OTHER AUDIT FINDINGS OR ISSUES   We generally discuss a variety of matters, including the application of accounting principles and auditing standards, with management each year prior to retention as the School's auditors. However, these discussions occurred in the normal course of our professional relationship and our responses were not a condition to our retention.
This information is intended solely for the use of the Board of Directors and management of [Name of Nonprofit] and is not intended to be and should not be used by anyone other than these specified parties.

[CPA Firm's Name]

EXHIBIT 4.11   *(Continued)*

management letter. Exhibit 4.12 is an example of a Communication of Significant Deficiencies and Material Weaknesses (SAS 115) letter.

Financial Reports

The auditor prepares the audit report and an accompanying Communication of Significant Deficiencies and Material Weaknesses if needed. Moreover, every nonprofit must file an IRS 990 Form with the Internal Revenue Service. Finally, a nonprofit that annually receives over $500,000 must prepare the Office of Management and Budget (OMB) Circular A-133 report.

THE AUDIT REPORT   Chapter 5, "Evaluate Financial Condition," includes a detailed discussion of the financial report's financial statements. The most important aspect of the financial report is the *opinion letter*, in which the

[CPA Firm's Letterhead]
[Date]

[Name and Address of Nonprofit]

In planning and performing our audit of the financial statements of [Name of Nonprofit] and for the year ended [Date], in accordance with auditing standards generally accepted in the United States of America, we considered the Council's internal control over financial reporting (internal control) as a basis for designing our auditing procedures for the purpose of expressing our opinion on the financial statements, but not for the purpose of expressing an opinion on the effectiveness of the [Name of Nonprofit]'s internal control. Accordingly, we do not express an opinion on the effectiveness of the [Name of Nonprofit]'s internal control.

A control deficiency exists when the design or operation of a control does not allow management or employees, in the normal course of performing their assigned functions, to prevent or detect misstatements on a timely basis. A significant deficiency is a control deficiency, or a combination of control deficiencies, that adversely affects the organization's ability to initiate, authorize, record, process, or report financial data reliably in accordance with generally accepted accounting principles such that there is more than a remote likelihood that a misstatement of the Council's financial statements that is more than inconsequential will not be prevented or detected by the organization's internal control.

A material weakness is a significant deficiency, or a combination of significant deficiencies, that results in more than a remote likelihood that a material misstatement of the financial statements will not be prevented or detected by the [Name of Nonprofit]'s internal control.

Our consideration of internal control was for the limited purpose described in the preceding paragraph and would not necessarily identify all deficiencies in internal control that might be significant deficiencies or material weaknesses. We did not identify any deficiencies in internal control that we consider to be material weaknesses, as defined above. However, we identified the following deficiencies in internal controls that we consider to be significant deficiencies.

Charge Card Bank Accounts

During our audit, we noted that reconciliations related to charge card bank accounts were not being performed in a timely manner. Due to this, the account balances were being inflated due to transactions remaining "in transit" that

EXHIBIT 4.12   Sample SAS 115 Communication of Significant Deficiencies or Material Weaknesses Letter

had actually cleared the bank. Sound internal controls require that all bank accounts be reconciled in a timely manner. We recommend that this account be reconciled on a monthly basis and adjusted for all cleared transactions. This is a repeat finding from the prior year.

Cash Disbursements

During our audit, we noted that several cash disbursements did not have adequate supporting documentation and/or the proper approval. Sound internal controls require that all transactions have support of adequate documentation; we recommend that every transaction have adequate supporting documentation. [Name of Nonprofit] has a policy in place for approvals; we recommend that be followed strictly by the guidelines set up.

Pledges Receivable

During our audit, we noted that pledges receivable are being accounted separately from the general ledger. We also noted that the subsidiary ledger being used to account for pledges receivable was not being reconciled to the general ledger in a routine manner. Sound internal controls require subsidiary ledgers be reconciled to the general ledger routinely. It is our understanding that the system will not allow for monthly reconciliations. We recommend, pledges be reconciled on a quarterly basis. While a repeat finding from the prior year, we have seen improvement.

Time Studies

During our audit, we noted that the National Office of the Boy Scouts of American recommends that time studies be performed once every three years. We believe that time studies are a crucial part of determining how to allocate expenses to their proper categories. Because employees can shift positions and responsibilities on an annual basis, we recommend that time studies be performed on an annual basis.

[Name of CPA Firm]

EXHIBIT 4.12 *(Continued)*

auditor can express four opinions regarding the financial statements' compliance with generally accepted accounting principles (GAAP).

1. *Unqualified ("clean") opinion.* The financial statements conform to GAAP.
2. *Qualified opinion.* The financial statements as a whole conform to GAAP, but with exceptions noted.
3. *Disclaimer of opinion (disclaimer).* The auditor disclaims expressing an opinion because of material (serious) departures from GAAP.
4. *Adverse opinion.* The financial statements do not conform to GAAP.

The desired opinion is, of course, an *unqualified* opinion, of which Exhibit 4.13 is an example.

[CPA Firm's Letterhead]
[Date]

[Name and Address of Nonprofit]

We have audited the accompanying statement of financial position of [Name of Nonprofit] as of [Date], and the related statements of activities, functional expenses and cash flows for the year then ended. These statements are the responsibility of the organization's management. Our responsibility is to express an opinion on these financial statements based on our audit.

We conducted our audit in accordance with auditing standards generally accepted in the United States of America. Those standards require that we plan and perform the audit to obtain reasonable assurance about whether the financial statements are free of material misstatement. An audit includes examining, on a test basis, evidence supporting the amounts and disclosures in the financial statements. An audit also includes assessing the accounting principles used and significant estimates made by management, as well as evaluating the overall financial statement presentation. We believe that our audit provides a reasonable basis for our opinion.

In our opinion, the financial statements referred to in the first paragraph present fairly, in all material respects, the financial position of [Name of Nonprofit] as of [Date] and the changes in net assets and its cash flows for the year then ended in conformity with accounting principles generally accepted in the United States of America.

[Name of CPA Firm]

EXHIBIT 4.13   Sample Unqualified Audit Opinion

In accordance with generally accepted auditing standards in the United States, the auditor audits four financial statements: the statement of financial position, the statement of activities, the statement of functional expenses, and the statement of cash flows The auditor is responsible for the opinion on the financial statements, and the nonprofit is responsible for their preparation. Because testing every financial transaction would be cost-prohibitive, the auditor reviews transactions on a *test basis*. Thus, the auditor can only give *reasonable assurance* that the financial statements are free *material misstatement*. In other words, the auditor is not responsible for undetected fraud. An unqualified opinion is denoted by the language, *"presents fairly in all material respects . . ."*

INDEPENDENT REVIEW REPORT   A less expensive option than an audit, a *review* provides assurance that the financial statements comply with GAAP and do not include material misstatements. Unlike in an audit, the CPA does not express an opinion on the financial statements. Exhibit 4.14 is an example in an independent accountant's review report.

COMPILATION REPORT   Another option for nonprofits in place of an audit is a *compilation*. The nonprofit either engages a Board member with accounting knowledge or an independent CPA firm to compile the financial statements but not to test accounts or verify that statements are in accordance with GAAP. Exhibit 4.15 is a sample compilation report.

AGREED-UPON PROCEDURE(S) REPORT   In an agreed-upon procedures arrangement, the nonprofit engages the CPA to examine one or more accounts, processes, or controls. For example, the nonprofit may want to know how to improve its cash disbursement process. The nonprofit hires an independent CPA to evaluate this process and provide recommendations. Exhibit 4.16 is an example of an agreed-upon procedure(s) report.

OFFICE OF MANAGEMENT AND BUDGET (OMB) CIRCULAR A-133 REPORT   If a nonprofit annually receives more than $500,000 in federal grants, the auditor must conduct the audit in accordance with OMB Circular A-133, following the *Generally Accepted Government Auditing Standards* (commonly referred to as the "Yellow Book"), issued by the Comptroller General of the United States. An A-133 financial report has five components in addition to the audit opinion:

1. The Independent Auditor's Report on Compliance and on Internal Control over Financial Reporting Based on an Audit of Financial Statements Performed in Accordance with Government Auditing Standards

[CPA Firm's Letterhead]
[Date]

[Name and Address of Nonprofit]

We have reviewed the accompanying statement of financial position of [Name of Nonprofit] as of [Date] and the related statements of activities and cash flows for the year then ended. A review includes primarily applying analytical procedures to management's financial data and making inquiries of [Name of Nonprofit]'s management. A review is substantially less in scope than an audit, the objective of which is the expression of an opinion regarding the financial statements as a whole. Accordingly, we do not express such an opinion.

Management is responsible for the preparation and fair presentation of the financial statements in accordance with accounting principles generally accepted in the United States of America and for designing, implementing, and maintaining internal control relevant to the preparation and fair presentation of the financial statements.

Our responsibility is to conduct the review in accordance with Statements on Standards for Accounting and Review Services issued by the American Institute of Certified Public Accountants. Those standards require us to perform procedures to obtain limited assurance that there are no material modifications that should be made to the financial statements. We believe that the results of our procedures provide a reasonable basis for our report.

Based on our review, we are not aware of any material modifications that should be made to the accompanying financial statements in order for them to be in conformity with accounting principles generally accepted in the United States of America.

[Name of Auditor]

EXHIBIT 4.14   Sample Independent Accountant's Review Report

2. The Independent Auditor's Report on Compliance with Requirements Applicable to Each Major Program and Internal Control over Compliance in Accordance with OMB Circular A-133
3. The Schedule of Expenditures of Federal Awards
4. The Notes to the Schedule of Expenditures of Federal Awards
5. The Schedule of Findings and Questioned Costs

IRS FORM 990   Unless required by a funder, a financial audit is optional, but the Internal Revenue Service (IRS) requires nonprofits designated 501(c)(3) to file annually IRS Form 990: *Return of Organization Exempt from Income*

[CPA Firm's Letterhead]
[Date]

[Name and Address of Nonprofit]

We have compiled the accompanying statement of financial position of name of nonprofit as of [Date] and the related statements of activities and cash flows for the year then ended. We have not audited or reviewed the accompanying financial statements and, accordingly, do not express an opinion or provide any assurance about whether the financial statements are in accordance with accounting principles generally accepted in the United States of America. Management is responsible for the preparation and fair presentation of the financial statements in accordance with accounting principles generally accepted in the United States of America and for designing, implementing, and maintaining internal control relevant to the preparation and fair presentation of the financial statements.

Our responsibility is to conduct the compilation in accordance with Statements on Standards for Accounting and Review Services issued by the American Institute of Certified Public Accountants. The objective of a compilation is to assist management in presenting financial information in the form of financial statements without undertaking to obtain or provide any assurance that there are no material modifications that should be made to the financial statements.

[Name of CPA Firm]

EXHIBIT 4.15   Sample Independent Accountant's Compilation Report

Tax, or one of its sister forms (990EZ, and 990-N).[9] Nonprofits with gross receipts less than $25,000 file form 990-N (e-Postcard) through the IRS website at www.irs.gov/ or by this link, http://epostcard.form990.org/. There is no charge to file this return. The e-Postcard asks for eight items:

1. Organization's legal name
2. Any other names used by organization
3. Mailing address of organization
4. Website address of organization, if one exists
5. Employer identification number of organization
6. Name and address of a principal officer
7. Organization's annual tax year
8. Answers to two questions:
   (a) Are your gross receipts normally less than $25,000?
   (b) Has your organization gone out of business?

[CPA Firm's Letterhead]
[Date]

[Name and Address of Nonprofit]

We have performed the procedures enumerated below, which were agreed to by the specified parties enumerated above to assist you with respect to the adequacy of accounting records of [Name of Nonprofit] on for certain accounts for the years ended [Dates]. This engagement to apply agreed-upon procedures was performed in accordance with standards established by the American Institute of Certified Public Accountants. The sufficiency of the procedures is solely the responsibility of the specified parties. Consequently, we make no representation regarding the sufficiency of the procedures described below, either for the purpose for which this report has been requested or for any other purpose.

Our procedures and findings are as follows:
Procedure:
We reviewed [insert procedure performed]:
Findings:
During our testing procedures, we noted the following:
Findings: [description of finding]

Recommendations: We recommend that [insert recommendations for findings]
We were not engaged to, and did not perform, an audit, the objective of which would be the expression of an opinion on the specified elements, accounts or items. Accordingly, we do not express such an opinion. Had we performed additional procedures, other matters might have come to our attention that would have been reported to you.

This report is intended solely for the information and use of the specified parties listed above, is not intended to be, and should not be used by anyone other than these specified parties.

[Name of CPA Firm}

EXHIBIT 4.16   Sample Agreed-Upon Procedures Report

Nonprofits with gross receipts more than $25,000 and less than $500,000 and total assets less than $1,250,000 file Form 990EZ, which is an abbreviated version of the 990. The core form is only four pages long. Some parts on the 990-EZ trace directly to parts of the 990; other parts on the 990-EZ are compilations of several parts of the 990. See the table below for these relationships:

990-EZ	990
Part I	Part VIII
Part II	Part X
Part III	Part III
Part IV	Part VII
Part V	Parts IV, V, VI
Part VI	Part IV, VII

Form 990 is due on the fifteenth day of the fifth month after the end of the fiscal year. Some donors accept Form 990 in lieu of an audit. Some nonprofits have qualified staff to prepare Form 990. Otherwise, they pay the auditor to do it. Thirty-seven states require nonprofits to submit the Form 990 to them. Twenty-six states require that an audit be submitted as well.[10]

Form 990 has a core form completed by all organizations, and schedules to be completed depending on the type of organization. The core parts of the 990 are shown below.

990 Part	Function
Part I	Summary of mission, governance, revenue, expenses, and fund balances
Part II	Signature block for officer and preparer
Part III	Expanded description of organization's mission and program services, with expense details
Part IV	Highly detailed checklist of required schedules helps organization determine which additional schedules to complete
Part V	Highly detailed list of questions to determine whether organization has complied with all other necessary IRS matters
Part VI	Information gathering about governance, management, and disclosure procedures within organization
Part VII	Compensation listed for officers, directors, trustees, key employees, and independent contractors
Part VIII	Revenue information for the year, in total and by type
Part IX	Expense information for the year, in total and by type
Part X	Balance sheet information, giving beginning and end of year data

Once filed, Form 990 is a public record, heavily scrutinized by watchdog organizations like Guide Star, BBBWise Giving Alliance, Charity Navigator,

American Institute for Philanthropy and Wall Watchers. These oversight agencies use the Form 990 to assess:

- Whether a nonprofit deserves its tax-exempt status
- Whether a nonprofit is meeting its programmatic objectives
- Whether a nonprofit is paying excessive salaries to its CEO and to top management

Concerned about financial improprieties, Congress directed the IRS to toughen its reporting requirements effective in 2009.[11,12] Exhibit 4.17 shows the major changes.[13]

In addition to these required changes, the IRS *recommends* that nonprofits adopt policies regarding conflict of interest, setting compensation, whistleblower protection, document retention and joint ventures with outside entities. Chapter 8, "Purchase Goods," discusses conflict of interest and whistleblower policies in more detail, including sample policies. Exhibit 4.18

EXHIBIT 4.17   Significant Changes to IRS Form 990

Required Changes

Compensation
Report the compensation of all current officers, directors and trustees, regardless of the amount.[14]
Report compensation more than $100,000 (formerly $50,000) to employees and vendors.

New Forms
Schedule C: Information regarding political campaign and lobbying
Schedule G: Information about fundraising and gaming[15]
Schedule H: Health care reporting of billings, collections, charity care, emergency room policies and use of management companies
Schedule I: Detailed listings of U.S. Grant recipients including payments to governments and other organizations
Schedule K: Additional information regarding schools
Schedule R: Detailed schedule of related party transactions

New Filing Requirements
The penalty for failing to file a Form 990 will be levied against the *individual* responsible for filing the form, not against the organization itself.
The Board must disclose whether it reviewed the 990 prior to its filing.
Nonprofit must make IRS Form 990 available to the public via the nonprofit's website or on a website like Guide Star's.
The nonprofit must disclose if it has a conflict of interest policy, whistleblower policy and a document retention policy.

EXHIBIT 4.18 Sample Records Retention Policy

The purpose of the Records Retention Policy is to:
1 Ensure protection of vital records in case of destruction by a catastrophic event
2 Assure compliance with state and federal laws governing retention of records
3 Maintain confidentiality of financial and other restricted records
4 Release storage space by disposing records no longer needed

Records will be kept according the schedule shown below. When authorized, records should be destroyed by being burned, shredded, or torn up to destroy the content of the documents or materials concerned. The chief financial officer may authorize the destruction of records not found in this scheduler.

Type of Record	Retention Period	Type of Record	Retention Period
Accounts payable and ledger	7 years	Bylaws	Permanent
Accounts receivable and ledger	7 years	Charter	Permanent
Auditor's reports	7 years	Construction and renovation	Permanent
Bank statements and deposit slips	Permanent	Contract bids	Permanent
Budgets	3 years	Minutes of Director meetings	3 years
Cancelled checks	7 years	Trademark Registration	Permanent
Contracts and leases (after expiration)	7 years		Permanent
General correspondence	3 years		
Legal correspondence	Permanent	Accident reports	7 years
Deeds, mortgages, and bills of sale	Permanent	Fire inspection reports	7 years
Depreciation schedules	Permanent	Insurance policies	Permanent
Endowment reports	Permanent	Settled claims	7 years
Expense distribution	7 years	Safety records	7 years
Financial statements	Permanent		
General journal and ledger	Permanent	Employment applications	
Petty cash vouchers	3 years	Retirement and pension records	3 years
Property appraisals	Permanent	Payroll, personnel, and time card (after termination)	Permanent
Property records, plans, costs, etc.	Permanent	Sickness and disability records	
Purchase orders	3 years		7 years
Tax returns-IRS and payroll	Permanent		7 years

is a sample records retention policy. However, before using this or any other sample, ensure that this schedule's retention periods are in accord with your state's document retention law.

Common Audit Terms

The following is a glossary of common audit terms.

- *Acceptance sampling.* Sampling to determine whether internal control compliance is greater than the tolerable deviation rate.
- *Audit trail.* A chronological sequence of audit records, paper or electronic, that verify summary ledger entries.
- *Audit adjustment.* Correction of a financial misstatement identified by the auditor.
- *Computer-aided auditing.* Computer-assisted audit tools and techniques (CAAT Ts) enable the auditor to analyze a large volume of data, not just a limited sample of them, to identify anomalies.
- *Confirmation.* Communication with outside parties to authenticate internal evidence.
- *Control deficiency.* The design or operation of an internal control prevents detecting or preventing misstatements on a timely basis.
- *Deviation.* Departure from a prescribed internal control.
- *Fieldwork.* Work done in the client's offices.
- *Generalized audit software.* Packaged software programs used in fieldwork to read computer files, select information, create data files and print records.
- *SAS 114 letter.* Letter to management and the Board identifying, and recommending corrective action to, significant deficiencies and material weaknesses found in the course of the audit.
- *SAS 115 letter.* Letter to management that evaluates the seriousness of internal control deficiencies.
- *Material misstatement.* A "misstatement" with false or missing information caused by fraud or error. "Material" means large enough to cause stakeholders, such as board members, to alter their decisions.
- *Material weakness.* Deficiency in internal controls that is a reasonable possibility of material misstatement.
- *PBC list.* The provided-by-client (PBC) list of space and services that the client will provide to the auditor to conduct the audit.
- *Work papers.* Schedules, analyses, transcriptions, memos, and confirmation results of balance sheets and income statements.
- *Significant deficiency.* Less severe than a material misstatement, the ability to report financial data reliably is so adverse that there is more

than a remote likelihood of a material misstatement of the financial statements.

- *Test count*. Count the client's physical inventory to match against the accounting record count.
- *Test data*. Run data through the computer to test the compliance of the controls in the software.
- *Tickmarks*. Footnotes in work papers represented by a symbol not a letter, indicating specified tasks have been carried out.
- *Trace*. Follow a transaction through the steps of a system.

CHAPTER 5

Evaluate Financial Condition

The financial report serves as the Rosetta Stone for evaluating financial condition. A financial snapshot as of the last day of the fiscal year, every financial report includes these three statements:

1. A statement of financial position
2. A statement of activities
3. A statement of cash flows

Voluntary health-and-welfare organizations must prepare a fourth, a statement of functional expense, which GAAP recommends, but does not require for the other types of nonprofits. To evaluate a nonprofit's financial condition, one must first be able to understand the financial statements. With this knowledge, one can compute ratios and other financial indicators to analyze financial condition.

Understand Financial Statements

To explain financial statements, we will use current financial statements of an actual nonprofit organization, Stop Hunger Now, Inc., which provides food and life-saving aid to the hungry and destitute all over the world. The organization is funded by contributions of cash, food, and equipment from individuals, corporations, and other nonprofits. Operating eight warehouses, the volunteer-based program sends high-protein, dehydrated meals to hungry people worldwide. The statements used reflect the finances of the warehouse in Raleigh, North Carolina. To explain many of the accounts in the statements, we refer to the financial report's notes to the financial statements. The Financial Accounting Standards Board (FASB) requires the auditor to explain specified accounting practices in the Notes to Financial Statements.[1] Exhibit 5.1 lists notes typically included in a financial report.

EXHIBIT 5.1   Notes to the Financial Statements

Type of Note	Description
Significant Accounting Policies	Accounting policies that materially affect the presentation of financial information, including:
	1. The basis of accounting (cash, accrual, modified cash, other) 2. The fixed asset capitalization policy 3. The inventory valuation method 4. The method to value donated assets and services 5. The definition of cash and cash equivalents
Donor-Restricted Contributions and Net Assets	Explanation of donor-restricted contributions and of the change in restricted net assets from the prior fiscal year
Contributions Receivable	Receivables pledged as collateral or otherwise limited for use, including a schedule of unconditional and conditional promises
Investments	The basis for valuing investments; the types of investments held; the cost and current fair value of investments; and realized and unrealized investment gains and losses[2]
Board- and/or Donor-Designated Endowment and Reserve	An explanation of the endowment or the reserve; the amount of change in the Board-designated unrestricted net-asset account
Property, Equipment, and Depreciation	The depreciation expense for the period; the depreciation method used; the balance in the major classes of depreciable assets
Leases	The value of outstanding capital and operating leases
Debt	The purpose of each debt obligation, its sources of repayment, the assets pledged as security, and the financing agreements
Pension and Other Postemployment Employee Benefits (OPEB)	The actuarial valuation method and the amount of funded and unfunded pension and OPEB (e.g., health care to the retired) liabilities
Cost Allocation Method	The method used to allocate indirect costs to operating programs

The Statement of Financial Position

The statement of financial position serves two principal purposes. First, it enables various stakeholders (e.g., management, donors, members, creditors) to assess a nonprofit's financial condition. Second, creditors use the statement to assess their likelihood of being repaid. Items reported in the statement of financial position include:

- Assets (what is owned)
- Liabilities (what is owed)
- Net assets (the difference between what is owned and owed)

FASB permits the statement to be presented in a (1) sequenced or (2) classified format. The sequenced format reports assets in order of their *liquidity* (i.e., how soon they can be converted to cash). For example, short-term investments are listed before less liquid property assets. Liabilities are listed according to their maturity date. For instance, a 30-day note payable is listed before a long-term bond.

The alternate method, *the classified balance sheet*, classifies assets and liabilities as current or noncurrent. A current asset, such as cash or a short-term investment, is convertible to cash within one year. A noncurrent asset will not mature for more than a year. If not shown on the statement, the notes to the statement of financial position must disclose:

- The liquidity of assets and liabilities
- The nature of temporary and permanent restrictions
- The contractual obligations regarding the use of particular assets

Exhibit 5.2 explains the number-coded accounts found in Exhibit 5.3, the Statement of Financial Position of Stop Hunger Now.

The Statement of Activities

The Statement of Activities, a nonprofit's operating statement, summarizes all financial transactions during the fiscal year that resulted in increases or decreases in net assets. The statement, which reports changes in unrestricted, temporarily restricted and permanently restricted assets, enables the reader to:

- Evaluate fiscal performance
- Assess the ability to continue services
- Evaluate managerial stewardship

EXHIBIT 5.2   Explanation of Accounts in the Statement of Financial Position

Code	Account	Explanation
1	Cash and Equivalents	All investments with an initial maturity of three months or less are considered cash and equivalents.
2	Promises to Give	Promised funds expected within one year. All are expected to be collected.
3	Notes Receivable	Notes receivable are reported at their fair market value. All are expected to be collected.
4	Investments	Interest earned on corporate stock is reported at its fair market value.
5	Property and Equipment	Assets valued over $500 are capitalized.
6	Lease Payable	This is a lease on a warehouse forklift.
7	Unrestricted Net Assets	Note the substantial decrease from 2007 to 2008.
8	Temporarily Restricted Net Assets	This is food held in the warehouse. In 2008, $308,615 in temporarily restricted food was sent to needy countries.

The statement can be presented in three ways: (1) a single column, (2) two separate statements,[3] or (3) a multicolumn. Exhibit 5.4 explains the number-coded accounts found in Exhibit 5.5, the Statement of Activities of Stop Hunger Now, which is presented in the multicolumn format.

The Statement of Cash Flows

With accrual accounting, the reporting period when a revenue or expense is recognized differs from the reporting period when the corresponding cash transaction occurs. The statement of financial position usefully indicates performance, but of equal interest is the amount of cash flow, which allows the reader to assess:

- The organization's ability to generate future cash flows
- The organization's ability to meet financial obligations
- The reasons for the differences between its cash receipts and payments

The statement of cash flows defines cash as:

- Currency
- Demand deposits with banks and other financial institutions
- Cash equivalents readily convertible to cash (i.e., close enough to maturity (less than three months) that a change in interest rates will not change their value).

EXHIBIT 5.3 Statement of Financial Position

Assets	2008	2007
Current Assets		
Cash and cash equivalents (1)	$103,125	$187,774
Promises to give (2)	2,987	2,750
Accounts receivable	8,773	–
Other receivable	246	246
Inventory	75,806	–
Prepaid expenses	35,689	7,579
Notes receivable, current portion (3)	57,606	45,000
Investments (4)	64,500	198,622
Total Current Assets	348,732	441,971
Property and equipment (at cost), net (5)	85,888	64,892
Other Assets:		
Notes receivable, less current portion	26,506	84,112
Deposits	5,140	2,639
	31,646	86,751
Total Assets	$466,266	$593,614
Liabilities and Net Assets		
Current Liabilities:		
Accounts payable and accrued expenses	$121,488	$ 41,587
Accrued vacation payable	13,181	4,946
Lease payable, current portion (6)	9,069	–
Total Current Liabilities	143,737	46,533
Total Liabilities	143,737	46,533
Net Assets:		
Unrestricted (7)	233,344	317,677
Temporarily restricted (8)	89,185	229,404
Total Net Assets	322,529	547,081
Total Liabilities and Net Assets	$466,266	$593,614

EXHIBIT 5.4   Explanation of Accounts in the Statement of Activities

Code	Account	Discussion
(1)	In-Kind Contributions	These are mostly contributed food and medical supplies that are shipped to third parties abroad for medical relief. In-kind contributions also include marketing assistance, public-relations support and a free warehouse.
(2)	Interest and Dividends	In 2008, the organization earned $11,563 in interest but lost $1,538 on the sale of investments.
(3)	Net Assets Released from Restrictions	Donor-restricted assets were held in warehouses that were for use in Africa, Central America, the Middle East and South Asia.
(4)	Program Services	Money spent on programs that directly benefit service recipients.
(5)	Management and General	Money spent to support program services that do not directly benefit clients.
(6)	Fundraising Activities	Expenses related to fundraising activities (e.g., events, mailings, professional-fundraiser expenses).
(7)	Changes in Net Assets	Notice the decline ($224,552) in net assets from 2007 to 2008.

There are two ways to present the statement, the direct and the indirect methods. Both have three cash categories:

1. *Operating activities.* Transactions involving (1) contributions and (2) pricing and delivering goods and services
2. *Investing activities.* Transactions affecting the purchase or sale of investments
3. *Financing activities.* Transactions involving borrowing and debt repayment

The direct method reports actual receipts and disbursements for each item of cash inflow and outflow. The indirect method begins with the *change in net assets* taken from the Statement of Activities (see Exhibit 5.5) and then adjusts for cash flows from investing and financing activities and the change in net assets such as:

- Depreciation expense
- Bad-debt expense

EXHIBIT 5.5   Statement of Activities

| | 2008 | | | 2007 |
	Unrestricted	Temporarily Restricted	Total	Total
Supports and Revenues				
Grants and contributions	$ 1,554,012	$165,396	$ 1,719,408	$1,235,567
In-kind contributions (1)	11,469,655		11,469,655	7,017,447
Sales revenue	1,255		1,255	
Interest and dividends (2)	11,673		11,673	16,716
Unrealized loss on investments				–461
(Loss) gain on sale of investments	–1,538		–1,538	2,000
Net assets released from restrictions (3)	305,615	–305,615		
Total Support and Revenues	13,340,672	–140,219	13,200,453	8,271,269
Expenses				
Program services (4)	13,035,300		13,035,300	7,833,458
Management and general (5)	176,859		176,859	145,243
Fundraising activities (6)	212,846		212,846	190,850
Total Expenses	13,425,005		13,425,005	8,169,551
Changes in Net Assets (7)	–84,333	–140,219	–224,552	101,718
Net Assets at Beginning of Year	317,677	229,404	547,081	445,363
Net Assets at End of Year	$ 233,344	$ 89,185	$ 322,529	$ 547,081

EXHIBIT 5.6   Explanation of Accounts in the Statement of Cash Flows

Code	Account	Discussion
(1)	Change in Net Assets	The net amount is shown in Exhibit 5.5, the Statement of Activities.
(2)	Net Cash Used by Operating Activities	In 2008, net cash decreased by $424,532, principally due to noncash revenue (stock contributed) and cash expenses exceeding cash revenues.
(3)	Net Cash Provided by Investing Activities	In 2008, net cash increased by $331,627 due to increased proceeds from sale of investments ($375,627). The organization had to sell investments to keep afloat due to borrowing more cash than it paid back.
(4)	Net Cash Provided by Financing Activities	In 2008, net cash increased by $8,298.
(5)	Cash and Cash Equivalents at the End of Year	The amount of cash and cash equivalents decreased from $187,774 to $103,125 from 2007 to 2008. The decrease should be a concern.

- Net realized and unrealized gains or losses on investments
- Realized (gain) on sale of investments
- Contributions of stock
- Changes in operating assets and liabilities

Exhibit 5.6 explains the number-coded accounts found in Exhibit 5.7, the Statement of Cash Flows of Stop Hunger Now.

Statement of Functional Expenses

FASB *requires* that voluntary health-and-welfare organizations prepare this statement but recommends that other types of nonprofits report the statement as well. The statement classifies expenses by function (e.g., program, supporting, fundraising) and by object/natural classification (e.g., salaries, supplies, travel) in a matrix format. Exhibit 5.8 explains the accounts found in Exhibit 5.9, the Statement of Functional Expenses for Stop Hunger Now.

Analyze Fiscal Condition

Various stakeholders—management, Board members, contributors, watchdog organizations—use the financial report and the IRS Form 990 to evaluate

EXHIBIT 5.7   Statement of Cash Flows

	2008	2007
Cash Flows from Operating Activities:		
Change in net assets (1)	$(224,552)	$101,718
Adjustments to reconcile change in net assets to net cash used by operating activities:		
Depreciation	23,277	13,141
Bad-debt expense	3,240	1,000
Unrealized (gain) loss on investments	–	461
Realized (gain) on sale of investments	1,538	(2,000)
Contributions of stock	(242,504)	(320,000)
(Increase) decrease in assets:		
Promises to give	(237)	72,250
Accounts receivable	(12,013)	–
Notes receivable	45,000	40,000
Inventory	(75,806)	–
Prepaid expenses	(28,110)	(2,839)
Other receivables	–	25
Deposits	(2,501)	–
Increase (decrease) in liabilities:		
Accounts payable and accrued expenses	88,136	(22,129)
Net Cash Used by Operating Activities (2)	(424,532)	(118,373)
Cash Flows from Investing Activities:		
Proceeds from sale of investments	375,627	236,000
Purchases of investments	(539)	(831)
Purchases of equipment	(43,502)	(31,264)
Net Cash Provided by Investing Activities (3)	331,586	203,905
Cash Flows from Financing Activities:		
Proceeds from borrowing activities	9,069	–
Payments on borrowing activities	(771)	(3,648)
Net Cash Provided by Financing Activities (4)	8,298	(3,648)
Net (Decrease) Increase in Cash and Cash Equivalents	(84,649)	81,884
Cash and Cash Equivalents at Beginning of the Year	187,774	105,890
Cash and Cash Equivalents at End of the Year (5)	$103,125	$187,774
Supplemental disclosure of cash flow information:		
Cash paid during year for interest	$3,515	$2,741

EXHIBIT 5.8   Explanation of the Accounts in the Statement of Functional Expenses

Code	Account	Discussion of the Account
(1)	Grants to Others	Notice the increase of $4,530,339 from 2007 to 2008.
(2)	Salaries: Others	Notice the increase in expenses for salaries for other than officers ($241,288) from 2007 to 2008.
(3)	Retirement	The organization has a simplified pension plan the contribution to which the Board determines annually.
(4)	Rent: Office	The office is leased monthly.
(5)	Rent: Warehouse	The warehouse is leased monthly.
(6)	Marketing, Public Relations and Advertising	The cost of brochures, posters, and press releases. They are expensed when the promotional activity takes place.
(7)	Depreciation	The depreciation of the office and warehouse equipment is charged to operations.
(8)	Travel	Notice the substantial increase in travel expenses from 2007 to 2008.

nonprofits' financial condition. With these reports, they can calculate telling indicators, including the following:

- Program efficiency ratio
- Fundraising efficiency ratio
- Liquidity ratios
- Margin ratios
- Funds and inventory management ratios
- Debt service ratios

These ratios are explained below. The dollar figures in the exhibits are taken from Stop Hunger Now's 2008 and 2007 IRS Form 990.

Program Efficiency Ratio

The *program efficiency ratio* calculates the percentage of funds expended directly on program services for clients or members. Funders would like to see as high a percentage of their money as possible spent on direct services, not indirect expenses like administrative salaries and related expenses. As a condition of funding, some funders place a cap on the amount of indirect expenses. Based on data in IRS Form 990, Exhibit 5.10 indicates:

EXHIBIT 5.9 Statement of Functional Expenses

| | 2008 | | | | 2007 |
	Program Services	Management and General	Fundraising	Total	Total
Grants to others (1)	$11,385,239			$11,385,239	$6,854,900
Program services—other	204,830			204,830	130,912
Salaries—officers	148,375	$ 30,038	$ 25,337	203,750	214,207
Salaries—other (2)	286,126	77,080	70,063	433,269	191,981
Payroll taxes	37,461	9,235	8,225	54,921	36,595
Employee benefits	28,985	7,146	6,364	42,494	26,479
Retirement (3)	8,192	1,659	1,399	11,250	8,655
Contract services	21,486	5,297	4,718	31,501	11,989
Rent—office (4)	4,093	1,009	899	6,000	6,000
Rent—warehouse (5)	82,894			82,894	48,664
Rent—equipment	2,333	575	512	3,420	795
Printing and reproduction		276	1,102	1,378	6,035
Marketing, public relations and advertising (6)	52,509	7,533	69,350	129,392	166,743
Bad debt	3,240			3,240	1,000
Bank service charges	1,795	442	394	2,631	2,165
Depreciation (7)	15,877	3,914	3,486	23,277	13,141
Dues and subscriptions	4,888	1,205	1,073	7,166	7,768
Insurance	12,711	3,134	2,791	18,635	10,338
Professional fees		11,781		11,781	16,482
Office supplies	18,191	4,485	3,994	26,669	18,095
Licenses & permits	4,633	1,142	1,017	6,792	2,972
Telephone and Internet	4,644	1,145	1,021	6,810	8,566
Travel (8)	43,606	10,750	9,574	63,930	45,803
Operation Sharehouse supplies	663,195			663,195	331,480
Miscellaneous	-7,093	-7,093		-7,093	3,006
Postage		6,107	1,527	7,634	4,780
Total Operating Expenses	$13,035,303	$176,860	$212,846	$13,425,005	$8,169,551

87

EXHIBIT 5.10   Program Efficiency Ratio

Ratio	Formula	Part on 990	Line on 990	Desired Trend
Program Efficiency	$\dfrac{\text{Program expenses}}{\text{Total expenses}}$	IX IX	$\dfrac{25}{25}$	Increasing

Stop Hunger Now	Formula	2007	2008
Program Efficiency	$\dfrac{\text{Program expenses}}{\text{Total expenses}}$	$\dfrac{\$7,833,458}{\$8,169,551} = 96\%$	$\dfrac{\$13,035,300}{\$13,425,005} = 97\%$

- How to calculate program-efficiency ratio
- The desired trend (increasing)
- The performance of Stop Hunger Now

The Better Business Bureau recommends that a minimum of 65 percent of expenses be spent directly on programs. The Charities Review Council of Minnesota recommends a benchmark of 70 percent. Some organizations, such as the United Way, calculate the percentage as a comparison of program expenses to total revenue. It recommends a percentage of 75 percent or higher.

Agency or Study	Program Efficiency Ratio Benchmark
American Institute of Philanthropy	60%
Better Business Bureau	65%
Charities Review Council of Minnesota	70%
James Cook Survey (Forbes, Oct. 28, 1991	76%

Based on these standards, Stop Hunger Now is perhaps doing too well. Spending 96 percent and 97 percent of its funds on programs in 2007 and 2008, respectively, the nonprofit is perhaps spending too little on fundraising and management.

Fundraising Efficiency Ratio

The fundraising efficiency ratio, which divides fundraising expenses by contributions (other than grants), measures fundraising expenses as percent of

EXHIBIT 5.11   Fundraising Efficiency Ratio

Ratio	Formula	Part on 990	Line on 990	Desired Trend
Fund-Raising Efficiency	Fundraising expenses	IX	25	Decreasing
	Total contributions (less government grants)	VIII	1h less1e	

Stop Hunger	Formula	2007		2008
Fund Raising Efficiency	Fundraising expenses	$190,851		$212,846
	Total contributions less government grants	$8,253,014[4] = 2.3%		$13,189,063 = 1.61%

total contributions. The amount of contributions and special-events revenues, not found in IRS Form 990, is found in the revenue ledger. Exhibit 5.11 shows how to calculate the fundraising ratio.

The American Institute of Philanthropy and the Better Business Bureau both recommend a fundraising-efficiency ratio of at least 65 percent.

Agency or Study	Fundraising Efficiency Benchmark
American Institute of Philanthropy	65% or more of revenue received
Better Business Bureau	65% or more of revenue received

Based on the ratios, Stop Hunger is again doing exceedingly well with over 98 percent of its contributions going to operations.

In evaluating fundraising efficiency, two factors may affect the fundraising efficiency ratio:

- A first-time fundraising event or campaign often incurs higher start-up expenses.
- Some fundraising methods are more expensive than others. For example, door-to-door solicitation is more expensive than phone calls, which are more expensive than direct mail, which is more expensive than electronic mail.

Sometimes a nonprofit misreports the amount of expenses, which may be the case for Stop Hunger Now, which reported few fundraising expenses in 2007 or 2008. Perhaps fundraising expenses were underreported. Surmising this is sometimes the case, the Urban Institute found that 37 percent of nonprofits with at least $50,000 in contributions reported zero fundraising costs.[5] On the other hand, fundraising may have been done by volunteers or a supporting foundation at no cost to the nonprofit.

Unrestricted Net Assets

The *unrestricted net assets ratio,* the bottom line if you will, is the amount held in reserve. Nonprofits maintain a reserve to cushion against an unanticipated decrease in revenues or increase in expenses. They may also maintain a reserve to save money to buy expensive equipment (e.g., a computer system) or a building. Some United Ways recommend that the reserve be at least three months of expenses. Though desirable, 61 percent of nonprofits had less than three months of available cash in 2010; and of these, 12 percent had no cash available.[6] No ratio, though, should be uncritically adopted. The amount in reserve will vary with a host of factors, including the organization's cash flow and mission. Exhibit 5.12 shows how to calculate the unrestricted net assets ratio.

The unrestricted net assets of Stop Hunger Now fell slightly, from 2.9 percent in 2007 to 2.4 percent in 2008, a razor-thin margin that should concern management and the Board. They should analyze the reasons for the decline and take action to restore the balance.

EXHIBIT 5.12   Unrestricted Net Assets Ratios

Ratio	Formula	Part on 990	Line on 990	Desired Trend
Unrestricted Net Assets	$\dfrac{\text{Unrestricted net assets}}{\text{Total expenses}}$	X I	27 18	Increasing

Stop Hunger Now	**Formula**	**2007**	**2008**	
Unrestricted Net Assets	$\dfrac{\text{Unrestricted net assets}}{\text{Total expenses}}$	$\dfrac{\$233,344}{\$8,169,551} = 2.9\%$	$\dfrac{\$317,677}{\$13,425,005} = 2.4\%$	

EXHIBIT 5.13   Days Cash on Hand

Liquidity Indicator	Formula	Line (Part) on 990	Desired Trend
Days of Cash on Hand	Cash and cash equivalents × 365 days / Total expenses less depreciation	1(X) & 2(X) × 365 / 18(I) to 22(IX)	Increasing

Stop Hunger Now	Formula	2007	2008
Days of Cash on Hand	Cash and cash equivalents × 365 days / Total expenses less depreciation	$187,774 × 365 / $8,169,551− / $13,141 / = 8.4 days	$103,125 × 365 / $13,425,005− / $23,277 / = 2.9 days

Liquidity Indicators

Cash is the lifeblood or any organization. Simply put, cash is necessary to pay day-to-day expenses. The indicators that measure liquidity/solvency include:

- Days of cash on hand
- The current ratio
- The quick ratio
- Net working capital

DAYS OF CASH ON HAND   The number of days of cash on hand is the number of days for which cash is available to meet daily expenses. Exhibit 5.13 shows how to calculate the amount.

The number of days of cash that Stop Hunger Now had on hand fell from 8.4 days in 2007 to 2.9 days in 2008. If this trend continues, the organization will not be able to pay its bills on time.

CURRENT RATIO   The current ratio measures the ability to pay current obligations. A ratio of 1.0 means that a nonprofit has just enough to pay its current liabilities. A healthy ratio for most organizations is between 2.0 and 4.0.[7] Exhibit 5.14 shows how to calculate the current ratio.

According to the benchmark, Stop Hunger Now still has a healthy current ratio, but the ratio plummeted from a robust 9.5 in 2007 to 2.4 in 2008.

EXHIBIT 5.14   Current Ratio

Liquidity Indicator	Formula	Line (Part) on 990	Desired Trend
Current Ratio	Current assets / Current liabilities	1(X) to 9(X) / 17(X) to 22(X)	Increasing
Stop Hunger	**Formula**	**2007**	**2008**
Current Ratio	Current assets / Current liabilities	$441,971 / $46,533 = 9.5	$348,732 / $143,737 = 2.4

QUICK RATIO   Akin to the current ratio, the quick ratio (which is also called the *acid test ratio*) measures the ability to meet short-term obligations with the most liquid (easily convertible to cash) assets like marketable securities and accounts receivable. Inventories are not included as an asset because they are relatively illiquid. Like the current ratio, experts recommend a quick ratio of 2.0 to 4.0.[8] Exhibit 5.15 shows how to calculate the ratio.

Stop Hunger Now's quick ratio is 1.9, which is slightly below the recommended amount.

NET WORKING CAPITAL   A measure of cash flow, not a ratio, net working capital should be positive, not negative. In deciding whether to make a loan to a nonprofit, bankers consider the amount of working capital to assess whether a nonprofit can make its payment obligations. Exhibit 5.16 shows how to calculate the amount of net working capital.

As with the other liquidity indicators, Stop Hunger Now's working capital fell from $395,438 in 2007 to $294,995 in 2008.

EXHIBIT 5.15   Quick Ratio

Liquidity Indicator	Formula	Line (Part) on 990	Desired Trend
Quick Ratio	Current assets − Inventories / Current liabilities	1 to 9(X) less 8(X) / 17(X) to 22(X)	Increasing
Stop Hunger Now	**Formula**	**2007**	**2008**
Quick Ratio	Current assets − Inventories / Current liabilities	$441,971 / $46,533 = 9.5	$348,732 − $75,806 / $143,737 = 1.9

EXHIBIT 5.16 Net Working Capital

Liquidity Indicator	Formula	Line (Part) on 990	Desired Trend
Net Working Capital	Current assets less current liabilities	1(X) to 9(X) less 17(X) to 22(X)	Increasing
Stop Hunger Now	**Formula**	**2007**	**2008**
Net Working Capital	Current assets less current liabilities	$441.971 − $46,533 = $395,438	$348,732 − 143,737 = $294,995

Days in Accounts Receivable

Days in accounts receivable measure the average number of days that accounts are receivable. The fewer days that accounts are receivable, the more cash is on hand. Thus, receivables should be vigorously collected. Exhibit 7.2 in Chapter 7, "Manage Cash Flow," explains how to expedite the collection of receivables. Exhibit 5.17 shows how to calculate days in accounts receivable.

The recommended benchmark is no more than 30 days in accounts receivable.[9]

Stop Hunger Now significantly betters this norm by having no outstanding receivables in 2007 and only 0.24 days in receivables in 2008.

EXHIBIT 5.17 Days in Accounts Receivable

Liquidity Indicator	Formula	Line (Part) on 990	Desired Trend
Days in Accounts Receivable	$\dfrac{\text{Accounts receivable} \times 365}{\text{Operating revenue}}$	$\dfrac{3(X) \text{ to } 7(X) \times 365}{12(I)}$	Decreasing
Stop Hunger Now	**Formula**	**2007**	**2008**
Days in Accounts Receivable	$\dfrac{\text{Accounts receivable} \times 365}{\text{Operating revenue}}$	$\dfrac{0}{\$8,271,269}$	$\dfrac{\$8,773 \times 365}{\$13,200,453} = 0.24$ days

EXHIBIT 5.18   Margin Ratios

Margin Ratios	Formula	Line (Part) on 990	Desired Trend
Total Margin	Revenues less expenses	12(I) less 18(I)	Increasing
	Revenues	12(I)	Increasing
Operating Margin	Revenue less expenses	12(I) less 18(I)	
	Operating revenues	12(I) less 11(1)	

Stop Hunger Now	**Formula**	**2007**	**2008**
Total Margin	Revenues less expenses	$\dfrac{\$8,271,269 - \$8,169,551}{\$8,271,269}$ = 1.2%	$\dfrac{\$13,200,453 - \$13,340,672}{\$13,200,453}$ = -1.7%
Operating Margin	Revenue less expenses	Same as above	Same as above
	Operating revenues		

Margin Ratios

Nonprofits need a sufficient margin (cushion) against fiscal uncertainties. The ideal margin depends on the amount of unrestricted net assets, the predictability of sales and other revenues and future economic conditions. The *total margin ratio* is revenues less expenses, then divided by revenues. The total-margin ratio may disguise problems, however. For instance, a one-time bequest to a nonprofit will inflate the ratio. More telling, therefore, is the *operating margin ratio*, which is operating revenues less expenses, and then divided by operating revenues. Exhibit 5.18 explains how to compute margin ratios.

The total margin and operating margins were the same in 2007 and 2008. Stop Hunger Now had an operating deficit of $224,552 in 2008, dropping the margins from positive 1.2 percent to negative 1.7 percent, which is a warning signal.

Funds Management Ratios

Some nonprofits sell goods and services. The *receivables/sales ratio* measures the extent to which credit has been extended for sales. The *payable/cost of goods ratio* is the percentage of goods billed, but not paid. The *sales/fixed assets ratio* measures the amount of equipment required to

EXHIBIT 5.19   Funds-Management Ratios

Funds Management Ratios	Formula	Desired Trend
Receivables/Sales	$\dfrac{\text{Accounts receivable}}{\text{Total sales}}$	Decreasing
Payables/Cost of Goods Sold	$\dfrac{\text{Accounts payable}}{\text{Operating expenses}}$	Decreasing
Sales/Fixed Assets	$\dfrac{\text{Sales}}{\text{Fixed assets less depreciation}}$	Increasing
Inventory Turnover	$\dfrac{\text{Monthly inventory sales}}{\text{Annual inventory sales}}$	Increasing

generate sales. The *billings/sales ratio* indicates the amount of expenses tied up in billings. The *inventory turnover ratio* divides the average monthly inventory sales by annual sales to determine the amount of inventory turnover. The more often the inventory turns over, the less money is tied up holding inventory items, and the more that can be spent on other purposes. This ratio is explained in more detail in Chapter 10, "Manage Fixed Assets and the Inventory."

The data to calculate these ratios are not available in the financial statements or in IRS Form 990. They must be culled from the subsidiary revenue and expense ledgers. Exhibit 5.19 explains how to calculate funds-management ratios.

Debt Service Ratios

Some nonprofits issue long-term debt. Debt service ratios, also known as *leverage* ratios, measure the extent to which an organization supports its activities by using debt. Two principal ratios are the debt and the debt-to-equity ratios. Generally, the debt ratio should not exceed 0.5 and the debt-to-equity ratio should not exceed 1.0.[10] Exhibit 5.20 shows how to calculate the two debt-service ratios.

Stop Hunger Now did not have any debt outstanding.

EXHIBIT 5.20   Debt-Service Ratios

Debt-Service Ratios	Formula	Line (Part) on 990	Desired Trend
Debt Ratio	$\dfrac{\text{Total debt}}{\text{Total assets}}$	20(X) 26(X)	Decreasing
Debt-to-Equity Ratio	$\dfrac{\text{Total debt}}{\text{Total net assets}}$	20(X) 22(I)	Decreasing

For Further Reading

Berger, Steven. *Understanding Nonprofit Financial Statements.* 3rd ed. Washington, DC: BoardSource, 2008. Excellent discussion of financial statements and ratio analysis.

CHAPTER 6

Prepare and Manage the Budget

All nonprofits, regardless of size and mission, should adopt an *operating budget* that estimates revenues and expenses for the next fiscal year. The operating budget conveys the organization's mission and priorities. One survey found that 85 percent of religious nonprofits have an operating budget.[1] In addition to the operating budget, nonprofits, depending on their size and resources, may prepare two other types of budgets: (1) a *cash flow budget* that projects monthly cash receipts and expenses over the fiscal year (discussed in Chapter 7, "Manage Cash Flow;" and (2) a *capital budget*, a multiyear estimate of capital expenses, such as buildings, land acquisition, vehicles, and equipment (discussed in Chapter 10, "Manage Capital Assets and Inventory").

Multiple stakeholders, including the Board, the CEO, staff, funders, and other constituents, such as clients, customers, and community partners, play a budgetary role. With input from key stakeholders, the budget process follows four steps:

1. The Board sets the policy direction.
2. Following the Board's direction, the CEO prepares the budget.
3. The Board reviews and adopts the budget.
4. The CEO and staff execute the budget.

Board Sets the Policy Direction

To set the policy direction, the Board should adopt a:

- Mission statement
- Strategic plan
- Budget policy

Each is discussed in this section.

Mission Statement

Each nonprofit should adopt a mission statement, articulating its *core values*. The Internal Revenue Service (IRS) requires 501(c)(3) nonprofits to submit an annual tax return called Form 990, including a mission statement identifying the nonprofit's:

- Purpose
- Goals
- Service recipients
- Activities[2]

A well-crafted mission statement is *highly* motivating. Many nonprofits do particularly ennobling work. Mindful of the good they are doing, employees, Board members, and volunteers are more willing to go "the extra mile." Furthermore, an inspirational mission statement is an effective marketing tool that attracts resources, both human and financial. Unfortunately, most mission statements are ineffective and, while most nonprofits have a mission statement, few employees know what it says. An ineffective mission statement may have one or more of the following characteristics:

- Too long to remember
- Full of jargon
- Uninspiring
- Narrow focus

Chief among these drawbacks is excessive length. Exhibit 6.1 compares the current mission statement of the United Way of America to that of the March of Dimes.

EXHIBIT 6.1   Sample Mission Statements

United Way of America	March of Dimes
To improve lives by mobilizing the caring power of communities.	To improve the health of babies by preventing birth defects, premature birth and infant mortality. We carry out this mission through research, community service education and advocacy to save babies' lives. March of Dimes researchers, volunteers, educators, outreach workers and advocates work together to give all babies a fighting chance against the threats to their health: prematurity, birth defects, low birth weight.

The United Way of America's mission statement is short, free of jargon, and inspirational. The March of Dimes' mission statement, though inspirational and jargon-free, is far too long to remember. It should be reduced to the first sentence: "To improve the health of babies by preventing birth defects, premature birth and infant mortality."

A second, telling weakness of many mission statements is that even if well crafted, the organizational culture does not reinforce the mission statement. Management should post the mission statement prominently in the workplace. Even more important, management, the Board, and staff should constantly remind each other and the public of their worthwhile mission and the people they serve.

Strategic Plan

Nonprofits should adopt a *strategic plan* to put the mission statement into action. Also referred to as a community scorecard, business plan, or service plan, the strategic plan envisions the future, articulating the nonprofit's *core values*, including:

- A caring attitude
- Respect for diversity
- Integrity
- A focus on the customer/client/member
- Responsiveness
- Financial sustainability

In times of fiscal distress, many nonprofits are financially vulnerable. Unlike governments, they do not have the coercive power to levy taxes. They rely on the generosity of donors, members, and grantors, who may reduce funding. A strategic plan takes a cold, brutal look at the future, making a *SWOT* analysis of the nonprofit's:

- *S*trengths
- *W*eaknesses
- *O*pportunities
- *T*hreats

Exhibit 6.2 is an example of the types of features that a SWOT analysis will reveal.

Based on the SWOT analysis, management and the Board should prepare an *action plan* that builds on the organization's strengths, takes advantage of its opportunities, remedies weaknesses, and heads off threats.

EXHIBIT 6.2   Sample SWOT Analysis

Strengths	Weaknesses
■ Adequate financial resources	■ No clear organizational mission
■ Appropriate technology	■ Management turnover
■ Professional management	■ Missing skills and competencies
■ Staff commitment	■ Lack of Board commitment
■ Entrepreneurial spirit	■ Poor customer relations
■ Modern buildings and equipment	■ Weak financial base
Opportunities	**Threats**
■ Expand services	■ Adverse demographics
■ Increased demand for services	■ Poor public image
■ New funding sources	■ Decreased governmental funding
■ Improve management capability	■ Declining volunteer interest
■ Reorganize	■ Decreased demand for services

Budgetary Policy

Based on the mission statement and the strategic plan, the Board adopts a budgetary policy that specifies:

■ The budgetary roles of the Board and CEO
■ The amount of funds to keep in reserve

BUDGETARY ROLES   The Board's fiduciary duty is to adopt policies that the CEO will administer. The CEO works for the Board, which evaluates his or her performance. Sometimes Boards defer too much to the CEO. For example, the Board of the United Way of Central Carolinas paid its CEO an excessively high, scandal-provoking salary of $1.2 million in 2008.[3] Similarly, the Board of the Kentucky League of Cities paid its CEO $307,044 in 2009, far in excess of the prevailing rate.[4] The CEO may accrue too much power when the Board is large and unwieldy to govern. A study in Indiana found that 47 percent of that state's nonprofits had Boards with 10 or members and 19 percent had between 15 and 29 members.[5]

To make large-sized Boards more manageable, nonprofits often create a *budget committee*, comprised of a subset of Board members, including preferably those with financial expertise. The committee acts as a liaison to the rest of the full Board and works with the CEO and CFO to prepare the budget, then submits it to the full Board for review and adoption.

Upon the CEO's recommendation, the Board decides salary and fringe benefit levels and the budget amount. During the fiscal year the CEO and CFO watch the budget, comparing budgeted to actual expenses and revenues. The CEO reports the status of the budget to the Board, usually monthly. If expenses are greater, or revenues lower, than budgeted, the CEO recommends ways for the Board to bring the budget back into balance by either cutting expenses or increasing revenues. Finally, at the end of the fiscal year, the Board evaluates program performance in light of service goals.

RESERVE POLICY   There are two types of financial reserves. An *undesignated reserve* cushions against a financial shortfall that could be caused by:

- An economic downturn
- Decreased memberships
- A large, unanticipated expense due to an act of nature (e.g., hurricane, tornado, wildfire)
- A breakdown of expensive equipment
- Reduced funding during the year (e.g., the unexpected termination of a grant)
- Unanticipated expenses (e.g., increased health care or utility costs)

Naturally, the larger the financial reserve, the more easily a nonprofit can weather such emergencies. Funders, though, take a dim view of too high a reserve. Quite understandably, they want a high percentage of their funds to be spent on clients and beneficiaries, not kept in reserve. Some, therefore, limit the amount of a reserve as a condition of funding. For example, some United Ways limit the undesignated reserve to 25 percent of the annual budget.

The second type, a *designated reserve*, earmarks funds for such purposes as:

- Equipment replacement
- Building repair
- Building acquisition
- Debt service

Because the amount of the reserve is sensitive, a Board should adopt a reserve policy such as that shown in Exhibit 6.3.

Budget Preparation

How the budget is prepared depends on the CEO's management style. A top-down, controlling management style centralizes budget making in the CEO's office. The CEO does not engage her or his program managers, instead

> The organization will retain sufficient funds to handle fiscal emergencies such as short-term cash flow problems, unanticipated funding reductions, and unanticipated expenses, according to the following conditions:
>
> 1. One-fourth (25%) of the unrestricted net assets shall be maintained as an operating reserve.
> 2. A second restricted reserve shall be maintained to replace capital assets. The reserve shall equal 20% of the approximate replacement cost of fleet vehicles and 1% of the cost of replacing facilities.

EXHIBIT 6.3   Sample Reserve Policy

telling them what their budget will be. In contrast, a collaborative, *bottom-up* management style solicits employee input and participation. Program managers prepare their own budgets and present them to the CEO, who has the final approval. The CEO encourages *all* employees, not just managers, to suggest ways that will improve effectiveness and efficiency. This budgeting discussion assumes a collaborative management style because it increases motivation and innovation.

The CEO prepares a budget calendar that lays out a budget preparation timetable, as in Exhibit 6.4.

The CFO compiles the budget calendar, budget request forms, and instructions into a *budget manual* used to orient new Board members and

EXHIBIT 6.4   Budget Calendar

Date	Action	Responsible Person(s)
2/1	Meet with the Board.	Board and CEO
2/15	Meet with the management team.	CEO and PMs
3/1	Project revenues.	CEO, CFO, and PMs
4/1	Make budget requests.	PMs
5/15	Approve the preliminary budget.	CEO and CFO
6/1	Approve the final budget.	Board
6/15	Incorporate Board-approved changes into the final budget.	CFO
6/30	Distribute approved budget.	CFO
7/1 to 6/30	Administer budget.	CEO, CFO, and PMs

Key:
Board: Nonprofit Board
CEO: Executive Director
CFO: Chief Financial Officer
PMs: Program Managers

staff to the budget process. The following sections discuss the steps shown in Exhibit 6.4.

CEO Meets with the Board

The CEO and Board meet to kick off the budget process. Sometimes held in a retreat setting, the Board conveys its priorities to the CEO. They give the CEO direction with respect to:

- The amount of merit and/or cost-of-living (COLA) increases, if any
- Fringe benefits to provide, including health care insurance, retirement compensation, leave benefits, compensatory time, and overtime
- Other post-employment benefits, such as health insurance to retirees
- Significant new program initiatives
- Fundraising campaigns

CEO Meets with Management Team

Each program manager, understandably, chiefly focuses on his or her program. As a nonprofit grows in size, program managers can become unfamiliar with each other's program goals, accomplishments, challenges, and aspirations. Such isolation can lead to "turf" protection. To increase cooperation, the CEO may meet with managers prior to their preparing budget requests. In the team-building session, program managers share their respective aspirations, accomplishments, and challenges. The dialogue builds a sense of togetherness and team spirit. In the session, the CEO communicates the Board's priorities as determined in their goal-setting meeting.

Forecast Revenues

The amount of revenues drives and underpins budget making. Nonprofits have seven principal types of revenues:

- *One-time revenue.* One-time award, usually to serve as seed money to attract subsequent funding
- *Competitive grant.* Annual or multiyear grant awarded competitively
- *Noncompetitive grant.* Annual or multiyear sole-source grant
- *Membership dues.* Membership fees and dues
- *Convention revenues.* Registration fees from conventions
- *Fundraising revenues.* Revenues from fundraising events and campaigns
- *Service fees.* Fees for services (e.g., tuition fees)

Forecasting Methods

There are four methods to forecast revenues:

1. *Qualitative method.* An "educated guess" about future revenues
2. *Deterministic method.* Plug data into a preset formula (e.g., the reimbursement rate times the number of clients served)
3. *Extrapolative method.* Use previous years' revenues to forecast next year's revenue. There are three extrapolative methods:
   A. *Penultimate year.* Assumes that the next year's budgeted revenue will be the same as the current year's.
   B. *Average change.* Multiplies the current year's budgeted revenue by the average percentage change in revenue over previous years, as shown here:

Example

	Year	Fees	Percent Change
	20 × 1	$129,256	
	20 × 2	137,011	+6%
	20 × 3	147,972	+8%
	20 × 4	156,333	+7%
Estimated	20 × 5	169,416	

Average Change (20 × 2 to 20 × 4) = 21%/3

    = 7% average annual change

Year 20 × 05 Estimate = 20 × 4 Fees × Average Change

    = $156,333 × 107%

    = $169,416

   C. *Moving average.* Predicts revenues with an erratic history, smoothing out annual differences by calculating average change for each point in a historical series. For instance, after reviewing 10 years of data, the revenues for years 1 through 3 would be averaged because the look to have the best fit. The average for this three-year period becomes the smoothed value for year 2. Then the values for years 3 and 4 are averaged to create the smoothed year 3 value, and so on.

   Microsoft Excel makes the moving-average calculation as follows:
   Step 1: Open an Excel file. Input the revenue data in Column A.

Step 2: Use the Data Analysis function.

Step 3: Use the Moving Average option in the Data Analysis tool.

Step 4: Select column A as your input range.

Step 5: Enter 3 as the Interval option because you are using three years.

Step 6: Select OK. You should see the Simple Moving Average Exhibits in column B.

4. *Break-even analysis.* Break-even analysis prices goods and services, using the formula:

$$\text{Break-even analysis} = \frac{\text{Fixed costs}\,(FC) + \text{Total variable costs}\,(VC)}{\text{Number of people served}}$$

Fixed costs remain the same regardless of the amount of service provided. For instance, rent, insurance, gas, and electricity costs remain fixed until more space is needed. *Variable costs* vary with the amount of service rendered. For instance, the more clients that a job counseling center sees, the higher are the variable costs, such as personnel, supplies, and equipment.

Example. Let us look at a break-even analysis example. Suppose you are going to establish a homeless center. You are seeking 100 percent funding from the county. The annual fixed costs of the shelter ($15,000) are for rent and utilities. The variable costs, $120 per person served in the shelter, pay for the cost of staffing, meals, and beds. The shelter holds 100 people. In your grant proposal, you estimate that you will serve 75 people in the first year and 100 people in the second year, with variable costs increasing to $130 per person in the second year. Calculate the funding needed in years 1 and 2 to break even.

Again, the break-even formula is

$$\frac{\text{Fixed costs}\,(FC) + \text{Total variable costs}\,(VC)}{\text{Number of people served}}$$

Year 1

$$\frac{\$15,000 + (75 \text{ people} \times \$120)}{75 \text{ people}}$$

That is,

$$\frac{\$15,000 + \$9,000}{75 \text{ people}} = \$320 \text{ per person}$$

Year 2

$$\frac{\$15,000 + (100 \text{ people} \times \$130)}{100 \text{ people}}$$

That is,

$$\frac{\$15,000 + \$13,000}{100 \text{ people}} = \$280 \text{ per person}$$

As shown in Exhibit 6.5, the revenue forecasting method varies with the type of revenue being forecast.

Make Budget Requests

Next, the CEO distributes the budget calendar, budget request forms, and instructions to program managers, who budget for salaries, fringe benefits, supplies, and capital items. The budget instructions specify:

- The salary increase, if any, to be given
- The amounts involved in calculating fringe benefits (e.g., Social Security, health care, pensions)
- Inflationary rates for particular goods
- Performance measures required to justify new and existing programs

  With this information, program managers budget for:

- Salaries
- Fringe benefits
- Capital outlay
- Existing and new programs

  These budget items are now discussed in more detail in the following sections.

Salary Requests

The Board should adopt a human-resource policy that includes provisions regarding employment procedures, compensation rates, and fringe benefits such as listed in Exhibit 6.6.

Organizations should pay wages and fringe benefits that fairly compensate employees for their efforts. Paying equitable rates reduces turnover and motivates employees. To determine fair compensation, a nonprofit should

EXHIBIT 6.5   Revenue Forecasting Methods

Revenue Type	Forecast Method	Discussion
One-Time Grant	Qualitative	Make a best guess about whether other agencies will fund the program, but be realistic. If future funding is unlikely, give affected employees sufficient advance notice of a program's discontinuance.
Competitive Grant	Qualitative	Whether a nonprofit will get a competitive grant, or have a grant renewed, is a subjective, qualitative assessment.
Noncompetitive Grant	Qualitative	Literally, "money in the bank," a "no-brainer."
Membership Dues	Extrapolative	Which extrapolative method is used depends on the revenue's history. With only one or two years of history, the penultimate method may be best. With several years of stable history, average change is best. With erratic revenue history, use the moving average method.
Convention Revenues	Qualitative or Extrapolative	If convention revenues have varied widely from year-to-year, use the qualitative method. If revenues have been predictable, use average change.
Fundraising and Capital Campaign	Qualitative or Extrapolative	The amount that will be raised in a first-time fund raising event or capital campaign is a qualitative, educated estimate. If there is stable revenue history, use the extrapolative method.
Fees	Break-even analysis, deterministic and extrapolative	Some fees are simply a matter of multiplying the number of service units by a set rate. For instance, grants will reimburse for services rendered to clients based on an agreed-upon reimbursement rate. On the other hand, if selling a product, the extrapolative method is used if there is stable revenue history.

periodically compare its compensation and fringe benefit levels to those of similar organizations. A large nonprofit may engage a consultant to conduct the *compensation classification* study. Ideally, the Board is financially able to grant employees an annual COLA increase to offset the effect of inflation. To decide the COLA amount, organizations typically use the annual change

EXHIBIT 6.6   Human-Resource Policy List

Policy Provision

Employment Procedures
Hiring, orientation, disciplinary, grievance, and termination procedures
Compensation
Salary and merit increases, overtime pay, and compensatory time procedures
Fringe Benefits
Group Insurance. Extent and type of insurance coverage, the organization's
    cost, employee's cost, and who is included and excluded
Retirement Plan. Extent and type of benefits, the organization's cost, employee's
    cost, and when an employee has vested benefits
Sick Leave. How sick leave is accumulated, the rate of accumulation, and the
    amount paid for·unused sick leave upon retirement
Annual Leave. How annual leave is accumulated, the rate of accumulation,
    notice to be given before taking leave, amount paid for unused leave upon
    termination, and maximum amount that can be accumulated
Administrative Leave. The amount of leave that can be taken for military duty,
    jury duty, and emergencies
Other Leave. The amount of leave that can be taken for maternity, paternity, and
    other purposes
Travel. Approval required for travel in and out of region, the mileage
    reimbursement rate, the per-diem reimbursement rate, how to make a travel
    advance, and the documentation required for reimbursement

---

in the Consumer Price Index (CPI), issued by the U.S. Department of Labor's Bureau of Labor Statistics. In addition to a COLA increase, the Board should reward high-performing employees with a merit increase if funds are available.

Fringe Benefit Requests

There are two types of fringe benefits: *mandatory* and *optional*. The national government *mandates* that nonprofits with 50 or more employees pay for:

- Overtime
- Social Security
- Unemployment compensation
- Family and medical leave
- Health care insurance

Moreover, all states, except Texas, require workers' compensation payments.

MANDATORY FRINGE BENEFITS

Overtime The Fair Labor Standards Act stipulates that employees be paid 1.5 times their basic hourly pay for the hours more than 40 that they work weekly. Executive, professional, administrative, and other highly paid workers, however, are exempt from the overtime provision. The employer must justify an exemption based on the type of work an employee performs, *not* on his or her job title. An excellent explanation of justifying exemptions can be found at the Federal Labor Standards Act home page at, "Exempt, Non exempt, Comp Time, and More," at http://www.flsa.com/overtime.html.

Social Security and Medicare The Federal Income Contribution Act (FICA), better known as Social Security, requires the employer to pay a flat percentage of wages established by federal statute. The current FICA rate is:

- Social Security   6.20% of wages
- Medicare   1.45% of wages
           7.65%

    The percentages are charged up to a salary cap, which is currently $106,800. Usually, the salary cap is annually adjusted upward to reflect the increase in the CPI.

Unemployment Compensation Overseen by the Department of Labor, the Social Security Act requires employers and the national government to contribute to a fund that temporarily compensates laid-off employees actively seeking employment.

Workers' Compensation Insurance Every state except Texas requires the employer to compensate workers for the medical and rehabilitation costs related to work-related injuries.

Family and Medical Leave The Family and Medical Leave Act requires employers with at least 50 employees to provide up to 12 weeks of unpaid leave for:

- The birth or adoption of a child
- Foster care
- Care of a sick child, spouse, or parent
- A serious health problem during any 12-month period

Health Care Insurance   The principal types of health care plans are:

- *Indemnity.* Employees freely chose their medical services and providers.
- *Health maintenance organization (HMO) and preferred provider organization (PPO).* The employer contracts with an HMO or PPO to provide employee health care.
- *Consumer driven.* A high-deductible plan combined with a health savings account or a health reimbursement account, which permits employees to set aside pretax money to pay for out-of-pocket medical expenses.
- *Voluntary employee beneficiary association.* An association, jointly funded by the employer and employee that pays for medical expenses.

To reduce health care costs, a nonprofit should adopt the *IRS Section 125 plan.* Named for its location in the Internal Revenue Code (IRC), the Section 125 plan provides tax savings by reducing employee medical premiums from gross salary calculation prior to calculation of federal income and Social Security taxes. Moreover, the reduction lowers the amount of Social Security and unemployment benefits that the nonprofit must contribute. Newly eligible employees may waive Section 125 when they choose the medical plan; otherwise, it can only be changed during the annual autumn enrollment period, for a January 1 effective date.

OPTIONAL FRINGE BENEFITS   Nonprofits can optionally provide the following benefits:

- Leave
- Pension plan
- Compensatory time
- Wellness program

Each is discussed in the following sections.

Leave   *Leave* includes time off work for holidays, vacation, sickness, military service, and family care.

Pensions   There are two types of *pension plans.* A defined-benefit plan guarantees a fixed pension benefit, based on the employee's age and number of years of service. Becoming more common, a defined contribution plan derives the pension amount from the amounts that the employee and the nonprofit have paid into the plan.

Compensatory (Comp) Time   *Compensatory* (comp) *time* is time taken off from work as compensation for extra time worked by employees who are exempt from receiving overtime under federal guidelines.

Employee Wellness   *Employee wellness* programs incentivize employees to be healthier. The nonprofit can offer programs to help the employee lose weight, stop smoking, and exercise more.

The program manager calculates the cost of salaries and fringe benefits to budget both for existing and new positions. Exhibit 6.7 is an example of a new position request form, which asks for:

■ The job class description
■ The position's source of funding
■ How the work is currently being performed
■ How the work will be performed if the new position is not approved

---

1. Job-class description
   a. If the request is for an additional position in an established job-class, what is the job-class title?
   b. If the request is for a new position with no job-class description, complete a "Job Analysis Questionnaire" furnished by the HR department.
2. Justification for the new position
   a. How will the position be funded?
   b. How is the work currently being performed?
   c. How will the work be performed if the new position is not approved?
3. How will the new position improve the level of service in your program?
4. What are the personnel expenses of this position?

FICA (7.65% of salary)
Health insurance ($6,000 per year)
Dental insurance ($80 per month)
Retirement (5% of salary)
Total personnel expenses

5. What are the other expenses of this position?
Vehicles
Tools
Equipment
Supplies
Total other expenses

EXHIBIT 6.7   Position Request Form

- The salary cost of the position
- The supplies and capital expenses needed to support the position

Budget for Capital Expenses

Capital assets have a longer life and higher value than operating assets. Capital-asset expenses include the purchase of land, buildings, equipment, vehicles, and the like. The Board sets the value (e.g., over $500) and life (e.g., over one year) of a capital asset. As discussed in Chapter 2, "Account for Transactions," a capital asset is capitalized (depreciated).

Capital items often have concomitant operating expenses, such as:

- Heating and cooling a building
- Fueling and maintaining a vehicle
- Repairing and maintaining a copy machine

In requesting a capital asset, the program manager should identify the subsequent operating costs associated with purchase. Moreover, the non-profit should create a reserve to replace equipment that becomes obsolete. For instance, computer hardware should be replaced about every three to five years. However, nonprofits with razor-thin reserves often do not set money aside for replacement.

Budget for Existing and New Programs

Nonprofits will prepare either a *line item* or a program-performance budget. A line-item budget simply shows expenses by line item with no performance measures. Exhibit 6.8 gives examples of line items.

In contrast, a program performance budget breaks expenses into programs and includes performance measures. Exhibit 6.9 is a sample of program expenses and performance measures.

Let us discuss each type of measure in more detail. *Inputs* are the time, materials, and equipment needed to accomplish work. Inputs are budgeted as objects of expenditure, also known as *line items*. Inputs give no indication of performance.

Many funders want to see measurable, significant results. There are four types of performance measures shown in Exhibit 6.10. The simplest measure of performance, an *output* measure, is a count of the amount of work performed. Though a good *workload* measure, outputs give no sense of the *quality* of work performed. To assess work quality, there are three types of measures. First, a *process measure* indicates *how well* work is performed:

- The error rate in processing forms and applications
- The time taken to process applicants
- The accuracy rate in placing clients

EXHIBIT 6.8 Line Item Examples

LINE ITEM EXAMPLES

101	PERSONNEL BENEFITS
181	FICA Tax Expense
182	Retirement
183	Health Benefits
184	Disability/Life
186	Workers' Compensation Ins.

TOTAL 101   PERSONNEL BENEFITS

102	PROFESSIONAL SERVICES
191	Audit

TOTAL 102   PROFESSIONAL SERVICES

200	SUPPLIES
210	Housekeeping Supplies
220	Food
230	Medical Supplies
231	Educational Training Supplies
232	Occupational Skills Training
240	Maintenance & Repairs Supplies
250	Automotive Supplies
260	Office Supplies

TOTAL 200   SUPPLIES

300	TRAVEL & CLIENT TRANSPORTATION
310	Travel
311	Agency Parking

TOTAL 300   TRAVEL & CLIENT TRANSPORTATION

301	COMMUNICATION
320	TELEPHONE
321	POSTAGE

TOTAL 301   COMMUNICATION

302	STAFF TRAINING
312	Training—Per Diem
391	Employee Training

TOTAL 302   STAFF DEV—TRAINING EXP

304	FACILITIES—UTILITIES/MAINT
331	Electricity
332	Water
333	Heat
351	Maintenance—Outdoor Vendors
352	Maintenance & Repairs—Equipment
353	Maintenance & Repairs—Vehicle
392	Garbage Collection

TOTAL 304   FACILITIES—UTILITIES/MAINT

400	FACILITIES—RENT
410	Rent

TOTAL 400   FACILITIES—RENT

450	INSURANCE AND BONDING
475	DUES & SUBSCRIPTIONS
490	Dues & Subscriptions

TOTAL 475   DUES & SUBSCRIPTIONS

480	LEASE—VEHICLE/OFFICE EQUIPMENT
411	Lease of Equipment
412	Rental Vehicle

TOTAL 480   LEASE—VEHICLE/OFFICE EQUIPMENT

Second, an *outcome measure* assesses whether the objective was *accomplished*. For example, did the nonprofit's program enable the customer to:

- Keep lost weight off
- Stay off drugs, cigarettes, etc.
- Remain in the job in which he or she was placed
- Not go back to jail
- Learn a marketable skill

EXHIBIT 6.9   Program Performance Budget

Program Name	Program Purpose	Measure	Budget
Preparation for Independent Living	Assist homeless young adults (age 16–21) with basic needs, employment, and rental assistance.	-Number placed in jobs -Number who attain a GED -Number able to sustain themselves in housing at the current rental rate	$325,000
Homesteaders	Help families stay together.	-Number of families that remain intact one-year after receiving service	$375,000
Restitution and Community Service	Provide supervised community service opportunities to enable youth to fulfill their court obligations.	-Percent of juveniles who satisfy the court order regarding community service and restitution of their victims	$275,000
Structured Day	Provide tutoring, remedial assistance, social and life skills to suspended students.	-How well students keep up with their school work during their suspension	$580,000
Boxing Gang Intervention Program	Develop boxing skills to teach teamwork, discipline, leadership, and healthy living.	-Measured physical fitness -Academic progress in school -Disciplinary actions -Compliance with parents -Youth not in gangs	$250,000
Youth Mentor Program	Mentor youth in one on one volunteer program to improve academic and social performance.	-Academic standing in school -Compliance with parents in the home	$383,661

EXHIBIT 6.10   Types of Performance Measures

Type of Measure	Description
Output Measures	Counts of the amount of work performed (e.g., number of clients served, amount of food distributed, members served, etc.)
Process Measures	Steps and the amount of time to perform a task
Outcome Measures	The ultimate service outcome desired
Efficiency Measures	Inputs (e.g., dollars or hours) divided by outputs or outcomes

Third, an *efficiency measure* determines the cost-effectiveness of a program by dividing inputs (usually expenses), by outputs or outcomes. For example, what is the cost:

■ Per client given counseling
■ Per person placed in a job
■ Per person given training
■ Per student graduating

Let us look at program justification in action. Many nonprofits receive local government funding, usually on a competitive process. Getting a grant, depends on the ability to demonstrate measurable success at a reasonable cost. Exhibit 6.11 shows the funding criteria and information that Wake County, North Carolina, uses to award funds. The funding criteria and weights include:

Funding Criterion	Weight
Community impact	30 points
Measurable outcomes	25 points
Organizational capacity	20 points
Fiscal planning	25 points

CEO Reviews Budget Requests

Next, the program managers submit their budget requests to the CEO, who typically meets with each manager to ask questions about their requests. Program managers often ask for somewhat more than they think they will get. The CEO modifies the requests to reflect the Board's priorities and the availability of resources.

PROJECT TITLE: _____ PROPOSAL # _____ TOTAL SCORE: _____

FUNDING REQUEST _____ TOTAL PROJECT BUDGET _____

POSSIBLE FUNDING RECOMMENDATION: ___ DEFINITELY ___ LIKELY ___ MAYBE ___ NO

Unsatisfactory Unclear Incomplete Insufficient 1	Minimal Weak Confusing Lacks some info 2	Basic Satisfactory, but some questions/concerns remain 3	Good Strong Well-planned 4	Exceptional Exemplary Model program No question remain 5
A. COMMUNITY IMPACT (30 points)				
1. Clearly describes all components of a project, reflecting a good understanding of the target population's needs, as well as any collaborative efforts			1 2 3 4	5
2. Identifies a target population, as well as the geographic area of the county to be served			1 2 3 4	5
3. Articulates the unmet need for the service with supporting statistics			1 2 3 4	5
4. Provides a well-conceived plan to maximize the target population's access to the proposed service			1 2 3 4	5
5. Differentiates proposed services from identical or similar services			1 2 3 4	5
			TOTAL =	_____
B. MEASURABLE OUTPUTS AND OUTCOMES (25 points)				
1. Indicates a reasonable number of clients to be served given the level of service			1 2 3 4	5
2. Provides realistic and meaningful, anticipated *measurable* outcomes			1 2 3 4	5
3. Demonstrates reliable and accurate methods of measurement			1 2 3 4	5
4. Describes appropriate strategies to achieve outcomes			1 2 3 4	5
5. Demonstrates past success through year-to-date or most recent actual data			1 2 3 4	5
			TOTAL =	_____

EXHIBIT 6.11 Nonprofit Funding Criteria.

1	2	3	4	5
Unsatisfactory Unclear Incomplete Insufficient	**Minimal** Weak Confusing Lacks some info	**Basic** Satisfactory, but some question remain	**Good** Strong well-planned Clear	**Exceptional** Exemplary Model program No questions remain
C. ORGANIZATIONAL CAPACITY (20 points)				
1. Demonstrates the program has appropriate facilities, etc.			1 2 3 4 5	
2. Demonstrates the program has qualified staff at a level that is adequate given the scope of services			1 2 3 4 5	
			TOTAL = _____	
D. FISCAL CAPACITY (25 points)				
1. Shows the program has diverse funding sources			1 2 3 4 5	
2. Shows all expenses			1 2 3 4 5	
3. Expenses are reasonable for scope of work			1 2 3 4 5	
4. There is a sufficient need to warrant new, additional, or ongoing Wake County funding for this program			1 2 3 4 5	
			TOTAL = _____	

TOTAL OVERALL SCORE _____

EXHIBIT 6.11 (*Continued*)

EXHIBIT 6.12   Budget Content List

Recommended Content

A transmittal letter from the CEO that outlines key policies, strategies, etc.
Summary information to the public
Precise, nontechnical, easy-to-understand language
A table of contents, index, and glossary of terms
Explanation of the programs
Performance measures
Charts and graphs that highlight key relationships
Discussion of the revenue sources and the assumptions underlying the revenue
    estimates
Discussion of accounting and budgeting changes
Index of statistical and supplemental data

Board Adopts the Budget

After the CEO's review, the CFO prepares the budget document for the Board's review and approval. The CEO's *letter of transmittal* to the Board summarizes the budget's highlights, including significant changes in income, expenses and programs. The letter should be written simply and clearly, and include informative charts, graphs, statistical information, and summaries. Exhibit 6.12 is a list of budget content features for you to keep in mind.

CEO Administers the Budget

At the CEO's direction, the CFO incorporates Board-approved changes into the final budget document, which is given to Board members, program managers, and funding agencies. The next task is to administer the budget, which includes four steps:

1. Control positions and expenses.
2. Monitor budgeted versus actual revenues and expenses.
3. Manage grants.
4. Seek funding.

Control Positions and Expenses

Before filling a vacant position, the CFO checks the budget to ensure that:

- The position is budgeted.
- Funds are available for the position.

If funds are not available for a position or a purchase in a line-item account, surplus funds may be available in another account. In that case, the Board can approve a transfer from the surplus account to the deficit account. Similarly, before issuing a purchase order, entering into a contract or paying an expense, the CFO checks the budget and accounting records to ensure that funds are available.

Monitor Budgeted versus Actual Revenues and Expenses

A budget is simply a *plan* for the fiscal year, during which revenues and expenses may actually be more or less than budgeted. The CEO should carefully compare budgeted to actual revenues and expenses, issuing a monthly report to Board members and program managers. If expenses and revenues do not meet budget projections, the Board may *amend* the budget. Sixty percent of faith-based organizations make such budget revisions during the fiscal year,[6] but only 40 percent monitor financial ratios periodically during the year.[7] Exhibit 6.13 shows budgeted versus actual revenues and expenses. At this point in the fiscal year beginning December 1, with nine months gone, the nonprofit should have spent about 75 percent of its budget. This comparison along with a comparison to prior year's experience indicates some possible red flag budget items.

If actual expenses are significantly *more* and/or revenues significantly *less* than budgeted, the Board must take corrective action. A budget shortfall can occur because of decreased revenues, increased expenses, or both. For instance, the economic downturn beginning in 2008 gravely affected many nonprofits' revenue streams. Fifty-two percent of nonprofits received less in contributions and 31 percent received less in grants.[8]

CUTBACK MEASURES When financially pressed, nonprofits must take *cutback measures* to decrease expenses and increase revenues. Examples include:

Measures to Cut Expenses
- Freeze hiring.
- Reduce capital expenses.
- Reduce electricity and heating usage.
- Reduce travel, training and professional memberships.
- Use volunteers in lieu of paid personnel.
- Use more temporary employees, who are not paid fringe benefits, except Social Security.

EXHIBIT 6.13   Monthly Budget Status Report as of September 30

	Annual Budget	YTD Actual	Percent of Budget	Percent Spent Prior Year
INCOME				
Charitable Foundations	$36,598	$27,449	75%	71%
Contributions	$33,000	$19,800	60%	68%
Government—Local	$328,288	$246,216	75%	75%
Government—Federal	$531,293	$398,470	75%	75%
Government—State	$931,791	$605,664	65%	70%
Medicaid	$103,182	$51,591	50%	59%
United Way	$224,509	$168,382	75%	75%
TOTAL INCOME	$2,188,661	$1,517,571	69%	70%
UNRESTRICTED NET ASSETS	$52,801			
EXPENSE				
100 Personnel Salaries	$1,446,014	$1,209,344	84%	75%
101 Personnel Benefits	$278,778	$226,995	81%	75%
102 Professional Services	$88,605	$79,745	90%	90%
200 Supplies	$57,009	$48,458	85%	81%
300 Travel and Communication	$21,399	$16,049	75%	69%
301 Communication	$38,806	$29,105	75%	75%
302 Staff Development— Training Expense	$39,040	$31,232	80%	75%
303 Facilities—Utilities/ Maintenance	$28,215	$22,572	80%	69%
400 Facilities—Rent	$164,063	$123,047	75%	75%
450 Insurance & Bonding	$47,999	$35,999	75%	75%
475 Dues & Subscriptions	$13,850	$9,695	70%	70%
480 Lease—Vehicle/Office Equipment	$17,034	$10,220	60%	68%
500 Capital Outlay	$650	$650	100%	100%
TOTAL EXPENSE	$2,241,462	$1,843,111	82%	77%
NET DEFICIT		–$325,540		

Measures to Increase Revenue

- Spend the operating reserve (if one exists).
- Hold fundraisers.
- Ask funders to send funds (e.g., a grant) sooner.
- Expedite the collection of accounts receivable.
- Borrow in anticipation of revenues.

MEASURES WHEN CONDITIONS WORSEN Should conditions worsen, more extreme measures are necessary:

- Furlough employees (i.e., require unpaid leaves of absence).
- Lay off employees.
- Reduce salaries (e.g., by 10%).
- Reduce fringe benefits (e.g., pensions).
- Borrow into a deficit position.
- Sell assets.
- Eliminate programs.

Laying off employees is the most severe measure. To decide which programs to reduce or eliminate, the Board should refer to its strategic plan and its *core values.* Programs contributing least to the core mission should be the first ones to be reduced. Exhibit 6.14 indicates the cutback measures that nonprofits took in 2009. Most common, nonprofits put a freeze on salaries and hires, collaborated with other nonprofits to provide services, developed a contingency budget in case more severe action was needed, relied more on volunteers, and cut staff and salaries.

Manage Grants

Nonprofits receive grants from governments, foundations, the private sector, and other nonprofits. Some grants are easy to administer; others are more problematic. For instance, some grants require that time spent on them

EXHIBIT 6.14 Nonprofit Cutback Measures Taken in 2009

Cutback Measure	Percent of Nonprofits	Cutback Measure	Percent of Nonprofits
Rely more on volunteers	39%	Speed up collection of receivables	19%
Freeze hires/salaries	48%	Reduce staff or salaries	35%
Use reserve funds	34%	Delay vendor payments	23%
Cut programs	36%	Reduce staff hours	26%
Collaborate on programs	52%	Reduce/refinance occupancy costs	14%
Reduce benefits	25%	Change mission or vision	9%
Sell assets	4%	Merge with another nonprofit	1%
Restructure/reduce services	4%	Develop a contingency budget	44%

Source: Nonprofit Finance Fund, *Nonprofit Finance Fund: 2010 State of the Sector Survey* (2010). Available at nonprofitfinancefund.org.

EXHIBIT 6.15   Grant-Funding Conditions

Grant	Amount	Length (years)	Fiscal Year Start	Payment Interval	Reimbursement Time
Federal Grants					
Homeless Youth	$140,000	3	Oct. 1	Monthly	Within 72 hours
Independent Living	199,963	5	Oct. 1	Monthly	Within 72 hours
HUD	60,506	2	Mar. 1	Monthly	Within 72 hours
Street Outreach	100,000	3	Oct. 1	Monthly	Within 72 hours
State Grants Governor's Crime Commission	90,000	2	June 1	Monthly	2 weeks
Juvenile Justice	857,299	1	July 1	Monthly in advance	
Local Grants					
City of Raleigh	28,000	1	July 1	Quarterly	Within 1 month
Wake County	63,138	1	July 1	Monthly	Within 3 to 4 weeks
Fee for Service					
Medicaid[a]	100,400	1	July 1	Upon being billed	1 to 6 months
Other Funding					
United Way	263,524	1	Jan. 1	Monthly in advance	
Duke Endowment	55,535	2	Mar. 1	Whole amount in Advance	

[a]Medicaid funds are continuing and are reimbursed upon being billed.

be recorded in five-minute intervals. Exhibit 6.15 indicates the revenues received by a nonprofit that serves troubled youth in Raleigh, North Carolina. Notice the variation in the funding source, length of the grant, fiscal year of the grantor, and payment and reimbursement periods.

The length of the grants varies from one to five years. The granting agencies' fiscal year also varies. Local governments and one state agency have a July 1 to June 30 fiscal year. Another state agency, the Governor's Crime Commission, which passes through federal money to nonprofits and local governments, has a fiscal year beginning on June 1. Three federal grants follow the federal fiscal year (October 1 to September 30), but the grant from the Department of Housing and Urban Development (HUD) begins March 1. Finally, the United Way and the Duke Endowment have fiscal years beginning January 1 and March 1, respectively.

The payment period is usually monthly after incurring expenses; but two agencies, the State Department of Juvenile Justice and the United Way, permit the agency to bill monthly *in advance* of expenses. Even better, the Duke Endowment pays the full amount of the grant in advance of expenses. Federal agencies reimburse electronically, reducing the reimbursement time to 72 hours or less. Less convenient, the local units reimburse within three to four weeks. Most problematic, Medicaid reimburses within a one-month to six-month period.

Also problematic is the fact that an agency may reduce funding during the nonprofit's fiscal year. For instance, viewing Exhibit 6.15, the State Department of Juvenile Justice normally pays the required 30 percent match for the grant. However, after the nonprofit had adopted its 2011 budget, the state still had not decided whether to require the nonprofit to pay the match, which would amount to 30 percent of $857,299, or $257,189 in additional expense.

Seek Funding

Many nonprofits constantly seek funding. About 33 percent of nonprofits have an in-house development officer, and about 16 percent hire a professional solicitor annually to raise funds.[9] To regulate fundraising, the National Association of Attorneys General and the National Association of State Charity Officials issued "A Model Act Concerning the Solicitation of funds for Charitable Purposes," which 38 states had adopted by 2008. The act has four requirements:

1. A 501(c)(3) nonprofit must register with the state if it hires a fundraiser.
2. The nonprofit annually must report its fundraising activities to the state.
3. The professional solicitor must register with the state.
4. The professional solicitor annually must report its activities to the state.

Fundraisers employ a wide array of fundraising methods, including telemarketing, direct mail, door-to-door solicitation, raffles, bazaars, and dinners; however, the overall amount of funds raised is rather small. In selecting a solicitor, the nonprofit should be concerned with the percentage of funds after expenses that it will receive. In 1988, the U.S. Supreme Court ruled in *Riley v. National Federation for the Blind* that a state cannot limit the percentage of funds that goes to fundraisers. Some states require solicitors to report the percentage of funds that they distribute to nonprofits. Among those states, the percentage of funds received by nonprofits varies, ranging from a high of 81 percent in Colorado to a low of 41 percent in North Carolina:

- Massachusetts. 65% in 2007[10]
- Connecticut. 67% in 2006[11]
- Colorado: 81% in 2008[12]
- North Carolina: 41% in 2008[13]
- New York: 61% in 2005[14]

Using these averages as a guide, a nonprofit should receive about 60 to 65 percent of the total raised. In some instances, the amount is justifiably less than the 60 to 65 percent benchmark. For example, initially establishing a donor list is more expensive at the outset of a fundraising campaign.

The nonprofit should be wary because some funders distribute *no* funds to the nonprofit.

Exhibit 6.16 is a list of best practices to follow in selecting a professional fundraiser.

EXHIBIT 6.16   Fundraiser-Selection List

Recommended Practice

Fundraiser Selection
Ensure the firm is licensed by the state.
Ask the fundraiser for references.
Ask the references about their experience, particularly the percentage of funds they retained.
Ask the references if they would hire the fundraiser again.
Narrow the field to three or four firms for a face-to-face meeting.

Contract Provisions
The duties and responsibilities of both parties
The compensation method: a flat fee or a percentage
The billing schedule
Additional expenses that will be reimbursed and up to what amount
The contract period
The right of prior approval of all materials, including the solicitation document
The nonprofit's exclusive control over funds in the nonprofit's bank account
A surety bond requirement or an irrevocable letter of credit
Who will pay for an unsuccessful campaign
Approval by the nonprofit of any subcontracting services
Regular reporting of contributions received
Conditions for contract termination

Ensure that the firm is state-licensed. Check the firm's references to evaluate its past performance. Narrow the field down to three to four firms, and then meet with the firms' principals to assess their capabilities. Include in the contract: standard contract terms, a surety bond requirement; and a process to settle accounts if the campaign loses money.

For Further Reading

Angelica, Emil, and Vincent Hyman. *Coping with Cutbacks.* St. Paul, MN: Amherst H. Wilder Foundation, 1997. Best feature is an inclusive list and discussion of cutback options.

Dropkin, Murray, Jim Halpin, and Bill La Touche. *The Budget-Building Book for Nonprofits*, 2nd ed. San Francisco: Jossey-Bass, 2007. Best feature is a set of budget worksheets that can be downloaded from a CD disc.

Maddox, David. *Budgeting for Nonprofit Organizations.* Hoboken, NJ: John Wiley & Sons, 1999. Introduction to operating, capital, and cash budgeting, including discussions of budget-cutting and human resource management.

CHAPTER 7

Manage Cash Flow

Cash is the mother's milk of nonprofits, but many nonprofits operate with razor-thin cash margins. In 2010, 61 percent of nonprofits had less than three months of available cash, 12 percent had no cash at all, and only 18 percent predicted a surplus for 2010.[1] For them, an accurate cash flow forecast prevents their entering a deficit position and having to borrow funds. Nonprofits can optimize their cash flow by adopting a cash management program that:

- Expedites the collection and deposit of cash in an interest-bearing instrument
- Delays disbursements for as long as legally possible

The cash-management program should:

- Take a revenue inventory
- Expedite cash flow
- Prepare a cash budget

Step 1   Take a Revenue Inventory

The revenue inventory charts each revenue source with regard to its:

- Collection history
- Legal basis
- Funding conditions
- Reliability

The CEO should be intimately familiar with each revenue source. The CFO should prepare a history of each revenue source, going back five years if possible. If the revenue is a grant, the CEO and CFO need to know its legal basis and its funding conditions (e.g., grant period, fiscal year, payment period, time to reimburse). Most important, the CEO should constantly assess each revenue's *reliability*; that is, how likely the revenue is to continue. Some revenues are easily predictable, but others are more uncertain, especially those sensitive to economic downturns. A funder may cut or terminate a grant in response to:

- Increased competition for funds
- A declining economy
- Poor performance by the grantee
- Reduced grant funding

Funding may be cut at the beginning of or during the nonprofit's fiscal year. For example, the national government, on a different fiscal year than nonprofits, may reduce or eliminate a particular grant. Cuts after adopting a budget confound cash flow projections.

The next sections discuss nonprofits' principal types of revenues, which include:

- Membership dues
- Contributions
- Grants
- Revenue from fundraising events
- Revenue from conventions

Membership Dues

Some nonprofits, particularly associations, rely heavily on membership dues. The objective is to retain existing membership and add new members. The CEO, with input from the Board, should set goals for membership retention and growth. If a nonprofit is not meeting its membership goals, it should ask whether any of the following is true:

- The goals are too optimistic.
- The annual membership fee is too high.
- Better marketing is required.
- The website should be improved to inform and attract members.

Even if the organization is meeting membership goals, management should periodically analyze the fee structure, asking whether to:

- Increase fees to offset inflation
- Charge differing fees for:
  1. Individuals and organizations
  2. Full and partial memberships
  3. Senior and junior members

Income from Contributions

Nonprofits, particularly churches, depend heavily on individual contributions. Individuals typically do not restrict how a nonprofit can spend its contributions. Notable exceptions, though, are United Way contributors, who can earmark all or part of their contribution for a particular program or programs. Effective fundraising practices aimed at individual contributors include the following:

- Periodically remind donors to contribute.
- Offer easy payment options (e.g., by credit, debit card or PayPal).
- Promptly acknowledge the receipt of and appreciation for a contribution.
- Periodically publish a newsletter highlighting the nonprofit's accomplishments and needs.
- Conduct direct mail, telemarketing, and door-to-door fundraising campaigns.

Management and the Board should annually evaluate the effectiveness of their contributions program with regard to the:

- Rate of repeat donations
- Ratio of collected to pledged contributions
- Ratio of fundraising expenses to fundraising income
- Change in funds contributed per donor
- Change in total contributions over time

Income from Grants

Governments, private foundations, firms, and nonprofits make two types of grants:

1. An *unrestricted grant* that the nonprofit can use for any purpose
2. A *restricted grant* that must be spent for a specified purpose

Although typically for one year, some grants are for several years. The granting agency usually requires strict adherence to its reporting and reimbursement procedures. Moreover, the grantor wants to see concrete, measurable program results. Failure to follow procedures or achieve outcomes can result in:

- Delayed funding
- Immediate termination of the grant
- Nonrenewal of the grant
- A financial penalty

Hence, management, especially program managers, should be *intimately* familiar with the regulations and procedures of each grant that they manage. They should establish a good working relationship with the personnel of the granting agency who oversee the grant. Good rapport enables both parties to resolve small differences easily before they become an irreconcilable impasse.

Income from Special Events

Running the gamut, special event fundraisers can include auctions, dances, meals, walks, food festivals, and the like. Typically, holding a fundraising event is a major undertaking, requiring a substantial time commitment from staff, volunteers, and Board members. Sometimes nonprofits undertake such an event too lightly, underestimate the time and commitment needed, and overestimate the likely revenues. Exhibit 7.1 is a special events management list of items to keep track of.

Appoint a special event coordinator to prepare a planning calendar, obtain necessary permits, and acquire special events insurance, if needed. The insurance policy should cover *specific* exposures, such as the food served, moving cars, parade marchers, and the like. (For a discussion of special events insurance, refer to Chapter 14, "Manage Risks.")

In the first event, start small. If it proves successful, then expand its scope next year. Wide stakeholder involvement is essential. Board members should support the event with both their time and treasure. Community support is also integrally important. For instance, an auction depends on the generosity of firms and individuals to donate goods and services. Finally, the

---

EXHIBIT 7.1   Special Events Management List

Recommended Practices

Appoint a special-event coordinator.
Create an event-planning calendar.
Realistically estimate the event's costs and revenues.
Start small. If the event proves successful, expand the scope next time.
Obtain the necessary permits and licenses.
Obtain special events insurance.
Negotiate with vendors to make a phased payment, if possible.
Use volunteers to the extent possible.
Solicit gifts from individuals and firms to auction off and/or give to participants.
Establish accounting controls over the receipt and disbursement of cash.
Engage the board in planning for, and contributing to, the event.

CFO should carefully account for receipts and disbursements, reconciling cash receipts with the number of tickets, and products sold.

Income from Conventions

Many nonprofits hold an annual convention or conference, the income from which can vary with the:

- Conference location
- Registration and other (e.g., travel) costs
- Quality of donor-sponsored activities and goods
- Conference quality, particularly its speakers and content

Some nonprofits view their annual conference as a moneymaker; others simply would like to break even. The financial performance of past conventions can be a good predictor of future success. Conventions held at the same venue annually (e.g., Las Vegas) typically have predictable attendance; however, predicting attendance at a new venue can be more uncertain.

Take care when negotiating terms with the conference hotel. Hotels often ask that the nonprofit guarantee to use a specific number of rooms and to pay all or part of the cost of any of those rooms not used. Likewise, take care when negotiating the rates for hotel services like audio-visual hardware, which can be shockingly expensive. Exhibit 7.2 discusses the provisions in a typical contract with a hotel and caveats to consider when negotiating the terms of the contract.

Step 2   Expedite Cash Flow

To optimize cash flow, collect and deposit funds in interest-bearing accounts *as soon as possible.* Exhibit 7.3 is an accounts receivable-collection list to use to expedite cash flow.

The practices listed in Exhibit 7.3 are now discussed in the next sections.

Billings

The CFO should establish written procedures to make billings, collections, deposits, and refunds. Send out bills *as soon as legally possible.* To track receivables, prepare an accounts payable aging schedule. The process, known

EXHIBIT 7.2   Hotel Contract Provisions

Contract Section	Discussion of the Contract Section	Caveat
Room Block	-The number of sleeping rooms reserved. The more booked, the more the hotel will reduce its standard rate and cost of meeting rooms.	-The hotel will charge a penalty for guaranteed rooms not used.
Guest Room Rates	-The nightly rate charged. -The stipulations and benefits including state and local tax rates, the date to which the room block will be held, parking facilities, and complimentary nights per room block, which is normally 1 night per 50 room nights sold. The hotel may upgrade the room to a suite as well.	-Compare the rate to the rates charged by other hotels in the area. If the rate is too high, attendees will go elsewhere.
Meeting Space	-The meeting room rental fee is based on the room block utilization. -The fee charge per room if the room block guarantee is not met. -The food and beverage charges. -Additional costs, such as tabletops for exhibition halls.	-Ensure the space is not too small or too large. -The rate increases significantly if the rooms fall below 50 percent of the guarantee. -Carefully examine menu and price options.
Cancellation Policy	-Penalties can range from 25 to 100 percent of the revenues the hotel did not realize for rooms, food, and beverages.	Make *realistic* estimates.
Other Terms	-Method of reservation. -Check-in and out procedures. -Early departure fee. -The billing method. -Boxes and materials charges. -Guarantees/dates owed. The hotel typically expects final numbers 72 hours in advance. -Loss and damage to merchandise of the group or attendees.	
Acceptance	-The contract is signed and returned to the facility.	

EXHIBIT 7.3   Accounts Receivable Collection List

Practice

Billings
Establish procedures regarding payments, collections, and refunds.
Bill for provided goods and services as soon as legally possible.
Prepare and review a monthly accounts receivable aging schedule.
Retain remittance billings to support accounts receivable accounting entries.
Maintain subsidiary accounts receivable records.
Post individual receivable records only from authorized documents.
Reconcile subsidiary accounts with the general ledger control account at least monthly.

Collections and Deposits
Deposit collected money daily by the bank's same-day deposit cut-off time.
Vigorously collect delinquent accounts, using all legal remedies.
Write off accounts after collection efforts have been unsuccessful.
Document why such an account was written off.
Authorize someone to make write-offs and adjustments.
Use electronic commerce.
Use a lockbox.
Use a zero balance account.
Collect payments within 30 days.

as *aging receivables*, records how long receivables have been outstanding, as shown in the following table:

Period	Outstanding Amount	Percent
30 days or less	$700,000	64%
31–60 days	$275,000	25%
Over 90 days	$125,000	11%
Total	$1,100,000	100%

Investment income is lost when billings are tardy. To determine whether billings have been delayed, select a representative sample of invoices. Determine whether the bills were promptly sent, and if not, ascertain the number days that bills were delayed. Use the formula below to determine the amount of interest income that was lost.

$$\text{Lost revenue} = \text{Dollar amount of late billings} \times \text{Prevailing interest rate}$$
$$\times \frac{\text{Number of days delayed}}{365 \text{ days}}$$

As discussed in Chapter 2, "Account for Transactions," the nonprofit should maintain a subsidiary account for each receivable account; post collections to account records; and reconcile the subsidiary records with the general ledger control account at least monthly.

Collections and Deposits

To earn same-day interest, funds must be deposited before the bank's same-day deposit cutoff time. Historically, this time was 2 P.M., but some banks are now more lenient, crediting deposits made at the end of the bank day. Other best practices include the following:

- Vigorously collect delinquent accounts using all legal remedies.
- Write off delinquent accounts for nonpayment only after making *all* possible collection efforts.
- Document in writing why the receivable had to be written off.

Two types of electronic commerce expedite collections. The automated clearinghouse (ACH) system, developed in the early 1970s as an alternative to checks, is a batch processing system designed for high-volume, low-value transactions including direct deposit of payroll and government benefit payments. ACH processes transactions usually in one to two days. An ACH transaction cost only a few cents.

A Fedwire (wire transfer), operated by the Federal Reserve, transfers large-dollar payments for same-day deposit. A wire transfer is considerably more expensive than an ACH transaction and its price varies. As an example, Bank of America charged $25 to send a wire and $12 to receive one in February 2011. To determine the minimum amount of a wire transfer needed to cover the transmission cost, use the formula that follows:

$$\text{Minimum amount} = \frac{\text{Cost of roundtrip wire transfer}}{\text{Interest rate}/360}$$

A lockbox also expedites deposits. Maintaining a post office box in the nonprofit's name, the bank collects and deposits checks during the day, enabling the nonprofit to earn same-day interest. There are two types of lockboxes. A *wholesale lockbox* collects high-dollar, low-volume payments; a *retail lockbox* collects high-volume, low-dollar payments. To determine whether a lockbox is cost-effective, compare the bank's lockbox service fee to the amount of additional interest that would be earned with same-day deposits.

A third bank service, a *zero balance account* (ZBA), sweeps cash into an overnight repurchase agreement or savings sweep account. To determine whether a ZBA is cost-effective, compare the added interest earnings to the ZBA service fee.

EXHIBIT 7.4   Cash Budget Estimation Methods

Cash Receipts	Estimation Method
Grants confirmed	Enter amounts in the months they will be received.
Grants anticipated	Enter grants anticipated whose starting date is still uncertain. Make best estimate of the month that funding will begin.
Individual contributions	Base the estimate on the amount of contributions received in the previous year or years.
Special events	Base the estimate on the amount of special events' revenues in the previous year or years.
Funds released from restricted	Enter funds that donors and/or the board will release from the restricted net asset account.
Fees at time of service	Base the estimate on the amount of fees collected in the previous year or years.
Accounts-receivable collection	Base the estimate on the amount of accounts receivables collected in the previous year or years.
Rent/facility use	Enter the amount of rent that users will pay for the nonprofit's facilities.
Ticket sales	Base the estimate on the amount of ticket sales in the previous year or years.
Contract services	Enter the amount that organizations have contracted to pay for nonprofit services.

Cash Disbursements	**Estimation Method**
Payroll	Enter monthly payroll expenses, adjusting for positions that will be added or deleted during the year.
Payroll taxes	Enter Social Security payments to employees and the national government in the months that payments will occur, adjusting for any change in positions during the year.
Benefits	Enter fringe benefit costs, adjusting for increases during the year (e.g., increased health care costs).
Rent	Enter the monthly building rental cost.
Office and printing	Base the estimate on the amount of office and printing expenses paid in the previous year or years.
Equipment leases	Enter monthly equipment-rental payments.
Insurance	Enter insurance payments in the month or months they will be paid.
Legal	Base the estimate on an annual contract agreement or on the legal expenses paid in the previous year or years.
Accounting and audit	Enter the amount to be paid under contracts for accounting and audit services.
Loan payment	Enter the principal and interest payments on outstanding loans or bonds.

Step 3   Prepare a Cash Budget

A cash flow budget projects cash receipts and disbursements over the fiscal year. The general ledger cash balance or the bank balance is the starting point for the forecast. To prepare a cash budget, the Nonprofits Assistance Fund provides an Excel spreadsheet, available at: http://www. nonprofitsassistancefund.org/. Exhibit 7.4 explains how to estimate cash receipts and disbursements.

Simply plug into the forecast the amount of confirmed grants and money released from a restricted account in the appropriate months and amounts. For instance, refer to Exhibit 6.15, Grant-Funding Conditions, which shows the payment period and reimbursement time for several grants and funding from the United Way and the Duke Endowment. Base other revenues' estimates on their collection history. Some revenues have a predicable collection pattern, while others have an erratic history that requires an educated guess.

The monthly payroll and fringe benefit payments are known. Adjust these amounts to reflect:

- A new hire or hires during the fiscal year
- An employee who will retire during the year
- If the position will be filled, the number of months that will likely elapse before filling the position

Some expenses (e.g., utilities, rent, insurance, Social Security, equipment leases) occur monthly. Other expenses occur at different times during the fiscal year (e.g., a capital purchase, audit fees, loan payments).

CHAPTER 8

Purchase Goods

The CFO is normally responsible for the purchasing system, which has two principal features: (1) a Board-adopted purchasing policy and (2) a procedures manual that covers the best practices listed in the list shown in Exhibit 8.1.

Adopt Purchasing Policy

The governing board should adopt a purchasing policy addressing the practices shown in Exhibit 8.1 and discussed in the sections that follow.

Conflict of Interest (COI)

A COI occurs when an employee or Board member enjoys monetary gain at the nonprofit's expense. Financial transactions between nonprofits and Board members are surprisingly extensive: 21 percent of nonprofits bought or rented goods, services, or property from a Board member.[1] To prevent a COI, the Board should adopt a *COI policy*, which half of all nonprofits have done.[2] Examples of a conflict of interest policy can be found at the following websites:

- *IRS COI Policy.* Appropriate for large nonprofits, can be found at www.irs.gov/instructions/i1023/ar03.html. Exhibit 8A.1 in Appendix A of this chapter is a copy of the IRS COI policy. Note that the policy intends to supplement, *not replace*, any applicable state and federal COI laws.
- *Independent Sector COI Policy.* This national nonprofit association's policy can be found at www.independentsector.org/uploads.
- *National Council of Nonprofits COI Policy.* This national nonprofit association's policy can be found at www.councilofnonprofits/org.conflict-of-interest.

EXHIBIT 8.1   Best Purchasing Practices List

Practices

Adopt Purchasing Policy Regarding
Conflict of interest
Whistleblower protection
Centralization of purchasing
Standardization of goods
Emergency purchase
Life cycle costing
"Green" purchasing
Purchase card usage

Order Goods
Prepare a specification.
Prepare a requisition.
Take quotations or bids.
Approve purchase orders and contracts.

Receive Goods
Count and examine goods to see whether they meet the ordered specifications.
Prepare receiving report.
Send receiving report to accounting.

Make Payment
Separate the duties of:
   -Purchasing, requisitioning, and receiving
   -Invoice processing and making entries to the general ledger
   -Preparation of cash disbursements, their approval, and making general-ledger
    entries
Receive invoices in central accounting office.
Review invoices for completeness.
Take discounts where possible.
Determine that funds are budgeted.
Limit disbursements and check signing to authorized personnel.
Prohibit signing blank checks in advance.
Set a reasonable limit on the amount that can be paid by facsimile signatures.
Separate facsimile signatures physically from blank checks.
Record machine readings to ascertain that all checks signed are properly
   accounted for.
Enforce controls to prevent duplicate payments.
Control and safeguard unused checks.
Retain records, checks, and supporting documents according to the
   record-retention policy.

Dispose of Goods
Follow Board-adopted policy regarding the disposal of goods.

EXHIBIT 8.2   COI Policy List

Provision
Upon their selection, Board members and management sign a statement, affirming their willingness to comply with the policy.
Prohibit staff and Board members from receiving a gratuity (e.g., a gift, favor, honoraria, etc.) from a firm doing business with the nonprofit.
Board members and management disclose any financial interest in a firm doing business with the nonprofit.
Board members and management recuse themselves from a decision that would benefit them.
Board determines, by majority vote, whether a COI occurred.
Reflect in the minutes the people present at a COI discussion and any vote relating to it.
If the Board believes that a Board member or employee has not disclosed a COI, provide him or her with the opportunity to rebut the charge.
Violation of the COI policy can result in (1) employee termination or (2) removal from the Board.
Specify in the Board's minutes the name or names of people found to have a COI.

Exhibit 8.2 lists the provisions to include in the COI policy.

A nonprofit must report in the IRS Form 990 whether it has adopted a COI policy.[3] The policy should require that employees and Board members disclose a financial interest in a company doing business with the nonprofit *unless* they have placed their financial interest in a blind trust. Recusal and divestiture will eliminate a possible COI. Board members should *recuse* (disqualify) themselves from making a decision that would benefit them, a family member or close associate. Typically, the Board can *waive* the recusal if the Board member can demonstrate that his or her benefit from the transaction will be insubstantial. Board members can also eliminate a COI by *divesting* themselves of a property that the nonprofit wishes to buy or lease.

The policy should also address the question of receiving a *gratuity*, which is a gift, monetary payment, favor, free meal, honoraria, and so on. Though legal, a gratuity gives the *appearance* of a COI. The nonprofit has two options: (1) ban gratuities altogether or (2) set a relatively low dollar threshold (e.g., $25) for an acceptable gratuity. In contrast to a gratuity, a *kickback,* which is a payment from a vendor in return for the nonprofit's business, is always illegal.

A COI policy will prevent such situations as those shown in Exhibit 8.3.

Potential conflicts of interest can be avoided by following best purchasing and hiring practices. For instance, a Board member can sell a product to

- Without taking competitive bids, the nonprofit buys supplies from a Board member.
- A Board member does not disclose that she is a silent partner in doing business with the nonprofit.
- The CEO lets a building repair project to a firm owned by his brother.
- The Board makes a loan to a fellow Board member.
- The CEO receives an annual $100 Christmas gift from one of the nonprofit's vendors.
- The CEO receives a $200 speaking fee for giving a speech to fellow nonprofits.
- The Board hires the wife of the CEO as the CFO without taking competitive applications.

EXHIBIT 8.3   Conflict of Interest Situations

the nonprofit *if* competitive written bids are taken and the Board member's product is the lowest priced. Similarly, a relative of the Board or management can be hired *if* the position was subjected to a rigorous recruitment and selection process that found the relative most qualified according to objective criteria.

Other situations, however, are not so clear. For example, should a Board member serve on another nonprofit Board that provides a similar service? It depends. If the other nonprofit is a collaborative colleague, there is not a COI. However, if the two nonprofits compete fiercely for funds, the Board member is put in an untenable position. For instance, when a Board member asks a friend for a major donation, which organization does she ask the friend to support? This is a situation of "dual loyalties" or "conflict of loyalties."

Whistleblower Protection

The Board should adopt a *whistleblower protection policy*. Nonprofits must report in the IRS Form 990 whether they have adopted a whistleblower policy.[4] The Sarbanes-Oxley Act makes it a federal crime for a firm or nonprofit to retaliate against an employee who reports suspected fraudulent activities. Sixty-seven percent of nonprofits have adopted a process for employees to report problems without fear of retaliation.[5] Exhibit 8A.1 in the Appendix of this chapter is a sample whistleblower policy. It has been prepared by the Nonprofit Risk Management Center, which advises the user to view the sample policy as a *starting point*.[6] Each nonprofit should adapt the policy to its special circumstances.

Centralization

Rather than permit each program manager to purchase goods, the purchasing policy should centralize procurement under a single person. Centralization enables the nonprofit to:

- Buy items in bulk, thus lowering unit costs
- Take more vendor discounts for early payment
- Permit suppliers to operate under a single set of rules and expectations

Standardization

The purchasing policy should require that goods be standardized to the extent possible. Standardization, buying like items in bulk, lowers both the costs of goods and purchasing expenses. Examples of goods to standardize include stationery, hand tools, gasoline, automotive parts, and supplies.

Emergency Purchase

An emergency purchase circumvents the normal purchasing process. An emergency purchase is permissible when health and safety are threatened. The purchasing policy should define what constitutes an emergency (e.g., a breakdown of the heating, plumbing, or cooling system) and authorize the person or persons who can approve an *emergency purchase order* (EPO). If an emergency occurs outside normal operating hours, and the authorized person is unavailable, the policy should permit someone at the scene of the emergency to issue the EPO.

Life Cycle Cost (LCC) Purchasing

Some Boards require LCC of energy-consuming goods. Traditionally, purchasing considers only the *initial purchase price*. In contrast, LCC considers the cost of *ownership*, including the:

- Initial purchase price
- Cost to operate the product or facility (e.g., repair, maintenance, energy costs) over its expected life
- Resale value, if any, of the product or facility

Using LCC, the initial purchase price of a good may be higher but the total cost of ownership will be lower. A common example of this is automobiles that cost more initially but have lower operating costs and higher resale value. The LCC method is applicable to *any* energy-consuming

EXHIBIT 8.4   LCC Example

	Compact Fluorescent Bulb	Incandescent Bulb
Initial Cost	$7.00	$0.25
Annual Operation Cost	$1.68	$8.71
7-Year Life Cost[a]	$10.58	$54.87
Life Cycle Cost	$17.58	$63.58

[a]After discounting for inflation
Source: Focus on Energy, focusonenegy.com.

product such as air conditioners, pumps, copy machines, and light bulbs. Exhibit 8.4 is an example of how to analyze the life cycle cost of two light bulbs, a 15-watt compact fluorescent bulb and a 60-watt incandescent bulb, assuming each light operates 1,400 hours per year (i.e., about four hours per day).

LCC is also applicable to building design and construction. In addition to a building's construction cost, the nonprofit also calculates the lifetime cost to heat, cool, and maintain the structure.

Green Purchasing

The Board may prefer to buy environmentally friendly ("green") goods. Exhibit 8.5 distinguishes between "green" and "ungreen" goods.

The CEO should prepare a cost-benefit analysis when considering green purchasing. Some green products are both ecologically friendly and cost effective; however, others are more expensive.

In addition to products, buildings can be built "green." The U.S. Green Building Council administers the Leadership in Energy and Environmental Design (LEED) standard for measuring building sustainability. The LEED rating system rates buildings with regard to their sustainability, water efficiency, energy consumption, and materials. The building design predicts the amount of energy and water costs that will be saved; however, these estimates are prospective. Actual operating experience sometimes reveals that the projections were overstated.

EXHIBIT 8.5   Green vs. Ungreen Goods

"Green Goods"	"Ungreen Goods"
Recycled paper	Disposable products
Two-way envelopes	Phosphate products
Alternative flexible fuel	Batteries with mercury
Energy-efficient light bulbs	Toxic cleaning products

EXHIBIT 8.6   Purchase Card List

Recommended Practice

Select a purchase card firm with competitive bids.

Select an issuer whose software is compatible with the nonprofit's accounting system.

Establish a dollar limit that can be charged monthly.

Establish procedures to purchase via the Internet, phone, and fax.

Establish procedures to issue, cancel, and handle cards and to deal with lost or stolen cards.

Require employees to acknowledge in writing that they have read and understand the procedures.

Reconcile purchase card transactions monthly.

Prepare receiving reports for purchased goods and retain sales receipts.

Establish agreements with banks, including the fee schedule.

CEO or CFO reviews and approves purchase card payments.

Purchase Cards

A purchase card, either credit or debit, cost-effectively enables the nonprofit to:

- Make a single payment, not more costly multiple payments
- Know the exact payment date, facilitating the cash flow forecast
- Receive an up-to-date report from the credit company or bank
- Reduce paperwork
- Instantly receive goods

On the other hand, the purchase card issuer charges a fee for credit, and sometimes debit, card service. The CEO should weigh the potential costs and benefits of purchase card usage. A purchase card is issued in an individual's or the organization's name. Management should carefully monitor purchase card usage to avoid misuse or fraud. Exhibit 8.6 is a list of recommended purchase card practices.

The policy should limit:

- The amount an individual can purchase daily and monthly
- The types of goods that can and cannot be purchased (e.g., not gasoline)

Typically, the policy *prohibits* using a purchase card to withdraw cash.

Order Goods

After adopting a purchasing policy, the next step is to order goods, which entails:

- Preparing a specification
- Preparing a requisition

- Taking quotations or bids
- Approving a purchase orders (P.O.s) and contracts

Specifications

The purchase specification is a request for an acquisition, which should be carefully prepared. A specification written too narrowly limits competition, whereas a specification written too vaguely undermines quality. There are five principal types of specifications. First, a *standard* specification is used to purchase frequently bought items. Second, a *brand name or equal* specification limits the purchase to a named brand or a brand substantially similar to the named brand. Prospective vendors should be very familiar with the brand name product. Third, a *design* specification sets dimensional and other physical requirements for the construction of buildings and other capital projects. Fourth, a *performance* specification defines the performance that the organization should accomplish with regard to such services as:

- Child foster-care placement (reunification, adoption, subsidized guardianship, etc.)
- Job placement
- Job retention
- Job training—skill mastery
- Recidivism in the criminal justice system
- Meals served

The rate of compensation may depend on how well the organization accomplishes its objectives. The contract may include incentives for superior performance and penalties for substandard performance. The fifth and final specification, *samples*, asks prospective vendors to submit a price and a sample of their product, which the buyer tests for performance.

Quotations or Bids

The next step is to take either quotations or bids. Upon recommendation by the CEO, the Board establishes a *bid limit* amount, over which the nonprofit must take competitive bids for a good or service. Items priced under the bid limit are bought by asking vendors to submit a price *quotation* over the phone, electronically, or in writing. Bids take considerably more time to process than quotations. The bid limit should thus be carefully set. A bid limit set too high unduly delays the delivery of needed supplies and equipment. In such a situation, the program manager may be tempted to circumvent the bid limit by a *splitting a P.O.* into two or more purchases priced under the bid limit. Conversely, a bid limit set too low can limit competition because purchasable items typically receive more bids than quotations.

A purchasing policy normally does not specify how many quotations to take. The objective should be to obtain as much competition as reasonable, taking at least three quotations if possible. If a program manager takes quotations, the CFO should reserve the right to ask for more quotations if he or she judges that a lower price can be obtained.

The CFO maintains a list of bidders, organized by major commodity groups, which should be updated regularly by adding qualified firms and dropping firms whose performance has been dissatisfactory.

The CFO sends an *Invitation for Bids* that includes the following provisions:

- *Who.* Name and telephone number of bidder
- *Specification.* Where and how to get a copy of the specification
- *Process.* The time and date of a pre-bid conference if required. The bid submission date. When the bid will be certified, evaluated, and awarded
- *Standard contract provisions.* A nondiscrimination clause, cancellation and termination provisions, conditions for accepting and rejecting deliveries, a COI clause, and pricing terms

For a construction project, the winning bidder typically posts three types of bonds:

1. A *bid bond* requiring compliance with the terms of the bid
2. A *performance bond* requiring the performance as stated in the contract
3. A *payment bond* requiring the contractor to pay subcontractors and suppliers

The firm forfeits the bonds if it does not meet the terms of the contract.

Bids are opened in a public meeting. The bidders' names, quantity of goods, unit price, total price, delivery date, and other pertinent information are formally recorded. The bid is awarded to the *lowest responsible* bidder. A responsible bid should:

- Meet the terms of the specification
- Offer the skills, labor, equipment, judgment, and resources required

If a bid proves irresponsible, the nonprofit must document in writing the reason for rejecting the bid.

Purchase Orders

A P.O. is a multiple copy form, authorizing the vendor to supply the order. A P.O. should be prenumbered to enable it to be matched against the requisition and the packing slip. Only an authorized person or people can approve a change to a P.O. or contract.

Receive Goods

Goods are received either at a central location or at the program that ordered the good. If the latter, the ordering program should authorize a person to receive goods. Goods should be very carefully inspected to ensure they meet the specification. Upon inspection, the receiver signs a receiving report, certifying that item or items have been delivered in the proper amount and condition. If part of an order is defective, the receiver can return the shipment in full or return only the substandard portion and revise the receiving report accordingly.

Make Payment

The vendor next sends an invoice to the CFO. To protect against fraud and theft, the following duties should be separated among personnel:

- Requisitioning and receiving goods
- Processing the invoice and making accounting general ledger entries
- Preparing and approving disbursements and making general ledger entries

Some vendors give a discount for timely payment. The discount is the amount of interest earned if a bill is paid before a specified time. The most common discount—2%/10, net 30—means a vendor will give a 2 percent discount if the bill is paid within 10 days; otherwise, the full price is due at 30 days. In essence, the vendor charges 2 percent of the invoice to extend credit 20 days.

Example. Assume an invoice with credit terms 2%/10, net 30. The interest charge is 2 percent of $1,000, the principal is $980, and the days of principal borrowed are 20 days of credit.

$$\text{Interest lost} = \frac{\text{Interest charge (in \$)}}{\text{Principal}} \times \frac{365 \text{ days}}{\text{Days principal borrowed}}$$

$$= \frac{\$20}{\$980} \times \frac{365 \text{ days}}{20}$$

$$= 37.23\%$$

The formula can be modified to calculate the cost of not taking the discount when the invoice amount is unknown:

$$\text{Interest lost} = \frac{\text{Cash discount (\%)}}{100 - \text{Cash discount (\%)}} \times \frac{365 \text{ days}}{\text{Days principal borrowed}}$$

$$= \frac{2\%}{100 - 2\%} \times \frac{365 \text{ days}}{20}$$

$$= 37.23\%$$

Either formula may be used to determine the interest rate for payment on dates other than the due date. For example, assume a nonprofit decides to pay a $1,000 invoice, with 2%/10, net 30 terms, 10 days after the due date:

$$\text{Interest lost} = \frac{2\%}{100 - 2\%} \times \frac{365 \text{ days}}{30}$$

$$= 24.83\%$$

Only authorized people can sign checks or electronic funds transfers. Authorized persons should issue a signed check only if substantiated by an invoice and not sign checks in advance of their scheduled payment date. To reduce time, the nonprofit may authorize use of a facsimile signature, which is a reproduction of the authorized person's signature. The device is either photographic, photostatic, or mechanical.

The nonprofit should (1) set a limit over which facsimile signature is not permissible; (2) adopt procedures to prevent duplicate payments and safeguard access to unused checks; and (3) retain checks, records, and supporting documents according to a Board-adopted or state-dictated record retention policy.

Petty Cash Purchases

Moneys are drawn from a petty-cash fund to purchase low-value, immediately needed items. The purchasing policy should limit the amount that an employee can withdraw from the petty cash fund. The limit is typically from $10 to $100. A custodian manages the petty cash fund, writing checks, and periodically reconciling the fund's balance to the amount withdrawn.

Dispose of Goods

Supplies are used up, but some capital items, such as computers and cars, have resale value. The purchasing manual should establish a procedure to dispose of such goods. Cars, for instance, may be sold at auction.

Appendix

Article I: Purpose

The purpose of the conflict of interest policy is to protect this tax-exempt organization's interest when it is contemplating entering into a transaction or arrangement that might benefit the private interest of an officer or director of the Organization or might result in a possible excess benefit transaction. This policy is intended to supplement but not replace any applicable state and federal laws governing conflict of interest applicable to nonprofit and charitable organizations.

Article II: Definitions

1. Interested Person
    Any director, principal officer, or member of a committee with governing board-delegated powers, who has a direct or indirect financial interest as defined below, is an interested person.
2. Financial Interest
    A person has financial interest if the person has, directly or indirectly, through business, investment, or family:
    a. An ownership or investment interest in any entity with which the Organization has a transaction or arrangement,
    b. A compensation arrangement with the Organization or with any entity or individual with which the Organization has a transaction or arrangement, or
    c. A potential ownership or investment interest in, or compensation arrangement with, any entity or individual with which the Organization is negotiating a transaction or arrangement.

Compensation includes direct and indirect remuneration as well as gifts or favors that are not insubstantial. A financial interest is not necessarily a conflict of interest. Under Article III, Section 2, a person who has a financial interest may have a conflict of interest only if the appropriate governing board or committee decides that a conflict of interest exists.

EXHIBIT 8A.1   Samples IRS Conflict of Interest Policy

Source: Internal Revenue Service, "Appendix A: Sample Conflict of Interest Policy," *Instructions for Form 1023—Additional Material,*
http://www.irs.gov/instructions/i1023/ar03.html.

Article III: Procedures

1. Duty to Disclose

   In connection with any actual or possible conflict of interest, an interested person must disclose the existence of the financial interest and be given the opportunity to disclose all material facts to the directors and members of committees with governing board-delegated powers considering the proposed transaction or arrangement.

2. Determining Whether a Conflict of Interest Exists

   After disclosure of the financial interest and all material facts, and after any discussion with the interested person, he/she shall leave the governing board or committee meeting while the determination of a conflict of interest is discussed and voted upon. The remaining board or committee members shall decide if a conflict of interest exists.

3. Procedures for Addressing the Conflict of Interest

   a. An interested person may make a presentation at the governing board or committee meeting, but after the presentation, he/she shall leave the meeting during the discussion of and the vote on, the transaction or arrangement involving the possible conflict of interest.

   b. The chairperson of the governing board or committee shall, if appropriate, appoint a disinterested person or committee to investigate alternatives to the proposed transaction or arrangement.

   c. After exercising due diligence, the governing board or committee shall determine whether the Organization can obtain with reasonable efforts a more advantageous ttransaction or arrangement from a person or entity that would not give rise to a conflict of interest.

   d. If a more advantageous transaction or arrangement is not reasonably possible under circumstances not producing a conflict of interest, the governing board or committee shall determine by a majority vote of the disinterested directors whether the transaction or arrangement is in the Organization's best interest, for its own benefit, and whether it is fair and reasonable. In conformity with the above determination, it shall make its decision as to whether to enter into the transaction or arrangement.

4. Violations of the Conflict of Interest Policy

   a. If the governing board or committee has reasonable cause to believe that a member has failed to disclose actual or possible conflicts of interest, it shall inform the member of the basis for such a belief and afford the member an opportunity to explain the alleged failure to disclose.

EXHIBIT 8A.1 *(Continued)*

b. If, after hearing the member's response and after making further investigation as warranted by the circumstances, the governing board or committee determines the member has failed to disclose an actual or possible conflict of interest, it shall take appropriate disciplinary and corrective action.

Article IV: Recordings of Proceedings

The minutes of the governing board and all committees with board-delegated powers shall contain:

a. The names of the persons who disclosed or otherwise were found to have a financial interest in connection with an actual or possible conflict of interest, the nature of the financial interest, any action taken to determine whether a conflict of interest was present, and the governing Board's or committee's decision as to whether a conflict of interest in fact existed.
b. The names of the persons who were present for discussions and votes relating to the transaction or arrangement, the content of the discussion, including any alternatives to the proposed transaction or arrangement, and a record of any votes taken in connection with the proceedings.

Article V: Compensation

A voting member of the governing board who receives compensation, directly or indirectly, from the Organization for services is precluded from voting on matters pertaining to that member's compensation.

A voting member of any committee whose jurisdiction includes compensation matters and who receives compensation, directly or indirectly, from the Organization for services is precluded from voting on matters pertaining to that member's compensation.

No voting member of the governing board or any committee whose jurisdiction includes compensation matters and who receives compensation, directly or indirectly, from the Organization, either individually or collectively, is prohibited from providing information to any committee regarding compensation.

EXHIBIT 8A.1   (*Continued*)

Article VI: Annual Statements

Each director, principal officer, and member of a committee with governing board-delegated powers shall annually sign a statement, which affirms such person:

a. Has received a copy of the conflicts of interest policy,
b. Has read and understands the policy,
c. Has agreed to comply with the policy,
d. Understands the Organization is charitable and in order to maintain its federal tax exemption it must engage primarily in activities that accomplish one or more of its tax-exempt purposes.

Article VII: Periodic Reviews

To ensure the Organization operates in a manner consistent with charitable purposes and does not engage in activities that could jeopardize its tax-exempt status, periodic reviews shall be conducted. The periodic reviews shall, at a minimum, include the following subjects:

a. Whether compensation arrangements and benefits are reasonable, based on competent survey information and the result of arm's length bargaining.
b. Whether partnerships, joint ventures, and arrangements with management organizations conform to the organization's written policies, are properly recorded, reflect reasonable investment or payments for goods and services, further charitable purposes, and do not result in inurement, impermissible private benefit or in an excess benefit transaction.

Article VIII: Use of Outside Experts

When conducting the periodic reviews as provided for in Article VII, the Organization may, but need not, use outside advisors. If outside experts are used, their use shall not relieve the governing board of its responsibility for ensuring periodic reviews are conducted.

EXHIBIT 8A.1 *(Continued)*

If any employee reasonably believes that some policy, practice, or activity of [Name of the Nonprofit] is in violation of law, a written complaint must be filed by that employee with the Chief Executive Officer or the Board President.

It is the intent of [Name of Nonprofit] to adhere to all laws and regulations that apply to the organization and the underlying purpose of this policy is to support the organization's goal of legal compliance. The support of all employees is necessary to achieve compliance with various laws and regulations. An employee is protected from retaliation only if the employee brings the alleged unlawful, activity, policy or practice to the attention of [Name of Nonprofit] and provides the [Name of Nonprofit] with a reasonable opportunity to investigate and correct the alleged unlawful activity. The protection described below is only available to employees that comply with this requirement.

[Name of Nonprofit] will not retaliate against an employee who in good faith, has made a protest or raise a complaint against some practice of [Name of Nonprofit], or of another individual or entity with whom [Name of Nonprofit] has a business relationship, on the basis of a reasonable belief that the practice is in violation of law, or a clear mandate of public policy.

[Name of Nonprofit] will not retaliate against employees who disclose or threaten to disclose to a supervisor or a public body, any activity, policy or practice of [Name of Nonprofit) that the employee reasonably believes is in violation of a law, or a rule, or regulation mandated pursuant to law or is in violation of a clear mandate of public policy concerning the health, safety, welfare, or protection of the environment.

My signature below indicates my receipt and understanding of this policy. I also verify that I have been provided with an opportunity to ask questions about the policy.

[Employee Signature]

[Date]

EXHIBIT 8A.2   Sample Whistleblower Policy

Source: Nonprofit Risk Management Center. Leesburg, VA 20176.

CHAPTER 9

Contract to Provide a Service

Nonprofits contract with governments, foundations, firms, individuals, and other nonprofits to provide a wide range of services, including:

- Human services, such as public health, mental health, housing, food, employment, and day care
- Educational services, such as a charter school, Head Start program, tutorial program, and the like
- Cultural services, such as an arts program, community theater, music group, or a museum

The granting agency contracts with the nonprofit to provide the service. Contracting is a three-step process that is described in this chapter:

1. Issue a request for proposals (RFP) or bids request.
2. Award the contract.
3. Administer the contract.

Issue RFP or Bids Request

The contractor will issue to the nonprofit an invitation for bids or an RFP. A bid, discussed in Chapter 8, "Purchase Goods," is awarded to lowest responsible bidder, which normally is the organization submitting the lowest price. In contrast, a winning *proposal* may not be the lowest priced. The contractor, though concerned with price, focuses on whether the nonprofit has the experience and ability to provide the service.

The contractor can issue a negotiable or nonnegotiable RFP. In a nonnegotiable RFP, the price that each nonprofit submits is fixed. In a negotiable RFP, the contractor negotiates with nonprofits to reach a price with a winning nonprofit. Exhibit 9.1 shows the RFP's provisions to which a nonprofit would respond.

EXHIBIT 9.1   RFP Provisions

Provision	Description
General Information	The agency contact person; whether a preproposal conference will be held; whether attendance at the conference is mandatory; the selection process; the agency's right to reject all offers
Scope of Service	A description of the service required
Nonprofit's Qualifications	(1) Related experience; (2) references; (3) evidence of financial stability, including most recent financial statements; (4) evidence of being insured and bonded; (5) resumes of staff who will do the work; (6) statement of the contractor's right to approve staffing replacements
Nonprofit Policies	Written policies concerning substance abuse, customer relations, customer complaints, and work inspection
Contractor's Responsibilities	The contractor will provide the nonprofit with parking, working space, storage for supplies or equipment, telephone access, etc.
Bonding	The nonprofit must have: (1) a *bid bond* (typically 5% of the contract price); (2) a *payment bond* ensuring the nonprofit's payment to its subcontractors; and (3) a *performance bond* ensuring against substandard performance
Evaluation criteria	Criteria for awarding the contract, including quality, price, and other elements

The heart of the RFP, the *scope of work* (SOW), specifies the nature of the work required. A performance contract, based on a performance specification, specifies expected service outcomes such as the number of:

- People housed in an overnight shelter
- Meals served to the needy
- Houses built or refurbished
- People inoculated
- Students earning their general equivalency diploma
- Mentally ill staying on their medication
- People placed in a job for x number of months

Award the Contract

Exercising due diligence, the funding agency investigates the experience and qualifications of the nonprofits submitting proposals. The contractor contacts the nonprofit's references to evaluate how well the nonprofit has performed on similar jobs.

The contract, following the RFP, should clearly define each party's responsibilities, the reporting requirements and the performance-evaluation criteria. The contract should be:

- Precise and accurate
- Simply written in the active voice
- Devoid of confusing terminology
- Consistent in its use of words, provisions, and numbering

Types of Contracts

There are three contracting models.[1] In the *competition* model, the contractor takes several bids or proposals and selects the lowest. In the *negotiation model*, the contractor contacts only a few nonprofits and does not specify the SOW in detail. After discussion with the nonprofits, the contractor selects one and negotiates a price and the SOW. In the third model, the *cooperation model*, the contractor contacts only *one* nonprofit, with which it enters into long-term contract awarded noncompetitively.[2] Arguably, this is the most common approach. One survey found that 73 percent of local units contracted with nonprofits for three years or longer.[3] Another study found that 82 percent of social service contracts were awarded noncompetitively.[4]

A contract entered into using the negotiation or cooperation model is a *relational contract*, which is based on mutual trust between the nonprofit and the contractor. The socially conscious mission of nonprofits reinforces contractors' trust in nonprofits. In a relational contract, the contractor and nonprofit fine-tune performance expectations through negotiation.[5]

Exhibit 9.2 shows common payment methods. A contract can have a performance incentive and/or a penalty provision. An incentive clause

EXHIBIT 9.2 Payment Methods

Payment Type	Provisions
Fixed price	An agreed-upon price is set. The contract is suitable for a measurable service with a predictable cost. The nonprofit assumes the risk for cost overruns.
Fixed price with incentive and/or penalty	Fixed price contract has a bonus for outstanding performance as defined in the contract and/or a penalty for substandard performance.
Fixed price with an inflation escalator	Fixed price contract has an inflation escalator provision to protect the nonprofit against an unanticipated, significant increase in labor or material costs.

EXHIBIT 9.3   Payment Methods to Human Service Nonprofits

Reimbursement Method	Percent
Cost reimbursable payments	53%
Fixed cost (flat amount)	48%
Unit cost payment/fee for service ($ per time unit)	35%
Unit cost payment/fee for service ($ per individual or family unit)	26%
Performance-based payment	17%

Source: Urban Institute, *Human Service Nonprofit and Government Collaboration* (2010).

specifies that the nonprofit can share in cost savings. A penalty provision financially penalizes the nonprofit for substandard performance. In times of high inflation, the contract may include an inflation escalator to reimburse for unexpected inflationary cost spikes.

Human service nonprofits use the other payment methods as shown in Exhibit 9.3. The most common payment method, cost reimbursement, pays all allowed expenses up to set limit. The fixed cost method pays a flat amount regardless of expenses. The unit cost reimbursement method pays a set fee per time unit or family/individual served. The performance based method bases payment on service outcomes.

Of the contracts reported in Exhibit 9.3, 60 percent required a match of 25 percent or more; 27 percent had to match 50 percent or more. Typically, grantors limit the amount that can be spent on administrative overhead. The limit is typically very strict. For 60 percent of the nonprofits, the limit was 10 percent or less.[6]

Administer the Contract

In the final stage, contract administration, the contractor usually assigns a *project manager* to oversee implementation, settle disputes, negotiate contract changes, and approve payments. A contract can be increased either bilaterally or unilaterally. A bilateral modification, signed by both parties, increases the contract based on a *change order*. A unilateral modification is only signed by the contractor.

A change order is a formal change to a contract, usually to the SOW. A competent project manager will carefully examine the suitability of the nonprofit's request for a change order. Sometimes, the service provider "low balls" (i.e., deliberately underestimates) its bid to get a contract with the intention of subsequently increasing its payments by means of change orders.

Sometimes problems arise while administering contracts. The Urban Institute identified five problems that nonprofits have contracting with

EXHIBIT 9.4   Problems with Government Contracting

Problem	Big Problem (%)	Small Problem (%)
Failure to cover full cost of contracted services	44%	24%
Too complex and too time consuming application requirements	37%	39%
Too complex and too time consuming reporting requirements	37%	39%
Governments changes to contracts and grants after they have been approved	26%	31%
Late payments	24%	29%

Source: Urban *Institute, National Survey of Nonprofit-Government Contracting and Grants* (2010).

governments. Exhibit 9.4 indicates the degree to which human service nonprofits perceived these problems to be a "big" or a "small problem."

In managing a contract, the nonprofit must be careful not to expend more than the contracted amount. If the contract is a unit (individual or family served) cost reimbursement, and the funder pays for the service in advance, the nonprofit must be careful to not spend the funds in advance of achieving the promised outcomes.

During the project, the project manager typically conducts an *after-action review* (evaluation and feedback sessions) after reaching an important event or milestone. In the event of a contract dispute, the project manager should try to resolve a problem. If the problem cannot be resolved, the funding agency will set a date for the nonprofit to correct the problem or face a penalty, which could be contract cancellation, after which the nonprofit forfeits its performance bond.

For Further Reading

Herman, Melanie. *Ready in Defense.* Washington, DC: Nonprofit Risk Management Center, 2003. For an excellent discussion of contracts, refer to Chapter 3, "Contracts, Contract Liability and Contract Risks."

CHAPTER 10

Manage Capital Assets and the Inventory

Capital assets include land, equipment, machinery, furniture, vehicles, and the like. Most nonprofits have capital assets, and some maintain an inventory of supplies. For example, food banks store food; the Salvation Army stores clothing and goods; most nonprofits store office supplies; and some store auto parts. An inventory management system safeguards such assets against theft and misuse.

Manage Capital Assets

As discussed in Chapter 2, "Account for Transactions," capital assets include property (land), plant (buildings), and equipment. A capital asset typically has an initial life longer than one year and has significant value, as defined by the nonprofit's capitalization policy. For most nonprofits, significant value is $500 or more. Exhibit 10.1 shows a list of recommended capital asset-management practices.

The CEO should designate an asset manager to have the overall custodial responsibility for the assets. If assets are considerable in number, the asset manager may designate people to be responsible for assets in the location where they work. The CFO should notify the asset manager of an asset's acquisition, relocation, sale, reassignment, or disposal.

To ensure independence, the duties of the asset manager should be separated from the jobs of taking the annual inventory, tagging assets, investigating the cause for missing assets and reconciling capital asset accounts.

To safeguard assets, insure them against misuse or theft. The nonprofit should make an annual count of capital assets. Sometimes, the nonprofit's auditor takes the inventory. If an asset is found missing, a missing asset form should be completed and an investigation conducted to determine its whereabouts. Suspected theft or vandalism must be reported to

EXHIBIT 10.1 Capital Asset Management List

Practice

Manage Assets
Designate an asset manager.
Tag capital assets when procured.
Assign a custodial responsibility for each asset.
Notify the asset manager when an asset is:
-Received
-Donated
-Relocated
-Sold
-Stolen, vandalized, or missing
-Reassigned to a different program

Separate the duties of the asset manager and the duty of:
-Taking the annual inventory
-Tagging assets
-Investigating missing assets
-Reconciling the capital asset-control accounts and making capital asset entries

Safeguard Assets
Insure assets.
Take an annual physical inventory of assets.
If an asset is missing, complete a Missing-Asset Form and investigate why the item
    is missing.
Report to law enforcement when an asset is stolen or vandalized.

Account for Assets
Maintain asset records that classify and identify individual items.
Capitalize the purchase price less the discount and expenses.
Record the cost of land, including its purchase price, legal and title fees, surveying
    fees, appraisal fees, and site-preparation costs.
Balance the asset subsidiary accounts with asset control accounts monthly.
Reconcile property records periodically with property accounts.
Report in the notes to financial statements the beginning balance, additions,
    disposals, and ending balance of assets.

Dispose of Assets
Periodically review the condition of capital assets to determine whether they are
    obsolete.
Dispose of goods according to the board-established policy.
Recognize gains and losses from the disposal of capital assets.
Record in the appropriate ledger the book value of the asset.

police. Finally, the CFO should maintain the accounting controls listed in Exhibit 10.1.

At some point, fixed assets wear out, break down, or become obsolete. Thus, the asset manager should periodically review the condition of assets to see whether they have become obsolete. Some goods (e.g., vehicles) have a residual value. The Board should adopt a policy specifying when and how to dispose of such goods. When an asset is sold, the CFO should record the transaction in the appropriate ledger.

Manage the Inventory

Inventory management has five aspects:

1. Stock the inventory.
2. Issue goods.
3. Safeguard the goods.
4. Dispose of assets.
5. Evaluate performance.

Exhibit 10.2 is a list of inventory management practices to follow.

Stock and Locate Items

The first step is to decide what and how much to stock, based on each item's usage rate, cost, and need. There is *no* need to stock a high-cost, little used, easily purchasable item; however, low-cost, fast-moving, high-priority items are *always* stocked. An item's location in the stockroom depends on its usage. For instance, fast-moving, commonly used items are located near the point of issuance.

Issue Goods

The inventory manager keeps a perpetual inventory record on each item, preferably in an electronic format. The record states the purchase price, items withdrawn, items received and the current number on hand. The inventory manager inspects received goods to ensure their quality and quantity and files a requisition as evidence of receipt. To reconcile perpetual inventory records with accounting records, a cut-off date is set for the receipt and issuance of goods at fiscal year-end.

Goods should be available when needed but not overstocked. To optimize the amount of goods on hand, use the *economic order quantity* (EOQ) method shown in this equation:

$$EOQ = \sqrt{\frac{2UO}{C}}$$

EXHIBIT 10.2   Inventory Management List

Practice

Stock Goods
Stock items.
Locate items in the storeroom.

Issue Goods
Maintain a perpetual inventory record on each inventory item.
Inspect received goods to ensure that the quantity and quality are as ordered.
Sign the requisition as evidence of receipt.
File approved requisitions.
Notify accounting of the receipt of goods.
Use receiving report or vendor invoice to record purchases on perpetual
    inventory records.
Establish a year-end cut-off date for the receipt and issuance of goods.
Use the economic order quality method to order goods.

Safeguard Goods
Limit access to perpetual inventory records.
Limit access to the inventory.
Insure inventories.
Bond employees responsible for managing the inventory.
Designate someone to approve an adjustment to inventory records.
Periodically check the accuracy of the inventory records.
Reconcile perpetual inventory balances against the general ledger and
    control accounts at least annually.
Take a physical inventory of goods at least annually.
Designate someone other than the asset manager to conduct the annual
    inventory.
Record the inventory count on perpetual inventory records.

Evaluate Performance
Set inventory performance objectives.

where

U = Annual usage
O = Cost of placing an order
C = Cost of carrying a unit in the inventory

Example
Meals on Wheels delivery vehicles use 1,600 oil filters annually. The cost
    of placing an order is $10.00. The unit cost is $7.00. The carrying
    cost is 20 percent of unit cost. The carrying cost per unit is $1.40
    (0.20 × $7.00). What is the EOQ?

$$EOQ = \sqrt{\frac{2UO}{C}}$$

$$= \sqrt{\frac{2(1,600)\$10}{\$1.40}}$$

$$= \sqrt{\frac{\$32,000}{\$1.40}}$$

$$= \sqrt{\$22,857}$$

$$= 150 \text{ oil filters}$$

The ordering frequency is derived from the EOQ using the next formula, which assumes 255 working days (260 days less 5 holidays),

where

N = Number of working days
U = Annual usage

Example

$$OF = \frac{N \times EOQ}{U}$$

$$= \frac{255 \times 150}{1,600}$$

$$= 24 \text{ days}$$

An order of 150 filters would be placed about every 24 working days.

Safeguard Goods

To safeguard goods from theft or misuse, allow only authorized people to access the storeroom and the perpetual inventory records. Insure the contents of the inventory against loss and purchase a fidelity bond covering the actions of people with access to the inventory. Permit only authorized personnel to adjust an inventory record. Take an annual physical inventory of the goods on hand, reconciling the amount counted in the physical inventory with the amount shown in the general ledger.

Evaluate Performance

A key inventory performance measure is the inventory turnover ratio, which is the annual usage of the inventory, divided by the average amount of inventory on hand, as shown in the next example.

Example

Let us assume an inventory last year had monthly amount of $200,000 in inventory on hand and had annual usage of $800,000. The inventory thus turned over four times during the year:

$$\text{Annual usage} = \$800,000$$
$$\text{Average monthly inventory} = \$200,000$$
$$= 4 \text{ inventory turns}$$

Let us assume the inventory turnover ratio increases from 4 to 8:

$$\text{Annual usage} = \$800,000$$
$$\text{Average monthly inventory} = \$100,000$$
$$= 8 \text{ inventory turns}$$

The amount of $100,000 ($200,000 − $100,000) is thus freed up for other purposes.

CHAPTER 11

Invest Funds

M ost nonprofits have very few funds to invest. Indeed, about half of all nonprofits, excluding foundations, derive less than 1 percent of their income from investments.[1] Living "hand-to-mouth," they depend on limited cash reserves and occasional short-term bank loans to maintain cash flow. Some nonprofits are not so cash starved, however. About 20 percent receive over 5 percent of their income from investments.[2]

Investing funds is a two-step process:

1. Adopt an investment policy.
2. Invest funds.

Exhibit 11.1 is a list of investment best practices.

Adopt an Investment Policy

The Board should adopt an investment policy to guide its investment decisions, the provisions of which are discussed below.

Investment Manager and Investment Committee

The investment policy designates an investment officer, usually the CFO, to manage the investment program. Nonprofits with substantial investments may create an investment committee to assist the investment manager.[3] The investment committee is comprised of Board members and/or citizens with financial expertise. To avoid a conflict of interest, the investment policy directs the investment manager and investment committee members to:

- Avoid personal business that conflicts with their committee responsibilities
- Disclose a potential conflict of interest (e.g., a financial interest in an institution with whom the nonprofit does business)
- Not invest in a business with which the nonprofit does business

EXHIBIT 11.1   Investment List

Practice

Investment Policy Provision
Designate an investment manager.
Appoint an investment committee.
Select an investment adviser.
Adopt the prudent investor rule.
Specify the investment mix.
Specify the amount of risk to assume.
Designate qualified financial institutions.
Possibly require socially responsible investments.
Adopt an investment strategy.

Investment Practice
Select the investment instruments.
Calculate interest returns.
Project cash flow.
Play the float.
Safeguard securities.
Report and account for investments.
Evaluate performance.

Investment Adviser

Large nonprofits, with a substantial amount to invest, may hire an investment adviser, who typically will only manage a substantial portfolio (e.g., over $300,000). To engage the services of an adviser, issue a request for proposals that specifies the following:

- Desired scope of work
- Qualifications of the investment adviser, including registration with the Securities and Exchange Commission (SEC)
- Supplying references
- Method of evaluating the adviser's performance
- Method of compensation

The nonprofit may give the adviser discretionary or nondiscretionary authority. With discretionary authority, the adviser can make trades without consulting the nonprofit. Nondiscretionary requires the adviser to obtain approval for individual transactions.

To evaluate prospective advisers' performances, the nonprofit should examine the return rates that they have earned managing similar clients' portfolios and compare those rates to standard performance indices such as the Standard & Poor's 500 equity investment index and the Russell 1000 fixed income instrument index.

The nonprofit should also check the investment advisers' form ADV. An adviser that manages $25 million or more in client assets must register form ADV with the SEC. Advisers managing less must register with the state. Form ADV has two parts. Part 1, found electronically on the Investment Adviser Public Disclosure website, contains information about any problems the adviser has had with regulators or clients. Part 2, available from the adviser, outlines the adviser's services, fees, and strategies.

Prudent Investor Rule

In *Harvard vs. Armory* (1830), the Massachusetts Supreme Court ruled that a trustee of funds should follow the *prudent man rule*:

> *Those with responsibility to invest others' money should act with prudence, discretion, intelligence and regard for the safety of capital as well as income.*

Over time, Congress codified the rule by enacting the Uniform Management of Institutional Funds Act in 1972, which 46 states have adopted. In 2006, Congress revised the Act into the now called *Prudent Investor Rule:*[4]

> *If the investment manager follows the "prudent investor" standard with due diligence, he or she is relieved of the responsibility for any loss in securities' value due to price changes.*

The nonprofit should adopt the prudent investor rule to protect the investment manager from unfairly bearing the responsibility for a decline in securities' values when he or she has exercised due diligence.

The Investment Mix

The investment mix describes how to allocate different types of investment instruments in the portfolio. Investment instruments vary regarding with regard to their:

- Rate of return
- Liquidity (convertibility to cash)
- Risk

EXHIBIT 11.2   Types of Risks

Risk Type	Explanation
Credit or Default Risk	Risk that payments on a security (interest or principal) will not be made under the original terms
Market or Price Risk	Uncertainty over the price at which a security can be sold prior to maturity in the *secondary* market
Liquidity Risk	Risk that a security cannot be sold quickly without experiencing a significant loss
Interest Rate Risk	Risk that a fixed interest rate security may have to be sold prior to maturity in a market where interest rates are rising, causing a loss of principal on the sale

The higher the rate of return, the higher is the risk. The higher the liquidity, the lower is the rate of return. The four types of risks are shown in Exhibit 11.2.

Most nonprofits minimize risk by taking a safety first, *SLY* investment approach, SLY standing for:

- *S*afety. First, protect against the default of principal and decline in stock price.
- *L*iquidity. Second, ensure liquidity to pay operating expenses.
- *Y*ield. Third, achieve a reasonable yield on investments.

The investment policy specifies the percentage of assets to invest in safe, fixed income securities versus more risky equities, whose value may decline with a fall in the stock market. The policy sets a total return goal (appreciation and income), such as 3 percent after inflation over a market cycle of three to five years and sets allowable investment ranges on the three main investment asset classes, such as shown in Exhibit 11.3.

The investment policy may further reduce risk by limiting the portion of the portfolio that can be held as shown below:

- Stock in any one sector of the economy (e.g., 25%)
- Stock in any one company (e.g., 5%)
- Investments in high risk securities
- Securities that have the same maturity date
- Long-term investments (e.g., only 5% can be held beyond 5 years)

EXHIBIT 11.3   Allowable Investment Ranges

Equities
Allowable Range—Minimum 20%; Maximum 40% of Total Assets
The equities will be high quality, domestic (U.S.) securities on the New York, NASDAQ or American Stock exchanges. The securities should have above average financial characteristics, e.g., price-to-earnings, return-on-equity, debt-to-capital ratios.

Fixed Income
Allowable Range—Minimum 40%; Maximum 65% of Total Assets
Bond investments will consist of taxable, fixed income securities with an investment-grade rating (Baa or higher) that possess a liquid secondary market. The maximum average maturity of the fixed asset portfolio will be 10 years, with not more than 25% of the bond portfolio maturing in more than 10 years.

Fixed Income
Allowable Range—Minimum 40%; Maximum 65% of Total Assets
The money market fund must be rated by at least one nationally recognized rating agency as in the highest category for short-term securities.

Qualified Financial Institutions

The investment policy should specify the financial institutions, depositories, and brokers/dealers qualified to do business with the nonprofit. To assess the qualifications of the firms, the investment manager should require the firms to furnish:

- A Consolidated Report of Condition, which is a quarterly report that allows regulators to monitor banks' financial condition
- Proof of certification by the National Association of Securities Dealers
- Proof of registration with the state
- Proof of having adequate insurance coverage

At least annually, the investment manager should evaluate each institution's creditworthiness to determine whether they should continue to do business with the nonprofit.

When placing an investment, the investment officer should seek competition, obtaining a competitive bid from at least three brokers or financial institutions. The nonprofit should then engage a bank's trust department as a third-party custodial agent to hold its marketable securities in safekeeping. The nonprofit should require that the bank annually provide a copy of its most recent internal controls report, prepared in accordance with Statement of Auditing Standard No. 70.

Socially Responsible Investing

Some nonprofits require *socially responsible investing* (SRI), which prohibits investments in firms that produce products (e.g., tobacco, alcohol, weapons, pornography) or services (e.g., animal testing, abortions, gambling) that the nonprofit considers socially repugnant. SRI can also prohibit conducting business with an oppressive government (e.g., China).

Investing in mutual funds makes SRI problematic, however, because their holdings include such a wide array of firms. Before adopting an SRI policy, a nonprofit should carefully weigh the benefits against the costs. One study found that nonprofits that avoid mutual funds lose from 3 percent to 4 percent in their annual investment return.[5]

Investment Strategy

The Board decides whether to pursue a *passive* or *active* investment strategy. A *passive* investment strategy, taken by most nonprofits, simply attempts to achieve the market average rate of return. Passive investing follows a *matching* strategy, buying securities that mature when funds are needed to pay expenses.

In contrast, an *active* investment strategy attempts to earn a higher-than-the-average market rate of return. An active investment strategy entails considerably more risk. Thus, a nonprofit following an active strategy should engage the services of a sophisticated, highly experienced investment adviser. Following an active strategy, the investor *rides the yield curve*, investing based on anticipated yield-curve changes. The most common yield curve is positive and upward sloping, which anticipates long-term rates will be higher than short-term rates. Preferring liquidity, investors accept a lower yield for short-term instruments.

INVEST FUNDS

Referring to Exhibit 11.1, best investment practices include the following:

- Select the investment instrument.
- Calculate interest returns.
- Project cash flow.
- Play the float.
- Safeguard securities.
- Report and account for investments.
- Evaluate performance.

The rest of this section discusses each.

Investment Instruments

A nonprofit can invest in three types of investment instruments: (1) fixed income, (2) equity (stock), or (3) an alternative. These are described in the remainder of this section.

FIXED INCOME INSTRUMENTS   There are seven types of fixed income investment instruments: (1) U.S. Treasury securities, (2) U.S. government agency obligations, (3) bank obligations, (4) commercial paper, (5) corporate notes and bonds, (6) money market mutual funds, and (7) short-term mutual funds.

1. *U.S. Treasury securities.* The U.S. government finances its national debt by issuing Treasury or T-bills, T-notes, and T-bonds. Each has the same credit standing but a different maturity date. Each week the national government offers a *T-bill*, due either in 13 weeks (91 days), 26 weeks (182 days), or 52 weeks. They are sold in minimum denominations of $10,000 and multiples of $5,000 above the minimum. They are sold on a discount basis, with a face value equal to 100.00 and at a price less than 100.00. For example, a $10,000 T-bill bought at 95 ($9,500) will return $10,000 a year later. The difference, $5,000, is the amount of the discount when the discount rate is 5 percent.

   A *T-note*, paying interest every six months, is issued with a fixed face amount (the par value); a maturity date; and coupon interest rate. T-notes start at $5,000 and increase in value in multiples of $1,000 for maturities of less than four years. Notes with maturities of greater than four years are available in minimum amounts of $1,000 and multiples of $1,000.

   A *T-bond* is a long-term obligation with a maturity of more than 10 years.

2. *U.S. government agency obligations (agencies).* Agencies—the Federal National Mortgage Association (Fannie Mae), the National Mortgage Association (Ginnie Mae), the Federal Home Loan Mortgage Corporation (Freddie Mac), the Student Loan Marketing Association (Sallie Mae), and Federal Farm Credit Banks—issue securities (called *agencies*) to finance their operations.

3. *Bank obligations.* Banks offer four types of interest-bearing instruments: (1) certificates of deposit (CD), (2) fixed time deposits, (3) banker's acceptances, and (4) repurchase agreements. Most states require that banks pledge collateral in the form of a U.S. government treasury or government-agency obligation to secure deposits over $100,000.

   A. *CD.* A CD is a deposit for a specified time in a financial institution documented by a certificate specifying its dollar amount, maturity date, and interest rate. A *nonnegotiable CD* must be held to maturity unless the issuer permits early redemption upon the depositor paying a lost interest income penalty. A *negotiable CD*, usually available in an amount of $100,000 or more, can be bought and sold in the secondary market before its maturity.

B. *Fixed time deposit.* Banks offer time deposits in passbook-savings, negotiable order of withdrawal (NOW), Super NOW and money market daily accounts (MMDA). A *passbook savings account*, offering the lowest interest rate, is not a transaction account (i.e., a check cannot be written on it). A *NOW account* is a transaction account that offers a somewhat higher interest rate than a passbook savings account. A *Super NOW account* offers a higher interest rate than a NOW account, but a lower interest than an MMDA account.

C. *Banker's acceptance (BA).* Often used to finance an international purchase, a BA is a time draft drawn by a customer against a bank. The bank "accepts" the draft to extend financing to the customer. Then the nonprofit buys the BA, whose collateral is the purchased merchandise.

D. *Repurchase agreement (repo).* The nonprofit temporarily buys a security with the agreement that the bank or securities dealer will repurchase it at a specific date.

4. *Commercial paper.* Corporations issue short-term unsecured promissory notes, known as commercial paper. Generally issued in $100,000 denominations, notes have maximum securities of 270 days, but most mature in a 30- to 50-day range.

5. *Corporate note or bond.* A corporate note has a maturity date ranging from 270 days to 10 years. A corporate note with a long maturity date is subject to the market risk of falling interest rates. A corporate bond typically does not mature until after one year.

6. *Money market mutual fund.* A money market mutual fund is a portfolio of money market instruments that requires a minimum investment, typically at least $1,000. Most permit a withdrawal on demand by check or electronic transfer but limit the size of the withdrawal.

7. *Short-term mutual fund.* A short-term mutual fund has a longer maturity and higher rate of return than a money market mutual fund. The average maturity of securities that comprise the portfolio is between one and three years.

Exhibit 11.4 shows the characteristics of fixed income instruments.

EQUITY INVESTMENTS The second type of investment is equities, of which there are two types: (1) stocks and (2) index funds. There are three types of stocks. *Common stocks* are securities that represent ownership in a firm.

EXHIBIT 11.4 Fixed Income Investment Instruments

Security Type	Security	Form	Minimum Denomination	Guarantee	Original Maturity Range	Interest-Payment Schedule
Bank obligations	Negotiable certificate of deposit (CD)	Payable to bearer	$100,000	Up to $100,000 by FDIC	7 days to 10 years	Semiannually or at maturity
	Nonnegotiable CD	Payable to bearer	Less than $100,000	Up to $100,000 by FDIC	7 days to 10 years	
	Time deposits[6]	Payable to bearer	No minimum	Up to $100,000 by FDIC	1 to 30 days	On withdrawal
	Banker's acceptance	Payable to bearer	$25,000 to $1,000,000	Bearer	30 to 270 days	Discount from par value
	Repurchase agreement	Secured transaction	$100,000 to $1 million	Counter party (securities as collateral)	Overnight to 90 days	Specified rate at maturity
U.S. Treasury securities	Treasury bill (T-bill)	Book entry	$10,000 and $1,000 increments	Full faith and credit of the U.S. government	3 months, 6 months, or 1 year	Discount from par value
	T-note and bond	Book entry	$5,000 and $1,000	Full faith and credit of the U.S. government	1 year to 10 years	Semiannually
U.S agency obligations	Agency bond	Book entry	$5,000 and $1,000	Moral obligation of the U.S. government	1 year to 10 years	Semiannually
Private sector obligations	Commercial paper	Unsecured promissory note	$100,000 for transactions or more	Bank's promise to pay, not by collateral	1 to 270 days	On the maturity date

The company's management acts as an agent for shareholders to protect their interests. *Preferred stock* differs from common stock in that preferred stockholders have priority claim on both earnings and assets. Preferred stockholders are paid their stock dividend in full before a dividend is paid to common stockholders. Finally, *convertible stocks* are debentures, bonds, or preferred stock that are changeable with another security.

An *index fund* is a mutual fund whose portfolio tracks a broad-based index, such as the S&P 500, thereby matching the market's overall performance.

ALTERNATIVE INVESTMENTS   The third type of investment is alternatives. "Alternative" to stocks and bonds, they include real estate, commodities, derivatives, contracts, and hedge funds. A *derivative* is a financial instrument whose price is "derived" from an asset (e.g., commodity, stock, loan, bond, residential mortgage) or from an interest index (e.g., the stock market index, the consumer price index, the exchange rate). A derivative transfers an asset's pricing risk to another party.

A *hedge fund* is a private partnership open to a limited number of investors. Hedging first began with farmers. The price a crop will fetch after harvesting may be higher or lower than the farmer expects. A *futures contract* hedges the farmer against a drop in prices by committing a merchant to buy his crop when it comes to market at a price agreed upon when the seeds were planted. In the 1970s, futures contracts expanded to hedge against variations in the price of currencies and interest rates. In 1982, futures contracts on the stock market became possible.

Closely related, but distinct from futures, are financial contracts known as *options*. The buyer of a *call option* has the right, but not the obligation, to buy an agreed-upon amount of a financial asset from the seller of the option at a certain time for a certain price. A buyer of a call expects its price to rise in the future. In contrast, a *put option* is the opposite. The buyer has the right, but not the obligation, to sell an agreed-upon quantity to the seller of the option. The third type of derivative, a *swap*, is a bet between two parties on the likely direction of interest rates. A *pure interest swap* allows the two parties to swap the interest payments they are receiving. A *credit default swap* offers protection against a company defaulting on its bonds.

Out of the range of most nonprofits, a hedge fund typically asks for a minimum of a six- or seven-figure investment and charges a management fee of at least 2 percent of the assets. Historically, hedge funds have provided a higher rate of return than other investments but are considerably more risky. A nonprofit should therefore avoid hedge funds and other alternative instruments unless managed by a knowledgeable investment adviser.

Calculate Interest Returns

The investment manager should be able to calculate the return on fixed income instruments. Examples follow.

TREASURY BILLS   A nonprofit buys a T-bill with a face value of $10,000 for $9,900. The bill matures in 91 days. Determine the yield,

where

> $SP =$ Selling price
> $PP =$ Purchase price
> $D =$ Number of days in the holding period

$$Y = \frac{SP - PP}{PP} \times \frac{360}{D}$$

$$= \frac{\$10,000 - \$9,900}{9,900} \times \frac{360}{91}$$

$$= 3.99\%$$

SIMPLE INTEREST SAVINGS ACCOUNT   If $1,000 is invested in a savings account for two years earning 2 percent interest annually, determine the future value at the end of one year, where

$$FV_n = PV(1 + i)^n$$

where

> $FV_n =$ Future value at the end of (n) periods
> $PV =$ Principal sum in dollars
> $i =$ Interest rate

Looking at Exhibit 11.5, Future Value of Interest Factors, the interest factor for two periods (years) and 2 percent interest is 1.0404.

$$FV = 1,000(1.0404) = \$1,040$$

ANNUITY   An annuity is a series of even, annual cash investments. If a nonprofit deposits $10,000 annually at an interest rate of 4 percent, how much interest will be earned at the end of three years if the interest is compounded annually?

$$SN = A(SAF_{i,n})$$

EXHIBIT 11.5 Future Value of Interest Factors

Periods, n	Interest Rate, i, %														
	1	2	3	4	5	6	7	8	9	10	11	12	13	14	15
1	1.0100	1.0200	1.0300	1.0400	1.0500	1.0600	1.0700	1.0800	1.0900	1.1000	1.1100	1.1200	1.1300	1.1400	1.1500
2	1.0201	1.0404	1.0609	1.0816	1.1025	1.1236	1.1449	1.1664	1.1881	1.2100	1.2321	1.2544	1.2769	1.2996	1.3225
3	1.0303	1.0612	1.0927	1.1249	1.1576	1.1910	1.2250	1.2597	1.2950	1.3310	1.3676	1.4049	1.4420	1.4815	1.5209
4	1.0406	1.0824	1.1255	1.1699	1.2155	1.2625	1.3108	1.3605	1.4116	1.4641	1.5181	1.5735	1.6305	1.6890	1.7490
5	1.0510	1.1041	1.1593	1.2167	1.2763	1.3382	1.4026	1.4693	1.5386	1.6105	1.6651	1.7623	1.8424	1.9254	2.0114
6	1.0615	1.1262	1.1941	1.2653	1.3401	1.4185	1.5007	1.5869	1.6771	1.7716	1.8704	1.9738	2.0820	2.1950	2.3131
7	1.0721	1.1487	1.2299	1.3159	1.4071	1.5036	1.6058	1.7138	1.8280	1.9487	2.0762	2.2107	2.3526	2.5023	2.6600
8	1.0829	1.1717	1.2668	1.3686	1.4775	1.5938	1.7182	1.8509	1.9926	2.1436	2.3045	2.4760	2.6584	2.8526	3.0590
9	1.0937	1.1951	1.3048	1.4233	1.5513	1.6895	1.8385	1.9990	2.1719	2.3579	2.5580	2.7731	3.0040	3.2519	3.5179
10	1.1046	1.2190	1.3439	1.4802	1.6289	1.7908	1.9672	2.1589	2.3674	2.5937	2.8394	3.1058	3.3946	3.7072	4.0456
11	1.1157	1.2434	1.3842	1.5395	1.7103	1.8983	2.1049	2.3316	2.5804	2.8531	3.1516	3.4785	3.8359	4.2262	4.6524
12	1.1268	1.2682	1.4258	1.6010	1.7959	2.0122	2.2522	2.5182	2.8127	3.1384	3.4985	3.8960	4.3345	4.8179	5.3502
13	1.1381	1.2936	1.4685	1.6651	1.8856	2.1329	2.4098	2.7196	3.0658	3.4523	3.8833	4.3635	4.8980	5.4924	6.1528
14	1.1495	1.3195	1.5126	1.7317	1.9799	2.2609	2.5785	2.9372	3.3417	3.7975	4.3104	4.8871	5.5348	6.2613	7.0757
15	1.1610	1.3459	1.5580	1.8009	2.0789	2.3966	2.7590	3.1722	3.6425	4.1772	4.7846	5.4736	6.2543	7.1379	8.1371
16	1.1726	1.3728	1.6047	1.8730	2.1829	2.5404	2.9522	3.4259	3.9703	4.5950	5.3109	6.1304	7.0673	8.1372	9.3576
17	1.1843	1.4002	1.6528	1.9479	2.2920	2.6928	3.1588	3.7000	4.3276	5.0545	5.8951	6.8680	7.9861	9.2765	10.7613
18	1.1961	1.4282	1.7024	2.0258	2.4066	2.8543	3.3799	3.9960	4.7171	5.5599	6.5436	7.6900	9.0243	10.5752	12.3755
19	1.2081	1.4568	1.7535	2.1068	2.5269	3.0256	3.6165	4.3157	5.1417	6.1159	7.2633	8.6128	10.1974	12.0557	14.2318
20	1.2202	1.4859	1.8061	2.1911	2.6533	3.2071	3.8697	4.6610	5.6044	6.7275	8.0623	9.6463	11.5231	13.7435	16.3665
21	1.2324	1.5157	1.8603	2.2788	2.7860	3.3996	4.1406	5.0338	6.1088	7.4002	8.9492	10.8038	13.0211	15.6676	18.8215
22	1.2447	1.5460	1.9161	2.3699	2.9253	3.6035	4.4304	5.4365	6.6586	8.1403	9.9336	12.1003	14.7138	17.8610	21.6447
23	1.2572	1.5769	1.9736	2.4647	3.0715	3.8197	4.7405	5.8715	7.2579	8.9543	11.0263	13.5523	16.6266	20.3616	24.8915
24	1.2697	1.6084	2.0328	2.5633	3.2251	4.0489	5.0724	6.3412	7.9111	9.8497	12.2392	15.1786	18.7881	23.2122	28.6252
25	1.2824	1.6406	2.0938	2.6658	3.3864	4.2919	5.4274	6.8485	8.6231	10.8347	13.5855	17.0001	21.2305	26.4619	32.9189
26	1.2953	1.6734	2.1566	2.7725	3.5557	4.5494	5.8074	7.3964	9.3992	11.9182	15.0799	19.0401	23.9905	30.1666	37.8568
27	1.3082	1.7069	2.2213	2.8834	3.7335	4.8223	6.2139	7.9881	10.2451	13.1100	16.7386	21.3249	27.1093	34.3899	43.5353
28	1.3213	1.7410	2.2879	2.9987	3.9201	5.1117	6.6488	8.6271	11.1671	14.4210	18.5799	23.8839	30.6335	39.2045	50.0656
29	1.3345	1.7758	2.3566	3.1187	4.1161	5.4184	7.1143	9.3173	12.1722	15.8631	20.6237	26.7499	34.6158	44.6931	57.5754
30	1.3478	1.8114	2.4273	3.2434	4.3219	5.7435	7.6123	10.0627	13.2677	17.4494	22.8923	29.9599	39.1159	50.9501	66.2118
31	1.3613	1.8476	2.5001	3.3731	4.5380	6.0881	8.1451	10.8677	14.4618	19.1943	25.4104	33.5551	44.2010	58.0832	76.1435
32	1.3749	1.8845	2.5751	3.5081	4.7649	6.4534	8.7153	11.7371	15.7633	21.1138	28.2056	37.5817	49.9471	66.2148	87.5651
33	1.3887	1.9222	2.6523	3.6484	5.0032	6.8406	9.3253	12.6760	17.1820	23.2251	31.3082	42.0915	56.4402	75.4849	100.6998
34	1.4026	1.9607	2.7319	3.7943	5.2533	7.2510	9.9781	13.6901	18.7284	25.5477	34.7521	47.1425	63.7774	86.0528	115.8048
35	1.4166	1.9999	2.8139	3.9461	5.5160	7.6861	10.6766	14.7853	20.4140	28.1024	38.5748	52.7996	72.0685	98.1002	133.1755

where

SN = Sum of the annuity

N = Amount deposited

$SAF_{i,n}$ = Looking at Exhibit 11.6, Sum of Annuity Factors $SAF_{4\%,\,3}$ (4% interest and 3 years) is a factor of 3.1216:

$$SN = \$10,000\ (3.1216) = \$31,216$$

ACCUMULATION OF FUTURE SUM EXAMPLE A nonprofit needs $200,000 at the end of four years to replace various pieces of capital equipment. How much should be set aside annually if an interest rate of 4 percent is earned? In Exhibit 11.6, Sum of Annuity Factors, $SAF_{4\%,4}$ (4% and 4 years) is a factor of 4.2465:

$$A = \frac{SN}{SAF_{i,n}}$$
$$= \frac{\$200,000}{4.2465}$$
$$= \$47,098 \text{ to be set aside each year}$$

Note to make each calculation, one could use a financial calculator on the Web, with which only the amount and period are plugged into the calculation.

Project Cash Flow

The investment manager should prepare a cash budget forecast based on anticipated receipts and disbursements. There are three types of cash flows:

1. *Certain flows.* Flows known in advance, such as debt payments, grants and pension payments
2. *Generally predictable flows.* Collections and disbursements based on a predictable cash flow history (e.g., payroll and utilities)
3. *Less certain cash flows.* Less predictable revenues and expenses (e.g., some grants, health insurance payments)

Chapter 7, "Manage Cash Flow," explains how to make a cash flow forecast.

Play the Float

Playing the float maximizes the amount of time that funds are available to invest. There are four types of float:

EXHIBIT 11.6 Sum of Annuity Factors

Periods, n	Interest Rate, i, %														
	1	2	3	4	5	6	7	8	9	10	11	12	13	14	15
1.	1.0000	1.0000	1.0000	1.0000	1.0000	1.0000	1.0000	1.0000	1.0000	1.0000	1.0000	1.0000	1.0000	1.0000	1.0000
2.	2.0100	2.0200	2.0300	2.0400	2.0500	2.0600	2.0700	2.0800	2.0900	2.1000	2.1100	2.1100	2.1200	2.1300	2.1500
3.	3.0301	3.0604	3.0909	3.1216	3.1525	3.1836	3.2149	3.2464	3.2781	3.3100	3.3421	3.3744	3.4069	3.4396	3.4725
4.	4.0604	4.1216	4.1836	4.2465	4.3101	4.3746	4.4399	4.5061	4.5731	4.6410	4.7097	4.7793	4.8498	4.9211	4.9934
5.	5.1010	5.2040	5.3091	5.4163	5.5256	5.6371	5.7507	5.8666	5.9847	6.1051	6.2278	6.3528	6.4803	6.6101	6.7424
6.	6.1520	6.3081	6.4684	6.6330	6.8019	6.9753	7.1533	7.3359	7.5233	7.7156	7.9129	8.1152	8.3227	8.5355	8.7537
7.	7.2135	7.4343	7.6625	7.8983	8.1420	8.3938	8.6540	8.9228	9.2004	9.4872	9.7833	10.0890	10.4047	10.7305	11.0668
8.	8.2857	8.5830	8.8923	9.2142	9.5491	9.8975	10.2598	10.6366	11.0285	11.4359	11.8594	12.2997	12.7573	13.2328	13.7268
9.	9.3685	9.7546	10.1591	10.5828	11.0266	11.4913	11.9780	12.4876	13.0210	13.5795	14.1640	14.7757	15.4157	16.0853	16.7858
10.	10.4622	10.9497	11.4639	12.0061	12.5779	13.1808	13.8164	14.4866	15.1929	15.9374	16.7220	17.5487	18.4197	19.3373	20.3037
11.	11.5668	12.1687	12.8078	13.4864	14.2068	14.9716	15.7836	16.6455	17.5603	18.5312	19.5614	20.6546	21.8143	23.0445	24.3493
12.	12.6825	13.4121	14.1920	15.0258	15.9171	16.8699	17.8884	18.9771	20.1407	21.3843	22.7132	24.1331	25.6502	27.2707	29.0017
13.	13.8093	14.6803	15.6178	16.6268	17.7130	18.8821	20.1406	21.4953	22.9534	24.5227	26.2116	28.0291	29.9847	32.0888	34.3519
14.	14.9474	15.9739	17.0863	18.2919	19.5986	21.0151	22.5505	24.2149	26.0192	29.3609	30.0949	34.4053	37.2797	34.8827	40.5047
15.	16.0969	17.2934	18.5989	20.0236	21.5786	21.5766	25.1290	27.1521	29.3609	33.0034	35.9497	39.1899	42.7533	40.4174	47.5804
16.	17.2579	18.6393	20.1569	21.7616	23.6975	23.6575	25.6725	27.8880	30.3243	33.0034	35.9497	44.5008	48.8837	48.6717	55.7175
17.	18.4304	20.0121	21.7616	23.4144	25.6454	25.8404	28.2129	30.8402	33.7502	36.9737	40.5447	44.5008	48.8837	53.7391	65.0751
18.	19.6147	21.4123	23.4144	25.1189	27.6712	28.1324	30.9056	33.9990	37.3790	41.3013	45.5992	50.3959	55.7497	61.7251	75.8363
19.	20.6109	22.8405	25.1169	27.6712	30.5390	33.7600	37.3790	41.4463	45.0184	48.0184	51.1591	56.9395	63.4397	70.7494	88.2118
20.	22.0190	24.2974	26.8704	29.7781	33.0659	33.0659	36.7856	40.9955	45.7620	51.1601	57.2750	64.2028	72.0524	80.9468	102.4436

178

21.	23.2392	25.7833	28.6765	31.9692	35.7192	39.9927	44.8652	50.4229	56.7645	64.0025	72.2651	81.6987	92.4699	104.7684	118.8101
22.	24.4716	27.2990	30.5368	34.2480	38.5052	43.3923	49.0057	55.4567	62.8733	71.4027	81.2143	92.5026	105.4910	120.4360	137.6316
23.	25.7163	28.8450	32.4529	36.6179	41.4305	46.9958	53.4361	60.8933	69.5319	79.5430	91.1479	104.8029	120.2048	138.2970	159.2764
24.	26.9734	30.4219	34.4265	39.0826	44.5020	50.8158	58.1767	66.7648	76.7898	88.4973	102.1741	118.1552	136.8315	158.6586	184.1676
25.	28.2432	32.0303	36.4593	41.6459	47.7271	54.8645	63.2490	73.1059	84.7009	98.3470	114.4133	133.3339	155.6196	181.8706	212.7930
26.	29.5256	33.6709	38.5530	44.3117	51.1134	59.1564	68.6765	79.9544	93.3240	109.1818	127.9988	150.3339	176.8501	208.3327	245.7120
27.	30.8209	35.3443	40.7096	47.0842	54.6691	63.7058	74.4838	87.3508	102.7231	121.0999	143.0766	169.3740	200.8406	238.4993	283.5686
28.	32.1291	37.0512	42.9309	49.9676	58.4026	68.5281	80.6977	95.3388	112.9682	134.2099	159.8173	190.6989	227.9499	272.8892	327.1040
29.	33.4504	38.7922	45.2188	52.9663	62.3327	73.6398	87.3465	103.9659	124.1353	148.6309	178.3972	214.5827	258.5833	312.0935	377.1897
30.	34.7849	40.5681	47.5754	56.0849	66.4388	79.0582	94.4808	113.2832	136.3075	164.4940	199.0209	241.3327	293.1990	356.7866	434.7451
31.	36.1327	42.3794	50.0027	59.3283	70.7608	84.8017	102.0730	123.3459	149.5752	181.9434	221.9132	271.1925	332.3149	407.7368	500.9568
32.	37.4941	44.2270	52.5027	62.7015	75.2968	90.8898	110.2181	134.2135	164.0370	201.1378	247.3236	304.8477	376.5159	465.8201	577.1003
33.	38.8890	46.1116	55.0778	66.2095	80.0638	97.3432	118.9334	145.9506	179.8003	222.2515	275.5291	342.4294	426.4831	532.0049	664.6653
34.	40.2577	48.0338	57.7302	69.8579	85.0670	104.1837	128.2588	158.6267	196.9823	245.4767	306.8374	384.5208	482.9033	607.5198	765.3852
35.	41.6603	49.9945	60.4621	73.6522	90.3203	111.4348	138.2369	172.3168	215.7106	271.0242	341.5894	431.6633	546.6807	693.5725	881.1699

- *Mail float.* The lag between mailing a check and its receipt by the payee (usually between 1 and 5 days)
- *Processing float.* The delay between the payee's receipt and deposit of a check (usually 1 day or less)
- *Availability float.* The delay between deposit of a check and when the bank credits the payee's account (usually between 0 and 2 days)
- *Federal Reserve float.* The lag between a check clearing from one Federal Reserve District to another (0 to 2 days)

To predict the number of days of float, the investment manager should track the history of transactions with other organizations. Today, the amount earned on the float is relatively small because Congress enacted "Check 21" in 2004, enabling banks to expedite transactions by converting checks into electronic images.

Safeguard Securities

The investment manager should establish a system that protects securities from loss, theft, or misuse, following a list like that shown in Exhibit 11.7.

The investment manager should record each security's date of acquisition, identification number, amount and physical location. A designated third-party trustee should hold the securities in the name of the nonprofit. The investment manager periodically verifies the accuracy of the types and

EXHIBIT 11.7   Safeguard-Securities List

Safeguard Measures

Store Securities

Register securities in the name of the nonprofit

Record the date of acquisition, identification number, purchase amount, interest dividend and physical location of each security

Bond individuals with access to securities

Periodically confirm that the amount and types of securities held by the safekeeping agent are accurate

Separate the duties of receiving and accounting for securities

Move Securities

Designate the person who can release securities from safekeeping

Release securities from the vault only upon proper authorization

Separate authorizing the release of securities from safekeeping securities and accessing the vault

Transport securities by armored truck

Require written and dual confirmation of a wire transfer

---

amounts of securities held by the safekeeping agent. Individuals who have access to securities must be insured by a surety bond. Only authorized personnel may release securities from safekeeping. An armored truck should be used to transport securities. Finally, written confirmation and dual authorization should be required for a wire transfer.

Report and Account for Investments

To account for investment transactions:

- Record the purchase of an investment in the general ledger on its transaction date
- Record investment income on a timely basis
- Allocate investment earnings to accounts
- Reconcile the subsidiary accounting records with the general-ledger control account

FASB Statement 124, Accounting for Certain Investments Held by Not-for-Profit Organizations, requires that a nonprofit report its investments in its financial statements at their *fair market value*. The practice, known as *mark to market*, records the current value of an investment (i.e., the amount for which an investment can be currently sold, *not* its original purchase price).[7] Exhibit 11.8 lists the investments to which FASB 124 applies.

Evaluate Performance

Management and the Board should set annual investment goals regarding (1) percentage of funds invested and (2) the interest rate of return.

EXHIBIT 11.8   FASB 124 Provisions

Instrument Type	Examples
Stocks and bonds	Creditor relationship with another organizations, e.g., corporate bonds
Debt securities	U.S. governments bonds, preferred stock, collateralized mortgage obligation
Equity securities	Common, preferred or other capital stock
Securities other than stocks and bonds	Mortgage notes, real estate, oil and gas interests, and private equity securities with a readily determinable value
Alternative investments	Hedge funds, offshore funds, real estate funds and venture capital funds

The rate-of-return objective can be set with reference to indexes such as the:

- S&P Index (for equities)
- Money market fund index
- *Public Investor* 10-bill index (fixed income)

One percentage of interest equals 100 basis points, thus an example of an investment return objective could be:

"To achieve a rate of return 40 basis points above the 3-month Treasury Bill rate."

Note that the IRS requires that foundations annually payout a minimum of 5 percent of their endowment value, but the payout is often more than 5 percent in practice.[8]

To evaluate investment performance, the investment manager compares the investment goals to the actual investment performance as shown in the example below

Example. At the beginning of the year, the Board set the objective to invest 95 percent of available funds and to achieve the *Public Investor* 10-bill index annual rate of return, which was 3 percent. In actuality, 94 percent of funds was invested at an average rate of return of 2.75 percent:

The actual performance was

$$\% \text{ Invested (94\%)} \times \text{Amount available (\$100,000)}$$
$$\times \text{ Interest rate (2.75\%)} = \$2,585$$

The projected performance was

$$\% \text{ Invested (95\%)} \times \text{Amount available (\$100,000)}$$
$$\times \text{Rate of return (3.00\%)} = \$2,850$$

Actual amount of earnings was $265 less than anticipated. ($2,850 − $2,585)

At least annually, the investment manager should report the performance of the investment program to management and the Board, detailing:

- The name, amount, price, and transaction date of each security purchased and sold

- Each security's percentage of the portfolio, its purchase date, its current market value, its unrealized gain or loss, and its annual income and yield (%) at maturity or time of sale
- The average weighted yield to maturity of investments compared to an appropriate benchmark(s)

For Further Reading

Higgins, David. *Essentials of Treasury Management*, 3rd ed. Bethesda, MD: Association of Financial Professionals, 2008. The treasury management bible for nonprofit and private sector managers. Mastery of the book's materials can result in becoming a Certified Treasury Professional.

CHAPTER 12

Manage Banking Relations

A nonprofit's bank is an important financial partner. Banks make payments and hold money. They may also give short- and long-term loans, safeguard securities, and provide investment services. Like any firm, banks vary with regard to the extent, quality, and price of the services they render. Banking relations include:

- Selecting the bank
- Managing banking services

Select the Bank

A nonprofit should periodically solicit proposals for banking services because competition encourages banks to "sharpen their pencil" to reduce prices. Some banks assign personnel who work exclusively with nonprofits, specializing in their banking needs. The banking services *request for proposals* (RFP) should include the provisions shown in Exhibit 12.1.

The various sections of the RFP are now discussed in detail.

Introduction

The introduction section specifies the contract timeline, including the dates to:

- Conduct the preproposal conference
- Submit proposals
- Interview prospective banks
- Award the contract

The introduction also sets forth the criteria for awarding the contract, including the:

EXHIBIT 12.1   RFP Provisions

Section	Provision
Introduction	Procurement timeline
	Award criteria
	Contract duration
	Bonding requirements
Scope of Services	Core services
	Secondary services
Proposal Evaluation	Aggregate banking-services costs or compensating balance interest rate
	Experience of bank team
	References
	Financial strength of the bank

- Price
- Bank's ability to provide services
- Bank's location
- Bank's financial condition

Though price is important, equally important is the *quality* of services that a bank can offer. Ideally, the bank should have a person experienced in nonprofit financial matters. Usually, a branch manager does not have such knowledge of nonprofit financial affairs. A bank's location is also a consideration. To minimize the expense of getting to the bank, the RFP should require that the bank be relatively close. Finally, the bank must be in sound financial condition.

The RFP should specify a multiyear contract (e.g., two to four years) to save the expense of annually soliciting proposals. Inflationary pressures increase the bank's costs, so the contract should permit the bank to increase its fees annually to reflect increases in the Consumer Price Index. Finally, the introduction section of the RFP should require that the bank take out a surety bond on employees who will handle money.

Scope of Services

The heart of the RFP, the scope of services, delineates services required for the bank. Banks offer core and secondary services, which are listed in Exhibit 12.2.

There are three types of banks. *Tier I* banks are national banks, which offer *all* the core and secondary services. *Tier II* banks are *regional* banks, which offer all core services, but limited secondary services. Finally,

EXHIBIT 12.2   Core and Secondary Bank Services

Core Services	Secondary Services
Bill payment	Zero balance account (ZBA)
Account reconciliation	Lockbox
Payroll	Credit: (1) short-term line of credit; (2) long-term credit (long-term loans, credit lease, bond agreement); (3) bond-credit enhancement (letters of credit); and (4) underwriting
Statements/Accounts analysis	Custodial services
Electronic funds transfer	Procurement cards
Security (positive pay, reverse positive pay, and Automated Clearing House block)	Investment assistance
Purchase-card payments	401(k) and 403(b) plan management
CD-ROM check imaging	Insurance including commercial property and liability, workers' compensation, life, medical, dental, and disability policies

Tier III banks are *locally owned* banks, which typically offer limited core and secondary services. Let us discuss core and secondary banking services.

Core Services

A nonprofit can bundle all of the core services into one RFP or unbundle some of them (e.g., purchase card payments) into a separate RFP.

Bill Payment

Banks pay bills by check or electronically. The CEO or a Board member approves a list of accounts payable that the bank pays.

Account Reconciliation

Banks offer full or partial reconciliation services. With *full* reconciliation, the nonprofit completely outsources account reconciliation to the bank, sending check-issuance data with which the bank reports:

■ Outstanding checks by check number
■ The amount of the checks issued
■ The date of the checks paid

With *partial* reconciliation, the bank provides a list of items paid and cleared, and the nonprofit makes the reconciliation.

Payroll

The bank calculates employees' gross pay and deductions, deposits pay into employees' bank accounts, and generates year-end W-2 reports. The bank typically charges for the service on a per-employee basis. Nearly all banks also offer *direct deposit* of payroll checks, reducing the costs of buying and issuing checks. Some banks also offer a *payroll card* service, enabling employees without a bank account to avoid a costly check cashing fee.

Statement/Account Analysis

The bank provides a monthly statement for each account that includes:

- Deposits in date order
- Paid items in check number order
- Wire transfers
- Interest rate summary

Electronic Funds Transfer (EFT)

Banks offer two EFT services. A Federal Reserve Communications System transaction is a one-day-turnaround wire transfer ("Fed Wire"). In contrast, an ACH transaction takes one to two days. The CFO can make a transfer by a telephone request to the bank or through the bank's on-line system.

Security

Because financial transactions are vulnerable to hacking and fraud, the bank offers three types of security service:

- *Positive pay.* Sometimes called *match pay*, this service protects against check fraud. After writing checks, the nonprofit transmits a payment file (check numbers, dates, and dollar amounts) to the bank. The bank matches the checks' serial numbers and dollar amounts against its file and pays only those checks that match.
- *Reverse positive pay.* More cumbersome than positive pay, the nonprofit must detect improper checks, sending them to the bank, which in turn returns them to the presenting bank.

- *ACH block.* The system blocks ACH transfers from clearing the bank account without the nonprofit's permission.

Purchase Card Payments

A nonprofit may permit its members and contributors to make payments by use of a purchase (credit or debit) card, which is discussed in Chapter 8, "Purchase Goods." Employees can also make purchases with a purchase card. A debit card automatically debits the checking account at the time of purchase. Some banks charge a monthly debit card fee; others do not. For credit card usage, the bank charges an annual percentage rate, which can be very expensive.

CD-ROM Check Imaging

The bank keeps images of checks for the current statement cycle, eliminating the need for check-storage space.

Secondary Services

The nonprofit should develop a *separate* RFP for each of the secondary services discussed in the following sections.

Zero Balance Account (ZBA)

A zero balance account, or ZBA, is a disbursement account that issues checks and initiates wire transfers and ACH transactions. Keeping the end-of-day balance in the account at zero, the bank sweeps funds into an overnight interest-bearing instrument. The nonprofit should determine if the increased interest earnings offset the bank's ZBA service fee.

Lockbox

A lockbox speeds up the collection process. The bank maintains a post office box in the nonprofit's name. Payers mail their remittances to this box, rather than to the nonprofit. The bank collects the payments daily and processes them for same-day deposit, eliminating the time to open mail and deposit funds and accelerating investments by several days. To decide whether to pay for a lockbox service, the investment manager should compare the bank's lockbox collection fee to the increased amount of interest earned on same-day deposit.

Credit

Banks offer short- and long-term credit as discussed in Chapter 13, "Borrow Funds." Short-term, the bank offers a line of credit, which is a dollar limit against which the nonprofit can borrow.

Types of long-term credit include:

- Long-term loan
- Capital lease
- Bond agreement

For a bond agreement, the nonprofit sells bonds to underwriters, who sell them to investors. The bank can act as the underwriter. To increase the credit standing of a bond, the bank can issue a letter of credit, irrevocably insuring payment of the bond's principal and interest.

Custodial Services

The bank sets up a third-party safekeeping agreement to:

- Maintain physical custody and safekeeping of financial assets
- Collect and remit income
- Collect the interest and principal to be paid on debt obligations
- Buy, sell, receive, or deliver securities upon specific instruction

The bank sends safekeeping receipts for each activity by e-mail, fax, or traditional mail within two days of the activity.

Investment Assistance

Chapter 11, "Invest Funds," discusses investment adviser services, including:

- Managing the investment portfolio
- Making a cash flow projection
- Assisting with the selection of depositories and brokers/dealers

401(k) and 403(b) Plan Management

The bank administers retirement accounts. In a 401(k) account, employees' contributions and the account's earnings are normally not taxable. The nonprofit usually matches the employees' contributions. A 403(b) plan is a tax-sheltered annuity plan.

Insurance Services

The bank may own a subsidiary company that sells insurance policies including directors and officers liability, workers' compensation, property, general liability and employee benefits, including group life, life, medical, dental, and disability.

Award the Contract

A nonprofit can compensate its bank one of two methods:

- *Direct payment.* The bank prices each service rendered and the nonprofit reimburses the bank periodically for charges incurred during that period.
- *Compensating balance.* The bank renders the services in return for the nonprofit maintaining a specified, minimum balance in a noninterest bearing account. This is called the *minimum compensating balance* (MCB) method, in which the nonprofit maintains an earnings credit using the following formula:

$$EC = CB \times (1 - RR) \times ECR(D/365)$$

where

EC = The total *dollar volume of credit used* to offset the service charges

CB = Average collected balance, which is the sum of the daily ending collected balances (both positive and negative) divided by the number of days in the analysis period

RR = The reserve requirement set by the Federal Reserve, which is the amount the bank must hold in an idle balance

ECR = The earnings credit rate, which is most commonly the 90-day Treasury bill rate

Let us assume:

CB = An average collected balance of $100,000

RR = A 10% Federal Reserve rate

ECR = A 90-day T-bill rate of 2%

Therefore,

$$
\begin{aligned}
EC &= \$100,000 \times (1 - .10) \times (.02 \times 30/365) \\
&= \$100,000 \times .9(.02 \times .08213) \\
&= \$100,000 \times .9 \times .0016426 \\
&= \$147,834
\end{aligned}
$$

EXHIBIT 12.3   Sample Account Analysis

Services	Monthly Volume	Charge per Service	Monthly Charge
Depository Services			
Account maintenance (8 accounts)			
Checks paid			
Items deposited			
Stop payments			
Returned checks charged to account			
Wire transfers:			
Incoming			
Outgoing			
ACH transactions:			
Incoming			
Outcoming			
Bank transfers between accounts			
Daily balance reporting			
Returned items			
Other Services			
ZBA checking			
ZBA payroll accounting			
Positive pay			

With the *direct fee method*, the bank's payment depends on its charge per transaction (submitted in its response to the RFP) and the monthly amount of account activity. The bank provides a monthly *account analysis* like that shown in Exhibit 12.3.

Financial Strength of the Bank

The nonprofit should select a financially sound bank because banks can fail. For instance, from 2007 to mid-September 2009, 120 banks failed.[1] To evaluate banks, the Federal Deposit Insurance Corporation (FDIC) uses the CAMELS system, an acronym that stands for rating a bank's:

- *C*apital holdings
- *A*ssets' quality
- *M*anagement capability
- *E*arnings rate

- *L*iquidity
- *S*ensitivity to market risk[2]

The FDIC rates a bank from 1 (best) to 5 (worst) on each criterion. An average score greater than 3 is considered unsatisfactory.[3] The FDIC identifies banks that warrant regulatory attention. The CAMELS ratings are unavailable to nonprofits because legally they must be kept confidential. However, rating agencies such as Moody's, Standard & Poor's, and Bankwatch publicly rate banks using similar criteria.

The FDIC historically has insured deposits up to $100,000; however, the FDIC raised the ceiling to $250,000 from 2009 to June 30, 2013, The nonprofit's contract with the bank should require the bank to collateralize deposits above the insured amount. Banks pledge U.S. Treasury securities, federal agency securities, and government-sponsored enterprise obligations to collateralize securities.[4] State collateralization laws vary, but most require or permit a bank to pledge collateral securities to secure deposits.[5] States that mandate collateralization monitor compliance. Where collateralization is optional, the nonprofit is responsible for monitoring compliance.

Manage Banking Services

After awarding the contract, the nonprofit should monitor the bank's services, account balances, charges, and activity volumes. The monthly bank statement reports the number of transactions (e.g., deposits, withdrawals, checks written, checks cleared), the collected balance for the period, earnings credits, and service charges. The CFO reconciles the bank statement by:

- Comparing the bank statement to the check register.
- Noting the checks, deposits, and withdrawals that have cleared.
- Subtracting service charges from the general ledger cash account.
- Adding to the general ledger cash account the credit amount the bank account(s) have earned for the nonprofit.
- The adjusted general ledger cash account should equal the bank statement's balance. If not, the nonprofit and/or the bank are in error due to (1) inaccurately entered data, (2) failing to identify all outstanding transactions, or (3) a mathematical error.

Banks typically require the nonprofit to report a reconciliation problem within 30 days.[6]

Exhibit 12.4 is a Sample Account Analysis Statement, and the following section explains its various elements.

EXHIBIT 12.4   Sample Account Analysis Statement

Average Monthly Balance Summary	Financial Activity
Average Ledger Balance	$35,103
(Less) Average Deposit Float	(4,726)
Average Collected Balance	30,377
Average Investable Balance	30,377
Less: Reserve Requirement (10%)	(3,037)
	$27,340

Services Provided	Units	Unit Price	Service Charge
Account Maintenance	1	$20.00	$20.00
Checks Paid	68	.07	4.76
Deposits	21	.30	6.30
Electronic Debit	10	.26	2.60
Electronic Credit	5	.26	1.30
Check/Debit Return	1	5.00	5.00
Check Fine Sort	67	.07	4.69
Photocopy of Check	2	7.50	15.00
Total Charges This Cycle			**$59.65**

Account Analysis Statement: Explanation

The following explains the different parts of an account analysis statement shown in Exhibit 12.4.

- *Average ledger balance.* The sum of the daily ending ledger balances (both positive and negative) divided by the number of days in the account-analysis period.
- *Average deposit float.* The sum of the daily dollar items in the process of collection divided by the number of days in the analysis period.
- *Average collected balance.* The sum of the daily ending ledger balances (both positive and negative) divided by the number of days in the account analysis period minus the average deposit float.
- *Average investable balance.* The balance in the account that the bank was able to invest in income-producing assets.
- *Reserve requirements.* The reserve balance that the Federal Reserve System requires, which is currently 10 percent.
- *Services provided.* The services provided and fees charged by the bank. These service charges are expressed as a per-unit price or flat monthly fee.

The *earnings credit* and *earnings credit rate* (ECR) are used to calculate the compensating balance needed to offset the service charges. The investable balance is multiplied by the ECR for the period. The ECR varies with the bank. Most common is the 90-day Treasury bill rate.

Common Banking Terms

The following is a glossary of common cash management terms used in this chapter and/or the documents referenced here.

Account analysis. Monthly statement provided to the nonprofit by a financial institution evaluating the adequacy of compensating balances maintained by the customer to offset services paid.

Account reconciliation. The act of a bank customer with a disbursing account inspecting its monthly rendered statement to determine whether there are any discrepancies on the statement.

Adjustment. Correction to a transaction when a bank deposit has been prepared incorrectly (e.g., addition error or missing item) or to an agency's disbursing account due to a posting error.

American Bankers Association (ABA) Transit-Routing Number. The number encoded in magnetic ink on the bottom of a check, assigned by the ABA, to specify the bank to which the check/warrant may be presented for collection.

Automated Clearing House (ACH). Organization housed within the Federal Reserve Bank (FRB) that acts as a clearinghouse for all ACH payments by exchanging ACH transactions among member financial institutions and providing for the settlement of funds.

Bad check. Any check dishonored by a paying bank for wrong endorsement, lack of endorsement, insufficient funds, account closed, stale date, etc.

Beneficiary. The name of a nonprofit that is the intended recipient of a wire transfer.

Certificate of deposit (CD). Receipt issued by a financial institution for a "time deposit" for a stated time and normally paying a stated interest rate.

Chargeback. A credit card transaction that has been refused by the cardholder's bank, resulting in the merchant's bank debiting its customer's bank account.

Collateralization of deposits. Pledging of collateral by financial institutions to secure deposits whose amount is in excess of the FDIC insurance coverage.

Collected funds. Funds deposited to a financial institution, where the funds are available for either withdrawal or investment.

Collection item. A check or other negotiable instrument that is not credited to the presenter's account until payment has been received from the payer bank. Bad checks are returned to depositing agencies as collection items, seeking reimbursement.

Compensating balance. Method to pay a bank for cash management services.

Dishonor. Refusal of a payer bank to honor a check presented for payment, usually due to a stop payment's having been placed on the item, or the item's not being on the agency's positive pay issuance file (e.g., counterfeit or stale dated).

Earnings credit allowance. Earnings generated by deposits that are applied toward monthly banking service fees. The earnings credit allowance is calculated in the bank's monthly account analysis.

Endorsement. The act of placing (either in writing or by stamping or typing) verbiage on the reverse side of a check or state warrant in order to make it a negotiable instrument.

Float. The time between the issuance of a check and the clearing of the item at the paying bank.

Magnetic ink recognition character (MICR). The data encoded with magnetic ink along the bottom of a check. The MICR fields include serial number, ABA transit-routing number, account number, and amount.

Next-day funds. Items deposited with a financial institution where the funds are not immediately available for either withdrawal or investment, but will be the following banking day.

Payer bank. The financial institution on which checks are drawn.

Post-dated check. A check payable on a future date. Checks issued with a future date cannot be honored by the banking industry until that date. There is no legal prohibition against writing a post-dated check.

Rejects. Checks that cannot be processed on bank-sorting equipment due to a problem with data.

Return. A bank transaction (or the item itself) where an item previously deposited or presented is returned due to noncollection. Examples of returns include bad checks and dishonored checks included in a cash letter.

Target balance. Desired balance a nonprofit customer attempts to maintain with a financial institution in order to compensate or offset the cost of services rendered. Also referred to as a *compensating balance.*

Uniform Commercial Code (UCC). The set of standardized state laws pertaining to the negotiation of checks, as they are presented though the commercial banking system for collection.

Watermark. A security feature contained on the reverse side of checks, representing a design printed in opaque ink, which can be seen only when viewed at an angle.

Zero balance account (ZBA). An account maintained with a financial institution (official depository) in which multiple deposits made to the account on a given day are totaled and "swept" as a single amount. Sometimes referred to as a *sweep account.*

For Further Reading

Fry, Robert Jr. *Who's Minding the Money?* 2nd ed. Washington, DC: BoardSource, 2009. Oriented to nonprofits that invest heavily, includes excellent discussions of the Prudent Investor Rule, investment risks, basic investment concepts, the role of an investment committee, and alternative investments.

CHAPTER 13

Borrow Funds

Nonprofits borrow funds to meet short- and long-term needs. They borrow long term to purchase a building or equipment such as computers, copiers, and vehicles. They borrow in the short term to cover a cash flow shortfall caused by, for example:

- Grant funds promised but not received
- An unexpected lawsuit judgment
- Declining membership funds
- An economic downturn
- An unexpected spike in costs (e.g., a health insurance-premium hike)
- An act of nature (e.g., hurricane, flood, tornado)
- The unexpected loss of a major funding source (e.g., a grant)
- Failure to collect receivables aggressively

Some nonprofits are chronically short of cash. For them, short-term borrowing is an everyday occurrence. Other nonprofits, enjoying a healthy cash reserve, borrow only in the rare event of a precipitous financial downturn. Sixty percent of nonprofits, however, had some form of debt in 2007.[1] Of these, 18 percent of nonprofits had issued municipal bonds that amounted to 57 percent of the total debt outstanding; and 52 percent had outstanding loans, lines of credit, leases and mortgages amounting to 43 percent of the debt outstanding.[2]

Issuing debt is a two-step process, select the debt instrument and purchase the debt, which are described in the following sections.

Select the Debt Instrument

A debt instrument has three features: (1) a funding period, (2) repayment conditions, and (3) security against default. A nonprofit has five debt options:

1. Line of credit
2. Loan
3. Mortgage
4. Bond
5. Lease

The features of each instrument are discussed in the following sections.

Line of Credit

Banks offer a *line of credit*—a *line*—that permits a nonprofit to borrow up to a preset amount over a one-year period. Interest accrues until the borrowed amount is repaid. The bank usually requires the nonprofit to pledge security in the event of default. For instance, if the line provides working capital, the bank usually requires the nonprofit to pledge its future revenues and/or assets. Normally, a bank can establish a line within a few days of application. The interest rate is usually the prime interest rate plus a percentage that depends on the type of security being pledged. There are three types of lines:

1. Uncommitted
2. Committed
3. Standby

An *uncommitted line* is informal (not put in writing). The bank can terminate it at any time. The bank charges interest on the borrowed amount. In contrast, a *committed line* is a formal written agreement conveying the line's terms and conditions. In addition to an interest fee, the bank charges a *commitment* fee, which is a percentage of either the total line *or* the line's unused balance. The bank can add an *overdraft provision* to an uncommitted or committed line, requiring payment of a finance charge for amounts charged over the credit line. Finally, a *standby letter* guarantees that the bank will lend funds if the nonprofit cannot pay a major expense.

A line of credit can be a double-edged sword. Some funders understandably take a dim view of the creditworthiness of nonprofits that depend extensively on lines. Funders do understand, though, that instances occur when taking out a line is acceptable. For instance, a nonprofit that depends on membership dues may experience a predictable, temporary cash flow shortage at the beginning of the fiscal year, or a nonprofit may take out a line in anticipation of forthcoming grant funds.

Furthermore, nonprofits sometimes take out a line to show banks that they are credit worthy. A bank will examine a nonprofit's repayment history to determine whether it is a good credit risk.

Loan

In contrast to a line of credit, a loan has fixed repayment terms. There are three types of loans:

1. Revolving credit agreement
2. Term loan
3. Swap

A *revolving credit agreement*, also known as a *revolver*, permits the non-profit to borrow and repay debt continually up to an agreed-upon amount. The bank charges a variable interest rate. The bank and nonprofit can renew the revolver annually for up to a five-year period. At the end of the revolver loan period, the nonprofit usually converts the revolver to a *term loan*. As with a committed line, in addition to the interest fee, the bank charges a commitment fee as a percentage of either the total line or the line's unused amount.

A *term loan* matures in 1 to 10 years. Repayment is usually made in equal monthly or quarterly payments based on a fixed or variable interest rate. Proceeds from a term loan are used to buy equipment, machinery, or a building. The security for the loan is the asset or group of assets (e.g., inventory or receivables) that the loan is financing.

A *swap*, exchanges a fixed interest rate obligation for a loan with a variable or floating interest rate. The bank may also offer the option to switch from a variable interest rate swap to fixed rate swap to eliminate the risk of rising interest rates.

Mortgage

A mortgage is a loan to purchase a building or land, which serves as the loan's collateral. The mortgage, which typically requires a down payment, is usually for a 20- to 30-year period, during which the nonprofit pays principal and interest based on a fixed or variable rate. A variable rate is typically a function of the prime lending rate.

Municipal Bond

Some nonprofits—such as private schools, colleges, nonprofit associations, and religious organizations—can issue tax-exempt *or* taxable municipal bonds, known as *municipals*. Municipal bonds issued on behalf of non-profits are called *501(c)(3) bonds*. Twenty-one percent of nonprofits had an outstanding balance of tax-exempt bonds in 2004.[3] A state or local government can also issue a tax-exempt bond on behalf of health care organizations, museums, colleges, private schools, and hospitals. Some states have created an agency to sell municipals on behalf of nonprofits. The state agency sells the tax-exempt bond to an underwriter, such as an investment bank, which then sells the bond to investors. The nonprofit, not the state, makes the principal and interest payments. To allow more nonprofits to issue tax-exempt bonds, underwriters can pool several nonprofits' bond issues.

If the nonprofit, not a state or local government, issues the bond, it must select an underwriter and bond counsel. The bond counsel furnishes an opinion guaranteeing the *tax-exempt* status of the bond. One or more of the three rating agencies—Moody's Investors Service, Standard & Poor's, and Fitch Inc.—assign the bond a rating. If not deemed creditworthy, a nonprofit can purchase bond insurance or a bank letter of credit to attain an acceptable credit rating.

Bond financing usually occurs in conjunction with a *capital campaign* during which the nonprofit attains pledged commitments. The principal and interest on the bond can be paid solely from both these pledges or from operating funds as well. Because the expense of securing the required bond counsel's opinion is relatively high, the bond must usually be for at least $1 million.

Taxable Bond

Only 501(c)(3) designated nonprofits can issued tax-exempt municipal bonds. However, there are about 500,000 other nonprofits not designated as 501(c)(3), including over 400,000 501(c)(4) member organizations. To finance a facility or other capital project, these nonprofits have the option of issuing a taxable bond. For instance, a nursing home or church might issue a taxable bond to build a facility.

Lease

A nonprofit may lease rather than purchase an asset. Leasing is cost effective when an asset such as a computer becomes technologically obsolete. Vehicles, too, are often leased. For instance, Meals on Wheels might decide to lease its delivery trucks. There are two principal types of leases. An *operating lease* leaves the asset's ownership with the lessor. A *capital lease* gives the nonprofit the option to purchase the asset at the end of the lease period. Leasing is advantageous when funds are not available to buy an asset outright, but leasing is more expensive than an outright purchase because of the interest cost.

Obtain Debt Financing

In deciding whether to make a loan, a bank heavily weighs a nonprofit's past repayment record. A nonprofit that repays its debt in a timely fashion and in full is more likely to get another loan, all other factors being equal. The nonprofit CFO should maintain a close, professional working relationship with his or her banking counterparts.[4] To obtain a line or a loan, the nonprofit should submit a financing proposal that includes an *executive* summary explaining the nonprofit's:

- Mission
- Core services and values
- Managerial capabilities
- Ability to repay the debt

An accompanying brochure and testimonials may enhance the application. In deciding whether to permit the loan or line, the banker reviews the following:

- Amount of the line or loan
- How the funds will be used
- Term of the line or loan
- Type of loan or line
- Repayment schedule (monthly, lump sum, interest-only initially)
- Repayment funding source
- Pledged collateral
- The nonprofit's debt repayment history

To assess the risk of nonpayment, the bank analyzes the nonprofit's financials, including the following:

- Balance sheet to determine the amount of unrestricted reserve funds
- Statement of activities to ascertain whether the nonprofit has stayed within its budget
- Cash flow projection to determine the availability of cash for repayment

The lender may deny a loan if it finds:

- A weak financial position
- Poor credit rating
- Insufficient collateral to secure the loan

A nonprofit typically uses it net operating revenue to repay a loan. If operating funds prove insufficient to repay a loan, a nonprofit may have to sell assets or refinance the loan. The lender may refinance a loan if the reason for nonpayment was truly unexpected. The lender, however, will not refinance if managerial incompetence caused the failure to repay.

For Further Reading

Yetman, Robert. "Borrowing and Debt," in *Financing Nonprofits*, edited by Dennis Young, 243–268. Lanham, MD: AltaMira Press, 2007. Good explanation of lines of credit, bank loans, mortgages, 501(c)(3) bonds and tax-exempt leases.

CHAPTER 14

Manage Risks

Nonprofits face the risk of loss due to accidents, fire, and theft. An effective risk management program produces a safe working environment, fewer accidents, lower insurance costs, increased productivity, and higher employee morale. The CEO should assign responsibility for the risk management program to a senior manager, typically the CFO. Some nonprofits also form a risk management committee to assist the risk manager. Risk management is a three-step process:

1. Identify the risk.
2. Treat the risk.
3. Administer the program.

These steps are discussed in the sections that follow.

Identify Risks

Organizations face five types of risks:

1. *Damage to property*. Due to carelessness, fire, natural causes and faulty equipment
2. *Loss of property*. Due to the dishonest acts of employees and the public
3. *Loss of income or increased costs*. Due to the malfunction of a revenue-producing facility
4. *Liability losses*. Due to accidents
5. *Loss of productivity*. Due to alcoholism, obesity, drug abuse, and smoking

Exhibit 14.1 indicates how to identify these five types of risks.

To determine the risk of damage to real and personal property, the risk manager should annually inventory capital assets, noting each asset's

EXHIBIT 14.1   Risk Identification Methods

Type of Risk	Risk Identification Method

Damage to Property
  a. Real property
  b. Personal (movable) property
	If the value of building is unknown, appraise it to determine its value.
	Use regional building cost indexes to update the insurable value of buildings.
	Maintain a fixed asset inventory.

Loss of Property
  a. Dishonest acts by employees
  b. By the public
	Calculate the amount of assets that employees manage.
	Determine the amount of cash, securities, and property that are vulnerable to theft.

Loss of Income or Increased Costs
  a. Loss of income
  b. Increased costs
	Estimate the funds needed to put the damaged facility into operation after a fire or act of nature.
	Estimate the increased costs to repair damage, rent, or purchase another building.

Liability Losses
  a. Auto related
  b. Other liability
	Calculate the amount of auto-related payments in the past five years.
	Calculate the amount of other liability payments in the past five years.

Productivity Losses	Estimate the amount of sick days and leaves of absence that have been excessive.

location, condition, type of construction, and value. As discussed in Chapter 10, "Manage Capital Assets and the Inventory," tag each asset and put each under the responsibility of a designated custodian. If the insurable value of a building is unknown, hire an appraiser to determine its value.

To insure against the risk of theft or embezzlement, the insurance industry sells a fidelity bond in an amount based on the dollar value of the assets that a person handles.

Some nonprofits, such as a day care or senior citizen center, charge a service fee. In the event of a fire or natural disaster, the nonprofit faces a loss of income and/or increased costs. To identify the amount of this risk, estimate how much the nonprofit would have to borrow to restore the facility or to find a suitable replacement.

To determine the auto-related liability risk, examine the past five years' history of losses. Adjust the average down for unusually costly accidents. Types of other liabilities include:

- Injury to employees, clients, or volunteers due to harmful acts
- Injury to employees or the public due to the failure to act professionally

Again, examine at least five years of history to estimate the amount of these risks.

Treat Risks

Once identified, there are four risk treatment options: (1) elimination, (2) reduction, (3) assumption by self-insurance or an insurance deductible, and (4) transfer. The most suitable best treatment option depends on a risk's (1) frequency and (2) severity (maximum loss from a single incident), as shown in Exhibit 14.2.

The four risk-treatment options are discussed in the following sections.

Risk Elimination

The best treatment option is to eliminate a risk altogether. Elimination is especially suitable for high-severity risks, examples of which include:

- A wading pool at a day care center
- Volunteers transporting disabled clients who require special care
- Hiring someone with a medical condition (e.g., a chronic back problem) that the job in question will likely aggravate

EXHIBIT 14.2   Risk-Treatment Options

Risk Category	Treatment Options
Category 1: Low frequency/Low severity	Assume the risk because the total amount of losses will be small.
Category 2: Low frequency/High severity	Transfer the risk to an insurance company or self-insure part of all of the risk because the amount of losses can be high.
Category 3: High frequency/Low severity	Assume the risk because the amount of losses will be low and predictable.
Category 4: High frequency/High severity	Avoid or transfer the risk.

- Hiring someone with poor driving record for a position that involves driving
- Failing to back up computer files at another site
- Failing to safeguard equipment, supplies, and vehicles from theft and vandalism
- Failing to include a contractual *hold-harmless clause* to transfer risk to another party

Risk Reduction

The second treatment option is to reduce the incidence and severity of risks. Every nonprofit, regardless of mission or size, should have a risk reduction program, including a safety policy. The Board-adopted risk management policy should specify the disciplinary actions to take against employees who violate the safety policy. A large nonprofit should form a *safety committee*, comprised of representatives from each program. Employees must "buy in" to the safety program, taking safety seriously. Exhibit 14.3 shows ways to reduce risk.

The next sections discuss in more detail the risk reduction practices listed in Exhibit 14.3.

DAMAGE TO PROPERTY   Adhere to a *preventive maintenance* program by regularly inspecting and maintaining equipment and vehicles. Inspect general operations (monthly), fire extinguishers (monthly), dangerous equipment (daily) and other equipment (yearly). Smoke alarms, whether AC or battery powered, should be pressure checked according to the manufacturer's schedule. When possible, equip buildings with a sprinkler system.

DAMAGE TO COMPUTERS AND RECORDS   Limit access to protected hardware and software; use intrusion-detection software; and update virus-protection software. For a more comprehensive discussion of IT controls, see Exhibit. 3.9, IT Controls List.

LOSS OF PROPERTY DUE TO DISHONEST ACTS   Carefully check the records of applicants for jobs that handle cash and other assets. When interviewing a prospective employee:

- Follow the screening guidelines in the interview guide.
- Prepare a documented job description for each position.
- Inform candidates of the reasons for an automatic disqualification.
- Ask *only* questions applicable to the position in question.
- Ask each applicant the *same* questions.

EXHIBIT 14.3   Risk Reduction Methods

Type of Risk	Risk-Reduction Method
1. Damage to Property	
a. Equipment and facilities	Schedule equipment downtime to perform preventive maintenance.
	Maintain boilers according to the manufacturer's specifications.
	Make a safety inspection of general operations (monthly), fire extinguishers (monthly), dangerous equipment (daily), and other facilities (yearly).
	Install sprinklers whenever possible.
	Inspect fire extinguishers monthly and pressure check according to the manufacturer's label.
	Replace smoke alarm batteries annually and smoke alarms every 10 years.
b. Computers and records	Maintain duplicates of records and computer files offsite.
	Update virus-protection software weekly or monthly.
	Secure and update employee passwords.
	Use uninterruptible power supplies.
	Maintain firewalls and intrusion-detection software.
	Comply with licensing terms.
	Limit employee access to hardware and software programs.
2. Loss of Property	
a. Dishonest acts of employees	Conduct a background check on applicants for financial positions.
	Separate the duties of check writing, making deposits, and bank-account reconciliation.
	Keep a duplicate record of checks.
	Prenumber and countersign checks.
	Assign custodial responsibility for fixed assets.
	Take an annual inventory of fixed assets.
	Deposit cash daily.
b. Dishonest acts of the public	Install crime deadbolt locks, burglar alarms, barred windows, safes, and vaults.
3. Liability	
a. Employee Liability	
(1) Human-resource	Follow best practices for hiring, promotion, discipline, grievances and appeals.
	Require a pre-employment physical.
(HR) management	Match job requirements' to employees' abilities.
	Include the FMLA policy in the Human Relations Handbook.
(2) Family Medical Leave Act (FMLA)[1]	Define employees' rights and obligations during family medical leave, including the right to reinstatement.

EXHIBIT 14.3   *(Continued)*

Type of Risk	Risk-Reduction Method
(3) Harassment	Adopt a policy that (1) defines harassment, (2) assures no retaliation for its reporting, and (3) assures confidentiality and that a thorough, impartial investigation will be made.
(4) Privacy	Notify employees that they have no right to privacy regarding their on-the-job use of e-mail, the Internet, voice mail, desks and lockers.
	Discipline employees for downloading inappropriate material.
(5) Workplace safety	Require employees to wear hard hats, goggles, special shoes, etc.
	Conduct safety training.
	Investigate accidents' causes to prevent future occurrences.
	Furnish ergonomically correct chairs and desks to avoid carpal-tunnel syndrome, back injuries and other related problems.
b. Public Liability (1) Auto-related	Regularly inspect vehicles to ensure they have an accident-report form in the glove box and that they are in good working order.
	Preventively maintain vehicles.
	Monitor use of employee-owned vehicles on nonprofit business.
	After an accident, require employees to have the police complete an accident report; get the other party's name, telephone number, insurance company and policy number; report the accident to the insurance agent or broker; not discuss the facts of the accident with anyone but the insurance company and attorney.
	Ensure that drivers have a valid license and safe driving record and take a defensive-driving course.
(2) Donors	Comply with IRS tax-exemption regulations.
	Secure donor records.
	Obtain donors' permission to send them mailings.
	Protect donors' privacy in Web-based records.
(3) Records retention	Keep detailed minutes of Board meetings.
	Approve prior meeting's minutes at next meeting.
	Adopt a record-retention policy.
(4) The Disabled	Configure the facility to meet the Americans with Disabilities Act's architectural standards.
(5) Volunteers	Screen volunteers before working in particular jobs (e.g., with youth, as drivers).

Twenty-three states have prepared pre-employment inquiry guidelines.[2] An excellent training resource is *The Staff Screening Tool Kit*, published by the Nonprofit Risk Management Center. The tool kit provides guidance to select and place volunteers and staff. It can be downloaded at www.nationalserviceresources.org/staff-screening.

The biggest risk of theft of assets occurs when financial duties are not separated. Please refer to Chapter 3, "Create the Internal Control System," for a comprehensive explanation of how to separate financial duties. Similarly, without a fixed asset control system, equipment and furniture are at risk of being stolen. Please refer to Chapter 10, "Manage Capital Assets and the Inventory," for a discussion of how to how to create a capital asset control system.

HUMAN RESOURCE (HR) MANAGEMENT   By far the biggest risk to a nonprofit is improper human resource management practices. Indeed, *92 percent* of the claims made against Board members and top management are employee related.[3] Most claims center on wrongful termination and sexual harassment. Employees can only be terminated after following due process. For instance, a manager cannot arbitrarily fire someone who has had consistently good performance evaluations *unless* a financial exigency can be shown. When considering disciplinary action, a nonprofit often is well served to consult with an employment lawyer. Also, take out adequate insurance against employee-related claims. Insurance coverage may be included in the commercial general liability policy or the directors' and officers' liability policy.

Exhibit 14.4 is a list of recommended HR management practices.

FAMILY MEDICAL LEAVE ACT (FMLA)   FMLA requires organizations to give their employees up to 12 weeks of unpaid pregnancy and after-birth leave if the nonprofit employs over 50 people and the person applying for the leave has worked at least 1,250 hours in the prior year. The nonprofit should include FMLA rights in the HR policy manual.

HARASSMENT   Harassment, sexual and otherwise, is a big risk exposure. Many employees are simply unaware of what constitutes harassment (e.g., an untoward touch or comment). Hence, in the HR policy, the Board should specify the following:

- A definition of harassment
- A provision that management will not retaliate against a complainant
- The procedure to investigate a complaint
- The disciplinary actions that can be taken

EXHIBIT 14.4   HR Management List

Practice

Policies and Procedures
Create an organization chart.
Distribute the HR policy and procedures manual to each manager.
Have legal counsel review the HR policy.
Do not permit employees to overdraw vacation or sick leave.
Prohibit nepotism and conflict of interest in hiring and promotion decisions.
Limit access to personnel and payroll records.
Post and adhere to the provisions of the Family Medical Leave Act.

Hiring
Perform a background check on people under consideration for a sensitive
    position.
Verify the work history and references of job applicants.
Include in the job application:
    -An equal-employment-opportunity statement
    -A truth clause (i.e., reserves the right not to hire or to terminate someone
    because he or she provides false or misleading information)
    -A provision permitting the nonprofit to check an applicant's criminal record
Require acknowledgment in writing from employees that they have received and
    understand the HR policy.

Discipline and Termination
Use progressive discipline to attempt to rehabilitate poor performers.
Give employees ongoing feedback, rather than just an annual performance review.
Document the reasons for termination in a written termination notice.
Deduct overdrawn vacation and sick leave when calculating final termination pay.
Collect keys, equipment, credit cards, etc. from terminated employees.

Payroll
Record payroll additions, separations, and deductions prior to the scheduled
    payroll cut-off date.
Maintain individual time-and-attendance records, reviewed and signed by
    employees' supervisors.
Reconcile the payroll register to the payroll account in the general ledger.
Require an authorized person to certify that the number of hours worked balances
    with the payroll register.
Require an authorized person to review and approve the payroll transmittals prior
    to cutting the payroll checks.

Vacation and Sick Leave
Maintain a record of vacation and sick leave.
Ensure the accuracy of the amount of employee vacation and leave days taken and
    available.
Require an authorized person to approve vacation and sick-leave requests.

EXHIBIT 14.4 *(Continued)*

Practice

Separate the Duties of:
Recording payroll in the general ledger and processing the payroll
Processing the payroll and processing personnel-action forms
Preparing the payroll, hiring, and firing employees and approving time reports

Performance Review
Give employees an annual performance evaluation.
Provide performance counseling.

PRIVACY Inform employees that they have no right to privacy regarding their e-mail and voice mail messages or access to their desk and locker. Take appropriate disciplinary measures against employees who download inappropriate material from the Internet.

WORKPLACE SAFETY The risk manager should investigate *each* accident to determine its cause and discover ways to prevent a future occurrence. Appropriate disciplinary action should be taken against those who violate safety practices. Along with the "stick," however, a nonprofit should offer a "carrot." Reward employees and teams who have achieved a sterling safety record. The reward can be *intrinsic,* such as a plaque, commendation, or award dinner); or it can be *extrinsic,* such as a cash payment and paid days off.

AUTO-RELATED LIABILITY Employees who drive at work should take a driving safety course and have a driver's license and safe driving record. Ensure that preventive maintenance is performed on the nonprofit firm's vehicles. In the event of an accident, require employees to:

- *Always* get a police accident report.
- Obtain the other party's name, telephone number, and insurance policy provider.
- *Immediately* report the accident to the nonprofit's insurance agent or broker.
- *Never* discuss the facts of the accident with anyone but the nonprofit's insurance agent and lawyer.

DONORS Protect the confidentiality of donors' records. Follow IRS regulations to ensure that donations are tax exempt. Obtain donors' permission to send them e-mail, faxes, and standard mail.

RECORDS AND RETENTION   Keep detailed minutes of Board meetings. IRS
Form 990 asks whether a nonprofit has a written document retention and
destruction policy.[4] Though not legally required, such a policy is strongly
recommended.[5] However, only 30 percent of nonprofits have adopted such
a policy.[6] Strictly adhere to the policy's record retention dates. The Sarbanes-
Oxley Act makes it a federal crime to alter or destroy records to prevent
their use in an official proceeding.[7] Exhibit 4.18 is a sample records retention
policy.

THE DISABLED   The Americans with Disabilities Act requires nonprofits to
provide disabled persons with access to public facilities.

VOLUNTEERS   While a great asset, volunteers also present a risk if they are
not carefully screened and trained. An excellent explanation of how to
screen volunteers is provided by a Canadian nonprofit consultancy, Insurance and Liability Resource Centre for Nonprofits, at insuranceinfo.
imaginecanada.ca/insuranceinfo.imaginecanada.ca/node/1020.

   Require volunteer drivers to provide proof of a valid driver's license and
current vehicle registration and check their driving records. Specify in writing that a poor driving record will disqualify them. Normally, a volunteer's
car-insurance policy is in effect in case of an accident. *However,* a volunteer's auto insurance policy often has low liability limits. For instance, a
state might require a minimum amount of $20,000 in bodily injury coverage
per person, $40,000 in bodily injury coverage per accident, and $10,000 in
property damage coverage per accident. However, if the financial responsibility exceeds these limits, the nonprofit can be held responsible for the
extra amount. Thus, the nonprofit's business auto insurance policy should
include secondary coverage in the event the nonprofit is made a party to a
legal action against the volunteer driver.

Risk Assumption

The third way to treat a risk is to assume it by (1) self-insurance or (2) an
insurance deductible. Large nonprofits, with considerable reserves, may opt
to self-insure all or part of particular risks. Typically, they assume risk up to
a high amount (e.g., $100,000) and transfer losses above the ceiling to an
insurance company. Assuming risk can be cost effective because insurance
companies:

- Have higher operating costs than a nonprofit
- Must pay taxes
- Typically earn a profit

To self-insure, the nonprofit creates a self-insurance fund. Deciding the amount of the fund is a technical calculation best made by a professional actuary. The Board should leave the self-insurance fund *intact*, no matter how inviting it might be as a funding source when financially strapped.

The second way to assume risk is by means of an *insurance deductible*. The nonprofit pays a percentage of a loss (the deductible amount), and the insurance company pays the remainder. The higher the deductible, the lower will be the premium. There are three types of deductibles:

1. *Straight deductible*. A fixed percentage or flat amount is deducted from each loss.
2. *Disappearing deductible* (used for a property loss). The insurance company pays an increasing percentage of a loss until it reaches an amount specified in the policy, after which the deductible disappears and the insurance company pays the full amount of the loss.
3. *Aggregated stop-loss deductible*. The nonprofit pays the full amount of a loss until it reaches an aggregated stop-loss limit, after which the insurance company pays 100 percent of the loss.

UNWITTING RISK ASSUMPTION   There are two ways that a nonprofit can *unwittingly* assume risk:

1. Insure property at its *actual cash value* (ACV) rather than its *replacement value* (RV).
2. Misuse coinsurance.

Properties and assets depreciate over time. Insuring a capital asset at its ACV incurs unnecessary risk. For instance, assume a building with an RV of $1,000,000 has depreciated by 50 percent. A policy written on an ACV basis will only insure one-half ($500,000) of the amount required to replace the building ($1,000,000).

A nonprofit also assumes too much risk by failing to understand the concept of *coinsurance*. A property is coinsured at a percentage of its value. Thus, the amount of insurance should be increased if a building's value *appreciates*. If not, risk is unwittingly assumed, as illustrated in the following example.

Example
A building, originally valued at $200,000, has appreciated to $400,000. If insured with an 80 percent coinsurance clause, 80 percent of the value ($320,000) should be insured. However, if the building is still insured at its original price ($200,000), then only $160,000 is insured. If the building incurs a $100,000 loss due to fire, for instance, then $50,000

in insurance benefits will be forgone. The formula for what the insurance company would pay is as follows:

$$\frac{\text{Amount of actual insurance}}{80\% \text{ of replacement value}} \times \text{Amount of loss}$$
$$= \text{Amount paid by insurance company}$$

Thus, in the example,

$$\frac{\$160,000}{\$320,000} \times \$100,000$$
$$= \$50,000$$

Risk Transfer

The fourth treatment option is to transfer risk to another party by means of the following:

- Hold-harmless clause in the contract
- Waiver of subrogation in the contract
- Insurance

A *hold-harmless clause* in a contract relieves the nonprofit from liability for a loss incurred during the execution of the contract. In essence, the clause transfers liability to the other party, which should have a *certificate of insurance* guaranteeing an adequate amount of insurance for the liability assumed.

In a legal sense, *subrogation* means that one party has the right to "step into the shoes" of the other party to bring a claim for damages. Property damage is the most common type of claim subrogated. For example, if a nonprofit's employee is in an accident where he or she is not at fault, the nonprofit's insurer will pay for the property damage to its vehicle. The insurer then becomes "subrogated" to the nonprofit's rights for the property damage. In other words, the insurer "steps into the nonprofit's shoes" and makes a claim against the other driver.

INSURANCE[8]   The most common way to transfer risk is to purchase insurance from an agent or broker. A broker, who is typically state-licensed, can purchase insurance for the nonprofit from *any* insurance company. In contrast, an insurance agent, also state-licensed, can purchase insurance only with companies with whom he or she has a contract. The insurance company pays a commission to the agent or broker. Brokers tend to serve various communities; agents tend to serve a particular community. Some agents specialize in personal insurance policies (e.g., homeowners and health insurance) and have relatively little experience with the commercial insurance lines that a nonprofit needs. Brokers have experience with commercial lines but may not be willing to handle small (e.g., less than $10,000) accounts. If seeking the services of an agent, ensure that he or she has extensive experience with commercial coverages.

Agents and brokers can provide four types of services:

1. Claims management
2. Safety consulting
3. Actuarial estimation
4. Training

There are three ways to engage the services of an agent or broker:

1. Request for proposals (RFP)
2. Market assignment
3. Conceptual competition

An RFP weighs both the price and the quality of services. Exhibit 14.5 describes the nature of the services that agents and brokers provide.[9]

The RFP selection method specifies the insurance policies the nonprofit will require. In contrast, the *market assignment* method asks several agents and/or brokers to submit a list of insurance companies that they represent.[10] The nonprofit then selects the insurance company or companies submitted by a single agent or broker or by two or more brokers or agents. With the third selection method, *conceptual competition*, the nonprofit negotiates an overall insurance coverage concept with an agent or broker prior to the agent or broker offering insurance policies.

EXHIBIT 14.5   Agent and Broker Service

Service	Description of Service
Purchase Insurance	Assist with preparing the insurance coverage specifications; negotiate the price of insurance policies; and assess and monitor the insurer's financial security.
Insurance-Program Management	Provide advice and counsel; prepare certificates of insurance; prepare insurance data for the annual financial audit; and meet periodically with the risk management committee and/or the Board.
Manage Claims	Handle claims; advise regarding claims settlement; monitor the performance of loss adjusters; and prepare loss and outstanding claims reports.

To select the agent or broker, the CEO and CFO need a sound understanding of the types of policies covering property damage and liability claims, which are listed and discussed in Exhibit 14.6.

Exhibit 14.7 explains the terms and conditions that are found in insurance policies.

In selecting an insurance company, the nonprofit should evaluate its financial condition. The leading cause of insolvency is having an inadequate loss reserve.[17] A helpful source is the insurance department of the state, which periodically analyzes companies' financials. Three rating agencies—A.M. Best, Standard & Poor's, and Fitch Ratings—also evaluate the financial strength of insurance companies. The rating agencies rate insurance companies as *secure* or *vulnerable*. Secure-rated companies have a strong ability to meet their financial obligations.

In summary, risk financing has four basic tenets:

1. Never risk a lot for a little price.
2. Never retain more risk that you can afford to lose.
3. Always consider the probability of a loss happening.
4. Never—*never*—view insurance as a substitute for a good loss prevention program.

Administer the Program

The risk manager administers the risk management program. Risk management includes the following duties:

- Record policies and correspondence.
- Investigate and report incidents.
- Review contracts.
- Handle claims.
- Litigate claims.
- Evaluate performance.

Policies and Correspondence

The risk manager should keep a copy of each insurance policy and the correspondence related to it. Such correspondence is needed if the nonprofit disputes the insurance company's performance. Never write or make notations on insurance policies. Any writing can have an effect on a dispute coverage.[18]

The state insurance commissioner specifies how long to archive records; but a claimant can file for a loss *after* a policy has expired and can request to *reopen* a closed case. For example, a child can reopen a claim after

EXHIBIT 14.6   Types of Insurance Policies

Type of Policy	Discussion
Property Damage	
Building and Contents	Should specify building's location, using a *per occurrence* deductible to insure against multiple losses from a single event. If the policy has a coinsurance clause, include an inflation cost index that automatically increases a property's value for inflation.
Business Interruption	Reimburses for the loss of income if a fire or act of nature renders a facility inoperable.
Computer	Offers broader coverage than the building and contents policy, including losses due to power surges, viruses, and computer drive crashes.
Earthquake and Floods	High-risk areas (e.g., San Francisco and New Orleans) should insure for these risks, which are typically not covered by the building and contents policy.
Boiler and Machinery	The policy covers accidents to boilers, refrigeration/air conditioning equipment, electrical power generators, and research apparatus.
Liability	
Commercial General Liability (CGL)[11]	Protects employees, Board members, and volunteers from third-party claims alleging property damage, bodily injury, personal injury, and advertising injury. Covers injuries from libel, slander, and contract liability. Typically excludes employment practices, however.
Improper Sexual Conduct	The CGL policy may exclude *sexual conduct* coverage. If so, purchase a separate improper sexual conduct policy that includes a provision to cover someone falsely accused of sexual abuse.
Business Auto	Covers liability (bodily injury and property damage) and first-party auto physical damage (collision and comprehensive). The policy should include anyone driving the vehicle with permission of the nonprofit. If the nonprofit does not own a vehicle, purchase hired and non-owned coverage to protect employees and Board members when they lease or rent vehicles or use their *personal vehicle* on official business. In the event of a loss, the employee's or volunteer's personal auto coverage is primary, but the business auto policy covers a loss in excess of employee's personal insurance.

EXHIBIT 14.6   *(Continued)*

Type of Policy	Discussion
Directors' and Officers' (D&O) Liability[12]	Covers claims against the organization, Board members, employees, and volunteers for mismanagement, including libel, slander, third-party harassment and discrimination, copyright infringement, and mismanagement. Include in the policy *employment practices liability insurance* (EPLI) or purchase a separate EPLI policy to protect against claims of sexual harassment, wrongful termination, failure to hire or promote, and discrimination.[13]
Workers' Compensation[14]	If a nonprofit has more than three employees, the federal government requires coverage; however, even a nonprofit with three or less employees should optionally purchase coverage if financially able.
Professional Liability[15]	Purchase this policy, *if* the CGL policy excludes volunteers who are professionals (e.g., doctors, lawyers, nurses). A malpractice provision protects against tort liability arising from negligent professional services.
Excess Liability[16]	When limits of a primary policy (e.g., CGL, business auto and professional liability) have been exhausted, this policy provides excess coverage, usually in $1 million blocks.
Umbrella Liability	Provides broader protection than excess policies because, in addition to excess coverage, the umbrella policy drops down to cover losses not covered by primary policies. Pays up to the umbrella limit.
Special Events	Covers special events such as parades, auctions, and meals that are not protected by the CGL policy. Coverage is limited to a particular exposure (e.g., food being served) at an event.
Cyber or Internet Liability	Property and commercial liability policies usually do not cover the loss of data when the computer system is breached. Pays to reenter data, repair or replace hardware, and recover data from a crashed file server.
Crime	The standard policy covers: (1) fidelity loss (due to employee dishonesty); (2) a loss on premises (e.g., money, securities, electronic records, etc); (3) a loss off premises due to theft, damage, or mysterious disappearance; (4) a forgery loss; (5) a securities loss; (6) computer-systems fraud; and (7) a counterfeit loss.
Fidelity Bond	Insures against theft and embezzlement. Most nonprofits purchase a *blanket position* bond that broadly covers positions (e.g., Board members, executive director, CFO), but not individuals.

EXHIBIT 14.7   Insurance Policy Provisions

Provision	Explanation
Declarations	The insured's name and address; the policy's duration; the coverage limit; the amount of the deductible and the premium
Insuring Agreement	Specifies policy coverage including:
	1. An indemnification clause specifying the basis for reimbursement
	2. An insurable interest clause indicating who can recover the loss
	3. A duplicate coverage clause preventing claimants from collecting for the same loss under multiple policies
	4. A subrogation clause indicating whether the rights of a negligent third party are retained or are transferred to the insurance company
Exclusions	Specifies the exposures *not* covered by a policy, such as earthquake or flood
Definitions	Defines the terms found in the insuring agreement and exclusions section
Conditions	Specifies conditions the insured must meet, such as:
	1. Notify the insurer of a loss.
	2. Cooperate with the insurer.
	3. Take reasonable steps to minimize losses.
Endorsements	Restrictions or modifications that add to the main coverage by revising a definition

reaching the age of majority. Thus, regardless of the state's time-retention limit, a nonprofit should retain insurance documents *indefinitely*.[19]

Incident Investigation and Reporting

In the event of an accident, the risk manager should complete an incident report form and *immediately* report a claim to the insurance company, requiring the insurance company to verify receipt of the notification. Some insurance companies require notification even if a claim is not made. The insurance policy usually specifies reporting the:

- Nature of the alleged wrongful act
- Alleged damages
- Name of the claimant(s)

Vehicle accidents can occur on and off a nonprofit's premises and at a nonprofit-sponsored special event. Accidents can involve employees, Board members, visitors, volunteers, and the public. The nonprofit should instruct its employees, Board members, and volunteers that in the event of an accident they should:

- Express concern for the other party, but *not* admit fault.
- Exchange names, telephone numbers, and insurance-company information with the other party.
- Notify the nonprofit's insurance agent and insurance carrier.
- Complete an accident report form.

Using a list like that shown in Exhibit 14.8, the risk manager should investigate an accident to determine its cause and to implement preventive and disciplinary measures when the nonprofit is at fault.

Contract Review

A poorly drawn contract poses considerable risks. The risk manager should therefore closely review *every* contract and lease agreement before signing. The nonprofit should require that only an authorized person enter into a contract. If someone other than the CEO can sign a contract, set a dollar limit above which the CEO must sign with the Board's approval. Exhibit 14.9 lists the provisions generally included in contracts.

Claims Handling

After notifying the insurance company of a claim, the risk manager should create a file to track the claim, including an accurate and complete record of each claim's correspondence and payments. The insurance company summarizes the premiums and losses that the nonprofit has paid over a three- to five-year period. At least annually, the risk manager should request a copy of this summary and match the nonprofit's records against the insurance company's.[20]

Claims Litigation

The nonprofit typically hears about a lawsuit only when served with a complaint or summons. After being served with the complaint or summons, the nonprofit should take the following steps:[21]

1. Note the date of the complaint or summons because it must be answered in 30 days.

EXHIBIT 14.8   Accident Review List

Practice

General Practice

Take a statement from the injured party or parties and from witnesses while their impressions are still fresh.

Put the injured person(s) at ease, explaining the purpose of the investigation.

Ask for the employee's account of the accident; do not interpret his or her remarks or make assumptions.

Repeat his or her version without editorializing.

Determine whether the employee was authorized and trained to do the task.

Determine whether the employee was adequately supervised.

Determine whether such an accident has happened before and what corrective action was recommended.

Take corrective measures to prevent a future occurrence.

Share the findings at a safety meeting with employees.

Vehicle Accident

Call the police department to get a copy of the accident report.

Require employees to limit their statement to the police to what they actually know.

Give the other party the claim number and adjuster's phone number.

Prohibit talking about an accident with *anyone* but the insurance company and attorney.

Accident on the Premises

If furniture or other equipment was involved, inspect it for a defect.

If the accident was a slip or fall, check the surface condition and the shoes of the person who fell.

Take a picture of the accident area.

Accident at a Special Event

Before the event, designate someone as the safety manager.

Clean slippery floors during an event to prevent a fall.

Keep a first-aid kit on hand.

After an accident, call the injured person to express concern but do not discuss the accident.

---

2. Immediately notify the insurance company.
3. Do not dispose of or tamper with *any* documents, no matter how harmful they may be to the nonprofit's case.
4. Talk with *no one* about the case other than the nonprofit's attorney and insurer.
5. Objectively recount the facts of the case to the insurer and attorney.

Litigating claims can be *very* stressful and frustrating. Sometimes the circumstances are such that the insurer will decide to settle a winnable case

EXHIBIT 14.9   Contract Provisions List

General Contract Provisions
Vendors and independent contractors must have a certificate of insurance
A hold-harmless clause
Name of the person (or outside counsel) who will review the legality of the
    contract
Name of the person who will review the insurance policies required by the contract
How the parties will notify each other
How the nonprofit or the other party will pay for a liability
How to terminate the contract with and without cause

Provisions for the Contractor
Contractor must pay its taxes and is not entitled to the nonprofit's employee
    benefits
Contractor will not engage in unlawful discrimination
Contractor will not assign the work to another contractor
All developments and creative ideas conceived in performance of the contract are
    the property of the nonprofit

Employment-Contract Provisions
CEO cannot compete with the nonprofit for a reasonable period after leaving the
    nonprofit
Board must approve the CEO's outside activities, such as consulting or serving on
    another nonprofit's Board
How to terminate the CEO's contract with or without cause
Amount of the CEO's severance benefits, if any, to pay upon termination

("make it go away") because the settlement will cost less than it would to
litigate.

The risk manager should evaluate the effectiveness of the claims management process using the formulas below:

Average Cost per Claim

$$\frac{\text{Total claims costs}}{\text{Total number of reported costs during a selected time period}}$$

Percentage of Open Claims

$$\frac{\text{Number of open claims}}{\text{Total claims reported}} \times 100$$

Average Claim Duration

$$\frac{\text{Total number of days open}}{\text{Total number of reported liability claims}}$$

Average Reporting Lag Time

$$\frac{\text{Total number of reporting days}}{\text{Total number of reported liability claims}}$$

Percentage of Litigated Claims

$$\frac{\text{Total number of claims in litigation}}{\text{Total number of reported liability claimss}} \times 100$$

Performance Evaluation

In addition to claims management measures, other performance measures include:

- *Auto accidents.* Number of incidents per 100 full-time workers or per number of miles driven
- *Non-auto accidents.* Number of incidents; number of lost workday cases; number of nonfatal cases without lost workdays
- *Severity of accidents.* Number of lost workdays per 100 full-time workers
- *Workers' compensation.* Experience modification factor (See discussion below.)

An organization that pays $5,000 in workers' compensation premiums qualifies to be experience rated. Experience rating adjusts the workers' compensation premium annually based on a nonprofit's prior years' payroll and loss data.[22] In 38 states, the National Council on Compensation Insurance performs the rating analysis. The other 12 states utilize their own rating bureau. In either case, the rating organization classifies each employee (e.g., clerical worker) according to the type of work he or she performs. Next, the rating agency multiplies the salaries of the employees in each job class by a rate based on the amount of risk associated with the position class. Then the expected losses for the nonprofit, based on this calculation, are compared to the nonprofit's prior years' *actual* losses. If the amount of the losses is less than expected, the rating bureau discounts the premium. If the loss rate is greater than the average, the premium is increased. This adjustment is the experience-modification rating, or just "the Mod." A Mod of 1.0 equals the expected loss. A Mod greater than 1.0 increases the premium; a Mod less than 1.0 decreases it. For example:

Expected premium	$5,000	$5,000
× Mod	1.2	90
Actual premium	$6,000	$4,500

Common Risk Management Terms

The following is a glossary of common risk management terms used in this chapter and/or the documents referenced here.

- *Agent.* One who solicits, negotiates, or sells a contract of insurance on behalf of an insurer.
- *Accident review.* Investigation of the causes of an accident to make changes to prevent a future occurrence.
- *Broker.* An independent representative who seeks and negotiates for insurance coverage on behalf of an insured.
- *Catastrophic loss.* A severe loss causing sizable financial and/or physical damage (e.g., damage from an earthquake, tornado, or hurricane).
- *Certificate of insurance.* A certificate of proof of having insurance.
- *Compulsory insurance.* Legally required insurance (e.g., workers' compensation insurance).
- *Contract.* An agreement between two or more parties characterized by mutual assent, competent parties, valid consideration, and a legal subject.
- *Contract review.* Scrutinizing a contract and lease agreement to limit liability and ensure legal compliance.
- *Condition.* Insurance policy provision that specifies conditions the nonprofit must meet (e.g., notify the insurer of a claim).
- *Contractual liability.* Duties and responsibilities for products or services assumed through a contractual relationship.
- *Damages.* The monetary value of a loss.
- *Directors' and officers' liability.* Liability of Board members, employees and volunteers of mismanagement including slander, libel, third-party harassment and discrimination, copyright infringement, and mismanagement.
- *Exclusion.* Risk exposure not covered by an insurance policy.
- *Frequency.* The number of times that a loss occurs (or is expected to occur) within any given time period.
- *Hazard.* A condition that increases the likelihood of a loss occurring from a given peril.
- *Hold harmless clause.* Contractual clause by which both parties agree not to hold the other liable for a loss.

- *Independent contractor.* An individual or company who has agreed to perform a job on behalf of another party.
- *Insurance.* A method of paying for losses by which one party assumes the responsibility to pay for another party's losses in exchange for the payment of premiums.
- *Liability.* The legal obligation to pay a monetary award for injury or damage caused by negligent or statutorily prohibited actions.
- *Limits of liability.* The most an insurance company agrees to pay in the case of loss. A "per occurrence limit" specifies how much the policy will pay per claim. An "aggregate limit" specifies the maximum amount that the policy will pay annually or during the policy term, regardless of the number of occurrences.
- *Loss history/loss experience.* The nonprofit's actual losses over an identified period.
- *Natural hazards.* Natural conditions that increase the risk of loss, such as earthquakes, wildfires, floods, hurricanes, tornadoes, landslides, etc.
- *Negligence.* The failure to act as a reasonable and prudent person would under similar circumstances.
- *Peril.* The cause of a loss (e.g., theft, accident, fire).
- *Professional liability.* Liability of professionals (e.g., attorneys, physicians, doctors) for damages resulting from their errors and omissions in performing professional services.
- *Real property.* Real estate, including buildings and land.
- *Retention/self insurance.* The amount of loss that a nonprofit will pay without insurance.
- *Risk.* The possibility of direct or indirect financial or physical loss to the entity.
- *Risk elimination.* Eliminate a risk by not providing a service or by taking preventive measures (e.g., backing up computer files).
- *Risk management plan.* A plan for identifying, eliminating, reducing, assuming, and transferring a nonprofit's risks.
- *Risk manager.* The employee responsible for managing the risk management plan.
- *Risk reduction.* Reduce the frequency and severity of a risk by following a safety policy.
- *Risk assumption.* Assume a risk by use of (1) self-insurance or (2) an insurance deductible.
- *Severity.* The financial impact of a loss on a nonprofit's financial stability and ability to fulfill its mission.
- *Special events insurance.* Insurance against claims resulting from injury at fundraising events such as auctions and meals.
- *Uninsurable risks.* Risks that currently cannot be financed by purchasing insurance.

- *Workers' compensation.* Mandatory benefits that state law requires employers to pay to their employees for injury, disability, death, or contracted disease arising in the course of employment, regardless of fault.

For Further Reading

Herman, Melanie, ed. *Coverage, Claims and Consequences: An Insurance
    Handbook for Nonprofits*, 2nd ed. Leesburg, VA: Nonprofit Risk Manage-
    ment Center, 2008. An exceedingly comprehensive account of insurance
    management, companies, and policies.
————. *Ready in Defense*. Leesburg, VA: Nonprofit Risk Management Center,
    2003. The book demystifies the core concepts associated with legal
    liability. Stresses how to prevent claims and lawsuits.

Notes

Chapter 1

1. Urban Institute, *National Center for Charitable Statistics, NCCS-GuideStar National Nonprofit Research Database: Special Research Version* (2005).
2. Kirsten Gronberg and Linda Allen, *The Indiana Nonprofit Sector: A Profile* (Bloomington, Ind.: The School of Public and Environmental Affairs, 2004).
3. Mary Feeney and Hal Rainey, "Personnel Flexibility and Red Tape in Public and Nonprofit Organizations: Distinctions Due to Institutional and Political Accountability," *Journal of Public Administration Research and Theory* 20 (2010): 801–826.
4. National Association of Schools of Public Affairs and Administration (NASPAA), *Guidelines for Graduate Professional Education in Nonprofit Organizations, Management and Leadership* (Washington, DC, 2006).

Chapter 2

1. Exempt are nonprofits whose cash position is little different from their accrual position.
2. The three forms include: (1) Form 990-N, when receipts are less than $25,000; (2) Form 990 EZ, when receipts are between $25,000 and a limit set by the IRS; and (3) Form 990 when receipts are above the limit.
3. For a more complete explanation of IRS Form 990, refer to http://www.irs.gov/.
4. See what was formerly FASB 95, Statement of Cash Flows, for a complete explanation.
5. This is a sample list. Many other accounting and fundraising software options are also available.

Chapter 3

1. Committee of Sponsoring Organizations (COSO), Treadway Commission, *Internal Control—Integrated Framework* (1992), http://www.coso.org/IC-IntegratedFramework-summary.htm.
2. Charles Landes, *Understanding SAS No. 112*, American Institute of Certified Public Accountants (1996), http://www.theiia.org/chapters/index.cfm/view.news_detail/cid/98/newsid/8375.
3. Association of Certified Fraud Examiners, *2008 Report to the Nation on Occupational Fraud and Abuse* (2008), http://www.acfe.com/documents/2008-rttn.pdf.
4. Ibid.

Chapter 4

1. Francie Ostrower and Marla Bobowick, *Nonprofit Governance and the Sarbanes-Oxley Act* (Washington, DC: Urban Institute, 2005).
2. Ibid.
3. Better Business Bureau, Inc., *Standards for Charity Accountability*, http://atlanta.bbb.org/Charity-Standards/.
4. Dorothy McMullen and K. Raghunandan, "Audit Committees and Financial Reporting Problems," *Journal of Accountancy* 182, no. 2 (1996): 79–81.
5. Ostrower and Bobowick, 3.
6. Peggy M. Jackson and Toni E. Fogarty, *Sarbanes-Oxley for Nonprofits* (Hoboken, NJ: John Wiley & Sons, 2005), 35.
7. The standards in Figure 4.9 paraphrase somewhat the actual language in the standards.
8. The eight standards are:
   SAS 104—Amendment to Due Professional Card in the Performance of Work Amendment
   SAS 105—Amendment to SAS No. 95, Generally Accepted Auditing Standards
   SAS 106—Audit Evidence
   SAS 107—Audit Risk and Materiality in Conducting an Audit
   SAS 108—Planning and Supervision
   SAS 109—Understanding the Entity and Its Environment and Assessing the Risks of Material Misstatement
   SAS 110—Performing Audit Procedures in Response to Assessed Risks and Evaluating the Audit Evidence Obtained
   SAS 111—Amendment to SAS 39, Audit Sampling

9. Excepted are religious organizations with gross income less than $25,000.
10. Jamie Usury, *Charitable Solicitation with Nonprofit Sector* (Salt Lake City, UT: Center for Public Policy & Administration, 2008).
11. Jennifer Hauge, "What's the Big Deal," *Risk Management Essentials* 17, no. 2 (2008): 1, 4–6.
12. Implementation is phased in over tax years 2008, 2009, and 2010, depending on the amount of gross receipts and assets.
13. Note these are only new changes. For a discussion of changed provisions as well, refer to this Moody, Famiglietti & Andronico, LLP, publication, Joyce Ripianzi, "IRS Releases Updated Final Form 990 Instructions," *Nonprofit Alert*, February 2009, http://www.bestbeancounters.com/mfa-news-and-resources/tax-alerts/NonprofitAlert-Feb09.pdf or Joyce Ripianzi, "IRS Releases New Form 990," www.mfa-cpa.com/, which cannot be found on the MPA site under that title?
14. Officers, directors, and employees earning more than $150,000 in reportable compensation or $250,000 in total compensation face more complicated reporting requirements.
15. There is a $5,000 threshold for itemizing individual fundraisers and events.

Chapter 5

1. For a more complete description of these and other notes to financial statements, refer to Russy Sumariwalla and Wilson Levis, *Unified Financial Reporting System for Not-for-Profit Organizations* (San Francisco: Jossey-Bass, 2000), 120–128.
2. Refer to Statement of Financial Accounting Standards, No. 124 for more guidance on investment reporting.
3. A statement of revenues, expenses, and other changes in net assets and a statement of changes in net assets.
4. The numbers in Exhibit 5.11, unavailable on the 2008 Form 990, are taken from the 2007 Form 990.
5. Kennard Wing, Mark A. Hager, Patrick Rooney, and Thomas H. Pollak, *Lessons for Boards from the Nonprofit Overhead Cost Project, Urban Institute*, 2004, http://urban.org/publications/411119.html.
6. Nonprofit Finance Fund, *Nonprofit Finance Fund 2010 State of the Nonprofit Sector Survey*, http://www.nonprofitfinancefund.org/docs/2010/2010SurveyResults.pdf.
7. Steven Berger, *Understanding Financial Statements*, 3rd ed. (Washington, DC: 2008), 46.

8. Ibid.

9. Ibid., 47.

10. Steven Finkler, *Financial Management* (Saddle River, NJ: Pearson, 2010), 547.

Chapter 6

1. John Zeitlow, Jo Ann Hankin, and Alan Seidner, *Financial Management for Nonprofit Organizations: Policies and Practices* (Hoboken, NJ: John Wiley & Sons, 2007), 255.

2. See Internal Revenue Service, *2010 Instructions for Form 990 Return of Organization Exempt From Income Tax*, http://www.irs.gov/pub/irs-pdf/i990.pdf.

3. Stuart Watson, "United Way Responds to Report on $1.2M Pay," *WCNC.com,* June 27, 2008.

4. Linda Blackford, "Executive Salaries High on the Charts, *Kentucky.com,* June 7, 2006, http://www.kentucky.com/klc/story/820337.html.

5. Kirsten Gronberg and Linda Allen, *The Indiana Nonprofit Sector: A Profile* (Bloomington, IN: The School of Public and Environmental Affairs at Indiana University, 2004).

6. Zietlow et al., 255.

7. Ibid.

8. Guidestar Publications, *The Effect of the Economy on the Nonprofit Sector* (Washington, D.C.: 2009).

9. Center on Nonprofits and Philanthropy, Urban Institute, *Who Raises Contributions for America's Nonprofit Organizations* (Washington, DC: 2004).

10. The Commonwealth of Massachusetts, Officer of Attorney General, *Attorney General's Report on Professional Solicitations for Charity in 2007* (Boston: 2008).

11. State of Connecticut Attorney General's Office, "Attorney General, DCP Commissioner Say Charitable Phone solicitors Pass on Smallest Amount since 2004," press release, November 13, 2007, http://www.ct.gov/ag/cwp/view.asp?A=2788&Q=404292.

12. State of Colorado Department of State, *2008 Annual Report: Charitable Solicitations: Colorado* (2008).

13. North Carolina Secretary of State, *Charitable Solicitation Division Annual Report* (2008).

14. New York Department of Law, *Pennies for Charity: Where Your Money Goes* (2006).

Chapter 7

1. Nonprofit Finance Fund, *Nonprofit Finance Fund 2010 State of the Nonprofit Sector Survey*, http://www.nonprofitfinancefund.org/docs/2010/2010SurveyResults.pdf.

Chapter 8

1. Francie Ostrower and Marla Bobowick, *Nonprofit Governance and the Sarbanes-Oxley Act* (Washington, DC: The Urban institute, 2007), 8.
2. Francie Ostrower and Marla Bobowick, *Nonprofit Governance and the Sarbanes-Oxley Act* (Washington, DC: The Urban Institute, 2006), 4.
3. See Form 990, Return of Organization Exempt from Income Tax, Part VI, line 12.
4. See Form 990, Return of Organization Exempt from Income Tax, Part VI, line 13.
5. Ostrower and Bobowick, 2006, 4.
6. Jason Zuckerman, "Whistleblower Protections in the Nonprofit Sector," *Nonprofit Risk Management Center,* http://www.nonprofitrisk.org/library/articles/employment091005.shtml.

Chapter 9

1. For an extensive discussion of the three models, refer to Ruth Hoogland Dehoog, "Competition, Negotiation, or Contracting: Three Models for Service Contracting," *Administration and Society* 22, no. 3 (1990): 317–340.
2. Ibid., 330.
3. Mary Marvel and Howard Marvel, "Shaping the Provision of Outsourced Public Services," *Public Performance & Management Review* 33, no. 2 (2009): 196.
4. Meeyoung Lamothe and Scott Lamothe, "Beyond the Search for Competition in Social Service Contracting: Procurement, Consolidation and Accountability," *American Review of Public Administration* 39, no. 2 (2008): 171.
5. Barbara Romzek and Jocelyn Johnston, "State Social Services Contracting: Exploring the Determinants of Effective Contract Accountability," *Public Administration Review* 64, no. 4 (2005): 437.
6. Elizabeth Boris, Erwin de Leon, Kate Berger and Nilena Nikolova, *Human Service Profits and Government Collaboration* (Washington, D.C.: Urban Institute, 2010), 10.

Chapter 11

1. Woods Bowman, Elizabeth Keating, and Mark Hager, *Investment Income in Financing Nonprofits* (Lanham, MD: AltaMira Press, 2007), 160.
2. Ibid.
3. Robert Fry, *Who's Minding the Money* (Washington, DC: Board Source, 2009), 43.
4. As of March 2009, 29 states had adopted this rule.
5. Christopher Geczy, Robert Stambaugh, and David Levin, "Investing in Socially Responsible Mutual Funds," (working paper, Social Science Research Network, October 2005), http://papers.ssrn.com/sol3/papers.cfm?abstract_id=416380.
6. Includes NOW accounts, Super NOW accounts, and MMDA accounts.
7. "AICPA Audit and Accounting Guide—Not-for-Profit Entities" addresses other investments not covered by FASB 124, including mortgage notes, oil and gas interests, and equity securities with a readily determinable value.
8. Commonfund Institute, *Principles of Nonprofit Investment Management: The Key Issues Facing Trustees and Financial Officers* (Wilson, CN: n.d.), http://www.commonfund.org/InvestorResources/Publications/Brochures/ Principles%20of%20Nonprofit%20Investment%20 Management.pdf.

Chapter 12

1. Cynthia Evangelisti and Kevin Lockhart, "Banking Due Diligence in the New Financial World," *Government Finance Review* 25, no. 5 (October 2009): 26–33.
2. Corinne Larson, "Credit Worthiness," in *Banking Services,* ed. Nicholas Greifer (Washington, DC: Government Finance Officers Association, 2004), 184.
3. David Higgins, *Essentials of Treasury Management,* 2nd ed. (Bethesda, MD: Association for Financial Professionals, 2008), 532.
4. For an extensive discussion of collateralization, refer to Larson, 187–195.
5. Larson, 188.
6. Susan Stevens and Lisa Anderson, *All the Way to the Bank* (St. Paul, MN: The Stevens Group, 1997), 39.

Chapter 13

1. Robert Yetman, "Borrowing and Debt," in *Financing Nonprofits,* ed. Dennis Young (Lanham, MD: AltaMira Press, 2007), 245.

2. Ibid.
3. Dwight Denison, "Which Nonprofit Organizations Borrow?" *Public Budgeting and Finance* 29, no. 3 (2009): 117.
4. Yetman, 263.

Chapter 14

1. The FMLA applies to organizations that have more than 50 employees who worked at least 1,250 hours in the past year.
2. Melanie Herman, *Ready in Defense* (Washington, DC: Nonprofit Risk Management Center, 2003), 54.
3. Erick Johnson, "Directors and Officers Insurance: What Every Board Member Should Know," *Association Now,* January 2009.
4. IRS Form 990, Return of Organization Exempt From Income Tax, Part VI, lien 14.
5. BoardSource and Independent Sector, *The Sarbanes-Oxley Act and Implications for Nonprofit Organizations* (2003, rev. January 2006), http://www.boardsource.org/clientfiles/sarbanes-oxley.pdf.
6. Francie Ostrower and Marla Bobowick, *Nonprofit Governance and the Sarbanes-Oxley Act* (Washington, DC: Urban Institute, 2006), 5.
7. See Sarbanes-Oxley Act 2002, Section 1102.
8. See Melanie Herman, ed., *Coverage, Claims and Consequences: An Insurance Handbook for Nonprofits,* 2nd ed. (Leesburg, VA: Nonprofit Risk Management Center, 2008). This text provides an excellent and comprehensive discussion of insurance. see.
9. Ibid., pp. 72–79 provides a sample RFP for insurance services.
10. Ibid., 81, experts recommend no more than 10 brokers and/or agents be contacted.
11. Ibid., 98–108, for an in-depth discussion of CGL.
12. Ibid., 121–136, for an in-depth discussion of D&O.
13. Ibid., 137–145 for an in-depth discussion of EPLI.
14. Ibid., 145–152, for an in-depth discussion of workers' compensation.
15. Ibid., 109–121, for an in-depth discussion of professional liability.
16. Ibid., 157–159, for an in-depth discussion of excess and umbrella liability coverage.
17. Ibid., 25.
18. Ibid., 52.
19. Ibid., 54.
20. Ibid., 61.
21. Herman, 2003, 91.
22. Usually the last three years.

Index